The Pursuit of Competence in Social Work

§§§§§§§§§§§§§§§§§§§§§§§§§§§§§§§§§

Contemporary Issues
in the Definition, Assessment,
and Improvement of Effectiveness
in the Human Services

all others concerned with improving
quality and efficiency of social work will
this book of value.

THE AUTHORS

RANK W. CLARK is professor, Depart-
t of Social Work, University of Mon-
.

ORTON L. ARKAVA is chairman and pro-
r, Department of Social Work, Univer-
of Montana.

he other authors are identified in the
t of the book.

Frank W. Clark

Morton L. Arkava

and Associates

⚜⚜⚜⚜⚜⚜⚜⚜⚜⚜⚜⚜⚜⚜⚜⚜⚜⚜⚜⚜⚜⚜⚜⚜⚜⚜⚜⚜⚜

The Pursuit
of Competence
in Social Work

Jossey-Bass Publishers

San Francisco • Washington • London • 1979

THE PURSUIT OF COMPETENCE IN SOCIAL WORK
Contemporary Issues in the Definition, Assessment, and Improvement of Effectiveness in the Human Services
by Frank W. Clark, Morton L. Arkava, and Associates

Copyright © 1979 by: Jossey-Bass, Inc., Publishers
433 California Street
San Francisco, California 94104
&
Jossey-Bass Limited
28 Banner Street
London EC1Y 8QE

Library of Congress Catalogue Card Number 79-83570

International Standard Book Number ISBN 0-87589-404-6

Manufactured in the United States of America

JACKET DESIGN BY WILLI BAUM

FIRST EDITION

Code 7910

The Jossey-Bass
Social and Behavioral Science Series

Preface

One of the chief characteristics of the social work profession is the variety of arenas in which practice is carried out. As Briar (1977, pp. 1529–1530) illustrates:

> Social workers are found at work in nurseries and homes for the aged, in schools and jails, in hospitals and summer camps, in emergency rooms and day care centers, in adoption agencies and community centers, and in countless other places that exist to serve people. And the utility of social work is not limited to the amelioration of problems that have already arisen. Many social workers are engaged in efforts to prevent problems and human suffering, and others attempt to enhance personal satisfaction and well-being, either through direct work with persons seeking to further their own self-development or through modifying social conditions that adversely affect certain individuals or groups. Social workers also practice as planners, community organizers, administrators and program

managers, program designers and developers, researchers, and as expert policy analysts on the staffs of legislative committees and in health and welfare agencies.

The numerous activities subsumed by social work practice have provided impetus for continuing debate on several major issues. Briar (1977, p. 1531) enumerates those issues as follows:

1. What is the core or foundation that all social workers have in common?
2. Where and when is professional specialization appropriate in social work?
3. What relative priority should be given to efforts directed to social change as compared to the amelioration of existing problems?
4. How effective are social workers, and what needs to be done to increase their effectiveness?

Debate has been sharpened further in recent years by economic and social events that in turn have created a demand for accountability for the expenditure of public funds and provision of the best possible services to clients by responsible professional practitioners. Citizens who once felt isolated from national and international events are confronted daily with energy, pollution, economic, and population problems. As the rate of change and the complexity of managing that change have intensified, individuals have become increasingly frustrated in their attempts to regain whatever control they imagined that they had in the past. Erosion of public trust and faith in the workability of major public institutions such as government, education, and welfare has calloused the national conscience. Because the United States economy currently is recession prone and plagued with unemployment and inflation, many taxpayers are unwilling to provide fiscal support for federal, state, and local government programs, even though the benefits of many of those programs may be desired. Sharp property tax increases resulting from inflation have triggered what may become a massive citizen revolt against public programs. Finally, a more skeptical, politically sophisticated, consumer-educated public is raising significant questions about the utility and expense of social welfare services and programs.

These developments have forced broad revisions in practice and professional education, including modifications in the nature of programs and services; legal, practical, and ethical challenges regarding the value of credentials; legal regulation of social work practice in the form of state licensing; and the relentless demand for accountability, raised within the profession and by social services program designers.

In addition to studying and debating the issues associated with internal pressures for accountability, the social work profession has responded to those demands with a variety of specific changes in its activities. For example, in the past decade the profession has developed a remarkable variety of sophisticated evaluation and intervention technologies. It has become more diverse in its range of services and expanded knowledge and skills required in specialized areas of practice. Baccalaureate-level training has been implemented to meet the increased need for professionally trained workers. Social work education programs have accommodated and responded to innovations in practice by offering a greater range of instruction in practice technologies and opportunities for increased specialization. A more comprehensive view of what constitutes the necessary range of practice competencies for social work has emerged concomitantly with current practice and educational concepts.

The title of this book, *The Pursuit of Competence in Social Work,* suggests that practice effectiveness in the diverse settings of social work will not be achieved rapidly or easily. Fundamentally, it is an incremental process of change directed toward optimizing educational and professional objectives. As such, the profession relies not so much on sudden inspiration as it does on hard work and careful evaluation. Providing clients with effective and humane services—those that seek, generate, and are responsive to relevant data-based information—is the principal mission of social work. The competent educator and practitioner will accept nothing less.

The contents of this volume were developed for discussion and review at the first Big Sky Summer Symposium, which was held at Big Sky, Montana, in August 1977. Distinguished practitioners and educators from several countries were invited to address the symposium's theme, "Competence in Social Work." Their papers, selected and edited for publication, are presented herein.

In Part One, "Legacy of the Past, Promise of the Future,"

Harry Specht in Chapter One traces the origins of the profession
from the late nineteenth century through the early years of this century when the first systematic description of social casework was developed by Mary Richmond. He reviews current models of social
work practice and related arguments concerning the generalist-
specialist dichotomy. He then presents an educational model in
which different types of educational content (both generalist and
specialist) are taught at different educational levels. Scott Briar in
Chapter Two describes the way in which the future of social work
is likely to be influenced through the use of new methodologies for
social diagnosis and social intervention.

Part Two, "Improving Practitioner Performance," illustrates
the range of viewpoints regarding the critical variables defining
social work competence. Frank W. Clark and Charles R. Horejsi in
Chapter Three explore the issues involved in using a skills orientation as the central feature of competence. They discuss the meaning
of skill, its relationship to competence, and the assumptions behind
skill orientations. In Chapter Four Harry Butler and Winifred Morphew Chambers recommend specific guidelines to improve and enhance practice competence. In their view, "The only course we can
follow if we wish our practice to come under the control of evidence
while adjusting for bias and unintended consequences is to use
systematic procedures to determine what ought to be done and
assess the consequences of our intervention." In Chapter Five Sonia
and Paul Abels examine competency-based education and compare
it with an alternative approach to the development of competent
practitioners—an approach based on "moral reasoning" as developed by Lawrence Kohlberg. Chapter Six by Claude Wiegand
describes six general categories of social competence that are offered
as a framework for education and practice in this helping profession. The components of competence in the form of identifiable
problem-solving skills could serve as a foundation for the competencies required for generalist practice. In Chapter Seven Betty L.
Baer describes a process aimed at identifying basic content for the
educational preparation of social workers. The resultant list of
competencies for entry-level workers constitutes an important step
in developing a coherent and systematic curriculum for professional
education in social work.

In Part Three, "Assessment Issues," Martin Bloom in Chapter Eight advocates the teaching of skills and competencies that will allow practitioners to measure the process and outcome of practice. Bloom offers for consideration a model of practice evaluation— namely, the single-system design—that focuses on objective outcome measures "that impinge on the *strategy of practice* itself. Thus, both ends and means of practice are included directly in these evaluative designs." David E. Cummins in Chapter Nine critiques the construct of competence from a research perspective and illustrates the fact that social work currently is working with imprecise measures of complex human phenomena: "We must avoid the promiscuous use of the phrase *social work competence* until we have a better idea of what we mean by it."

Part Four, "Linking Field Performance and Curriculum Design," analyzes methodologies to make training in professional schools responsive to actual field practice. In Chapter Ten, using a task analysis framework, Robert J. Teare provides an objective and detailed look at tasks of human services workers employed in public welfare. His analysis is based on objective data and contains a unique description of the current dimensions of public welfare practice. Teare's research provides an unusual contribution to the field because it objectively captures those practice dimensions appearing to constitute public welfare practice. Such data provide a basis for objective analysis of practice competencies by clear specification of practice in one setting and are "designed to bridge a gap that exists between practice theory and job design." In Chapter Eleven Michael J. Austin describes a system for studying the competencies of generalist practice and how functionally derived worker tasks can be used in curriculum building. As Austin notes, "The concepts of tasks, roles, and functions reflect a beginning attempt to locate categories of common meaning and areas for collaboration." His contribution provides a curriculum development model that utilizes information regarding actual worker tasks and identifies the need for developmental research in this area.

In Part Five, "Generalist Skills," B. Jeanne Mueller and Constance E. Shapiro in Chapter Twelve present a detailed description of the generalist approach to the role of case manager. They include a description of a baccalaureate-level educational program and a detailed discussion of teaching methods and related procedures used to evaluate the competency of student social workers. Katharine Hooper Briar in Chapter Thirteen describes the instructional tools that she has used in teaching interviewing to undergraduate social work majors (tools such as self-observation via video playback, role playing, and cognitive rehearsal) to help them acquire competence in interpersonal skills. Charles Zastrow and Ralph Navarre, in Chapter Fourteen, offer a method of assessing and developing social work competence. The competence criterion they selected is "the ability to counsel and relate to people." The approach they employed uses videotaped role playing as the principal method of developing and assessing counseling skills. A sophisticated method for training and assessing interviewing skills is provided by David Katz in Chapter Fifteen. He illustrates one means by which a laboratory approach to interviewing can serve the needs of competency-based education and empirical investigations regarding the dimension of the competence.

In Part Six, "Specialist Skills," Jean M. Kruzich in Chapter Sixteen describes the specialized competencies required for practice in the role of human services administrator. She describes the tasks of administrators in a public welfare setting and relates those tasks to the development of specialized practice competencies. Chapter Seventeen also is based on an analysis of data concerning administrators. Robert W. McClelland and Carol D. Austin specify general administrative competencies and describe a method used to assess them. They relate the findings to social work practice and education. Another range of specialized competencies is presented by Joan B. Jones and Susan C. Richards in Chapter Eighteen. They describe the development of a program designed to train BSW-level social workers in the specialized skills of financial counseling. Eleven major competencies essential to money management are identified and related to social work education.

Part Seven, "Competence in New Organizational Settings," emphasizes the fact that contexts such as culture, political dynamics, and economics play a part in defining social work competence. In Chapter Nineteen Peter Hookey reviews the development of generalist human services agencies in England, the Netherlands, Sweden, and the United States. He describes the integration of social work agencies with other professions and the resulting non-specialized, multidisciplinary human services agencies. He then assesses the implications of service integration for education, pointing out that "integrated service generalists need to be prepared to function as creative conceptualizers and planners of various forms of integrated service networks."

The authors whose original works are contained in this volume challenge the reader to consider the processes of competence specification and empirical investigation as developing movements within the profession. We have invited points of view divergent in scope, theoretical orientation, and methodology to stimulate inquiry and debate and thereby enrich the further development of competence in social work.

Acknowledgments

We wish to acknowledge the valuable contributions of the many persons who assisted in the development and production of this volume. At the outset, Fern Berryman and Gerry Shannon were instrumental in helping us prepare for and staff the Big Sky Summer Symposium, from which this book evolved. Their commitment, energy, and uncommon sense have not been forgotten.

To members of the University of Montana Department of Social Work we extend thanks for their assistance with the symposium.

Lynne Holder and Pat Washburn typed the final manuscript. We appreciate their competence and perseverance.

One person associated with this collection was irreplaceable. Genie Brier, of the University of Montana, edited the manuscript. Completion of the lengthy project demanded extensive after-hours' work. In addition to clarifying what was written, she kept us organized and on schedule. We are grateful.

Missoula, Montana   FRANK W. CLARK
February 1979   MORTON L. ARKAVA

Contents

Part Two: Improving Practitioner Performance

Part Three: Assessment Issues

Part Four: Linking Field Performance and Curriculum
Design

The Authors

FRANK W. CLARK, Ph.D., is professor, Department of Social Work, University of Montana, where he teaches basic helping skills and social work methods for individuals and families.

Clark received his A.B. degree from Whitworth College in 1961 and his M.S. and Ph.D. degrees from the University of Oregon in 1965 and 1968, respectively. His professional interests include competency-based education in social work, practice with individuals and families, social policy and mental health, behavior modification, and human sexuality. He is a frequent consultant to faculties and organizations on curriculum renewal, competency-based education, and objective settings. Currently he is regional chairperson of the American Association of Sex Educators, Counselors, and Therapists and has served as editorial board member of the Banff International Conferences on Behavior Modification (1970–1974). He founded and organized the Big Sky Summer Symposium Series.

He and his wife, Lana Clark, have three children—Chris, Matt, and Leah. He enjoys racquetball, hiking, and skiing, alternated with music and quiet contemplation.

MORTON L. ARKAVA, Ph.D., is chairman and professor, Department of Social Work, University of Montana.

Arkava received his A.B. and M.S.W. degrees from the University of Connecticut in 1960 and 1962, respectively, and his Ph.D. degree from the University of Wyoming in 1967. He also attended Washington University for advanced study in social work research. His professional activities have included board membership on the Council on Social Work Education (1971–1975) and membership on the Undergraduate Standards Committee of the Council on Social Work Education (1970–1974). He has written books on competency-based education, behavior modification, and psychological testing and has published numerous research articles on assessment in social work and foster care.

Arkava is married to Leone Wicks and has two children, Linda and Diane. His leisure-time interests include running, hiking, and hunting.

PAUL ABELS, Ph.D., is professor, School of Applied Social Sciences, Case Western Reserve University.

SONIA LEIB ABELS, M.S.W., M.A., is associate professor, Department of Social Sciences, Cleveland State University.

CAROL D. AUSTIN, Ph.D., is instructor and project associate, School of Social Work, University of Wisconsin at Madison.

MICHAEL J. AUSTIN, Ph.D., is professor, School of Social Work, University of Washington.

BETTY L. BAER, M.S.S., is associate professor, School of Social Work, West Virginia University.

MARTIN BLOOM, Ph.D., is professor, School of Social Work, Virginia Commonwealth University.

KATHARINE HOOPER BRIAR, D.S.W., is assistant professor, Department of Sociology, Anthropology, and Social Welfare, Pacific Lutheran University.

SCOTT BRIAR, D.S.W., is dean and professor, School of Social Work, University of Washington.

HARRY BUTLER, Ph.D., A.C.S.W., is dean and associate professor, School of Social Work, San Diego State University.

WINIFRED MORPHEW CHAMBERS, Ph.D., is a free-lance philosopher of science for Video Learning, Inc., San Diego, California.

DAVID E. CUMMINS, Ph.D., is assistant professor, Department of Social Work, University of Montana.

PETER HOOKEY, Ph.D., is assistant professor, School of Social Work, University of Illinois at Urbana-Champaign.

CHARLES R. HOREJSI, D.S.W., is professor, Department of Social Work, University of Montana.

JOAN M. JONES, D.S.W., is assistant professor, School of Social Welfare, University of Wisconsin at Milwaukee.

DAVID KATZ, Ph.D., is associate professor, George Warren Brown School of Social Work, Washington University.

JEAN M. KRUZICH, M.S.W., M.P.A., is project director, Social Welfare Administration Project, School of Social Work, University of Minnesota at Minneapolis.

ROBERT W. McCLELLAND, M.S.W., M.P.H., is clinical assistant professor, School of Social Work, University of Wisconsin at Madison.

B. JEANNE MUELLER, Ph.D., A.C.S.W., is professor, College of Human Ecology, Cornell University.

RALPH NAVARRE, M.A., M.S.W., A.C.S.W., is assistant professor, Department of Social Welfare, University of Wisconsin at Whitewater.

SUSAN C. RICHARDS, M.S., is lecturer, School of Social Welfare, University of Wisconsin at Milwaukee.

CONSTANCE H. SHAPIRO, Ph.D., A.C.S.W., is instructor, College of Human Ecology, Cornell University.

HARRY SPECHT, Ph.D., is dean and professor, School of Social Welfare, University of California at Berkeley.

ROBERT J. TEARE, Ph.D., is director of research, School of Social Work, University of Alabama at Tuscaloosa.

CLAUDE F. WIEGAND, M.S.W., is associate professor, Faculty of Social Work, University of Regina.

CHARLES ZASTROW, Ph.D., is associate professor, Department of Social Welfare, University of Wisconsin at Whitewater.

The Pursuit
of Competence
in Social Work

*Contemporary Issues
in the Definition, Assessment,
and Improvement of Effectiveness
in the Human Services*

I 𝕏

Generalist and Specialist Approaches to Practice and a New Educational Model

Harry Specht

𝕏𝕏𝕏𝕏𝕏𝕏𝕏𝕏𝕏𝕏𝕏𝕏𝕏𝕏𝕏𝕏𝕏𝕏𝕏𝕏𝕏𝕏𝕏𝕏

The generalist approach to social work practice provides an appropriate and useful orientation for an *introductory* education for the profession. With this professional orientation, students can be given a beginning knowledge about practice for direct and indirect services, some skill training in its application, and information about social welfare policies and programs. Following achievement of competence at this level, professional development should focus on specialized elements in practice: *in-depth knowledge and skill* in regard to human growth and development, social welfare policy, methods of practice, and research in social work and social welfare. At an advanced level, education for the profession should develop

Note: I would like to express appreciation to Neil Gilbert and Henry Miller for their helpful comments, suggestions, and ideas for this chapter.

1

competence at *synthesis and development of knowledge* for the profession. At this stage, knowledge and skill are general.

These comments will be expanded in the concluding section of this chapter. It will be useful, though, to explain first how this particular conception of professional education is related to earlier models and other current conceptions of social work education.

Early Conceptions of Practice

The origins of the profession of social work lie in the late nineteenth century, with nurses, settlement workers, and the "friendly visitors" of the Charity Organization Societies—mostly middle- and upper-class young women who engaged in charitable activities to help lower-class people. These activities evolved into what has become known as social work. Because these activities usually were ancillary to the work of other professionals, carried out in well-established institutions such as schools, hospitals, and charitable societies, early social work actually was a collection of subprofessional specializations (Bartlett, 1970, pp. 20–36). These origins laid the basis for the organization of the profession up through the 1940s. During most of that period, social work was organized along functional area lines, which became known as fields of practice, and most social work training and professional organizations followed suit. Thus, by the 1920s there were five fields of practice: family, child welfare, medical, psychiatric, and school social work. Social group work and leisure-time services, community organization, corrections, and public assistance were added in later years (Bartlett, 1970).

Mary Richmond was the first person to formulate these activities in a systematic fashion. Her books *Social Diagnosis* (1917) and *What Is Social Casework?* (1922) represent landmarks in the literature of "scientific helping." "Social diagnosis," she said, is "the attempt to make as exact a definition as possible of the situation and personality of a human being in some social need—of his situation and personality, that is, in relation to the other human beings upon whom he in any way depends or who depend upon him, and in relation to the social institutions of his community" (Richmond, 1917, p. 357). Richmond's definition of social diagnosis presents a conception of social work practice that is as useful today as it was at the beginning of the century. Interestingly, she preferred the words *social treatment* over *social casework,* and the former was the term of choice of many social workers until the 1920s (Richmond, 1930b). *Social treatment* carried with it a much broader conception of the target of social work action than the term *social casework,* because it placed the focus on the person and the situation rather than on the case alone. Her conception of the "situation and personality of a human being in some social need" required an understanding of the client and his family, friends, relatives, work situation, and community social agencies.

Richmond's work is not theoretical in a technical sense; it is more of a how-to-do-it guide. But in those early years of the profession, no one else had put together these thoughts in one volume. Her rationalization of social treatment was part of a general movement in philanthropic work. She lived in the age of developing rationalization in industry; only a few years before she wrote her books, Henry Ford had organized the first industrial assembly line. It was not surprising, then, that the philanthropic organizations (financed largely by the great philanthropists of business and industry) would support the development of systematic and rational methods of handling charitable activities. At the same time as the publication of Richmond's books, the community chest and council-of-social-agencies movements were taking shape, reflecting in the donation to charitable funds the same motive force at work in the rationalization of social casework (Gilbert and Specht, 1977b).

The theoretical underpinnings of late nineteenth- and early twentieth-century social work were largely unarticulated. Major ideas came from scientists like Charles Darwin and Herbert Spencer; physicians like Benjamin Rush, Emil Kraepelin, and Henry Meyer; and political scientists like Adam Smith and Robert La Follette. The vision of society that underlay philanthropic activity was one in which the fortunes of mankind were determined largely by physical and biological forces that a benevolent and enlightened upper class could attempt to control by social engineering, using many of the new tools of science that were emerging rapidly in that day. The science of eugenics and the newly developing sciences of society—such as sociology, anthropology, and psychology—were of great interest to social workers of those days. Like the developments taking place in industry, these sciences were preoccupied with mechanics; the social sciences were based essentially on the philosophical assumptions that underlay the more fixed social class structure of the times, a structure in which the responsibility for helping "the poor"—that is, the majority of society—lay with the upper classes.

In the late 1920s, an explicit theory of human behavior, mostly Freudian, was integrated into social work thinking as a means of explaining and directing practice. This was a daring and innovative step, because Freudian theory was neither popular nor widely understood. It gave social casework a basis for understanding and interpreting human responses to social forces that theretofore had been lacking in the profession. Freudian and other psychologically based theories were the first theoretical systems used by social workers; and, regardless of the limits of these kinds of theories, they provided a powerful knowledge base for the development of professional practice.

Another significant stream of activity in the development of social work and social welfare was the work of the social settlements. Settlement leaders like Jane Addams and Florence Kelley were more interested in social reform and social legislation than in charity and scientific helping. In a sense, their methods of work were unscientific because they required immersion in the community rather than objectivity; they lived with and experienced with their clients, and they were somewhat put off by the detachment and cautiousness that professionalism appeared to generate. Not until the 1930s and 1940s, when social group work methods and community organization practice were incorporated into social work, were the settlements absorbed into the community of social work agencies, because these new methods were more compatible with the existential here-and-now orientation of the settlements.

The first formal training for social work began at the end of the nineteenth century as in-service training for groups such as the Charity Organization Societies. Training programs in colleges and universities were introduced at the beginning of the twentieth century. All this early training essentially was education for social casework (Lubove, 1965).

Although Richmond's work had laid the basis for a generic

form of social casework practice, professional education for the fields of practice continued into the 1940s. The notion underlying generic casework is that there are basic concepts that all social work practitioners use.* This idea represented a step forward in social work because it meant that the profession was not merely a series of adjunctive activities carried on in separate institutions such as schools and hospitals. Rather, certain *general* principles and concepts of helping could be applied across institutional areas. Generic practice, therefore, was an increment to the developing body of social work knowledge. This body of knowledge, in the 1920s, consisted largely of the principles and methods described by people like Richmond (1917) and Cannon (1951) and Freudian-type theory as interpreted by people like Marcus (1929), Towle (1931), and Robinson (1930).

Along with development of ideas about generic social casework practice and the introduction of explicit theory, two new specializations developed in social work in the 1930s and 1940s: social group work and community organization. These specializations were based in theoretical and philosophical systems of thought different from those of social casework. Social group work was rooted in the philosophy of John Dewey and associated with schools of progressive education. It was concerned largely with how social groups (that is, family, peer groups, social clubs, and community groups) affect socialization and social development. Social group workers like Coyle (1948) and Wilson and Ryland (1949) brought to the field of social work an interest in the capacity of the social group to support individuals and solve social problems. They were more interested in education for citizenship and development of social capacities than in treatment of social illness (Papell and Rothman, 1966). Community organization was not concerned with the kinds of therapeutic interventions undertaken by social caseworkers. It came into social work more as a function than a professional practice. That is, the community chests and councils of social agencies (which constituted the major part of the field of com-

---

* The notion of a generic casework was introduced formally to the profession by the report of the Milford Conference in 1929. The Milford Conference was a consortium of social workers who had begun in 1923 to discuss social work practice (American Association of Social Workers, 1929).

munity organization up to the 1950s) were the fund-raising and
fund-distributing subsystem of the field of social welfare, concerned
primarily with philanthropic fund raising for voluntary agencies
(Gilbert and Specht, 1977b). In these early years, social group
workers and community organizers tried to make their modes of
practice look as much as possible like social casework, the predominant mode of practice in the field. Thus, social group work
gradually became more clinical and less focused on citizenship training and community action; and much of the literature on community organization described it as a social work method concerned
predominantly with "intergroup work" processes and development
of healthy social relationships (Gilbert and Specht, 1977b).

The Depression of the 1930s had a great impact on the institution of social welfare. The Social Security Act of 1935 marked
the entry of the federal government into the social welfare field on a
large scale. Since that time, government has become the major
source of support for social welfare and social service programs of all
kinds. The immediate effect of this shift in sources of support for
social welfare was to nudge the profession in the direction of more
clinical types of work and away from serving poor and disadvantaged populations. As the federal government assumed primary
responsibility for income maintenance programs for the poor, the
voluntary agencies, which hired most of the professional social
workers, shifted their focus to other types of social services, such as
family counseling and leisure-time services. This, too, was a period
in which social workers were extremely concerned about profes-
sionalization; the clinically oriented types of services were particularly attractive because of the more clearly developed and high-
status technologies available in the medical and psychiatric fields.

In the 1930s and 1940s, there was no broad public acceptance of the psychotherapeutic arts of social caseworkers or of some
of the ideas borrowed from progressive education by social group
workers. A beachhead for the ideas of Freud, Horney, and Dewey
had been established in the middle-class intellectual and artistic
communities; by and large, however, these were not popular treat-
ments. Most people did not seek them out, and there was no basis
on which to build support for them in programs serving the masses.
Some social workers did work in public assistance programs at that

time, but the majority of "professionals" (that is, MSWs) did not. Psychiatric social work was where it was at for most social workers in the 1930s and 1940s. In terms of status and prestige, after psychiatric social work came child welfare and medical social work.

The disengagement of most professional social workers from the poor may be somewhat difficult to understand from the perspective of the late twentieth century. Today it is fairly well established that income support, social services, and psychotherapy are necessary and useful to all social classes in the community. But at the beginning of the century, income support services and social treatment were something that the upper class provided for the "worthy" poor, based on sentiments of *noblesse oblige* and the sanctity of charitable giving. Psychotherapy, for the most part, was for the rich only.

When income support types of philanthropy were taken over by government, and the private agencies moved into psychosociotherapeutic types of work, questions about social class bias in the social services simply were not raised. The concept of social class in American life was first studied by sociologists in the 1930s. The term *social class* entered professional vocabularies in the 1940s; it was not until the 1950s, with the publication of Hunter's (1953) *Community Power Structure,* that ideas about differential distributions of social resources and power became an issue for professional discussion and action by social workers, city planners, sociologists, political scientists, and other professionals and academics. Alinsky (1946), writing in the 1940s, was an exception, but his ideas did not achieve currency in the professions until the 1960s.

For all these reasons, professional social work in the 1930s and 1940s drifted in the direction of clinical treatment and psychosociotherapeutic types of work, and most social work professionals were employed in agencies that did not serve the neediest population groups.

By the 1940s social casework, social group work, and community organization had become the three major specializations in social work, with social casework by far the largest. At that time, a person considering a career in social work was confronted with a much simpler set of choices than those existing today. A "professional social worker" was a person with an MSW degree, and the majority of MSWs were social caseworkers who worked in clinically oriented settings. A smaller number were social group workers, most of whom worked in leisure-time agencies such as settlement houses, community centers, and youth services. A small group was in community organization and was composed predominantly of older, "seasoned," male professionals who usually worked for community chests and health and welfare councils.

These divisions were reflected in the several professional organizations of social workers. The American Association of Social Workers, organized in 1921 and composed principally of caseworkers, was the largest professional organization. The American Association of Group Workers, organized in 1936, was a smaller fledgling organization for social group workers. The Association for the Study of Community Organization, established in 1946, was a comparatively informal group. (Community organization was recognized by the Council on Social Work Education as a legitimate specialization in social work education only in 1962. Until then, students could take courses in community organization, but they would have had to be trained first in social casework or social group work.)

In 1955 the different social work organizations (seven in all) combined to form the National Association of Social Workers (NASW), a clear indication that the social casework–social group work–community organization trinity in social work was not to remain for long the pattern of organization of the profession. Even so, the specialization of social casework appears to be a viable entity today. The *Social Casework* journal still is considered an important one in the field, and, despite the unification of professional social workers in NASW, societies of clinical social work for social workers in private practice are growing in size and influence. There is now a National Federation of Societies of Clinical Social Work, which publishes its own journal and engages in other professional activities to promote private practice (Levin, 1976).

Elements of Change in Social Work Practice

The social upheaval of the 1960s—largely a revolution in human rights—brought about significant changes in American society, which in turn effected some changes in social work practice. The civil rights revolution began in 1954, when the United States

Supreme Court declared school segregation unconstitutional. The Warren Court's decision sparked the latent power of the black community and kindled large-scale demonstrations to protest numerous grievances. The movement for blacks' rights to equal access to public facilities and opportunities to jobs and education was supported by many Americans. The sit-ins, marches, civil disobedience, and other forms of nonviolent action in the following years were supported by social workers as professionals and citizens.* The initial successes of the civil rights movement were reflected in the Economic Opportunity Act of 1964, the Civil Rights Act of 1964, and the Elementary and Secondary Education Act of 1965. The legislation enforced constitutional rights to access to public facilities and voting and created programs to increase opportunities for education and jobs for minority groups and other deprived people. However, early results of the civil rights movement left many people frustrated; it was apparent that these programs would not make an immediate impact on the American minorities' source of anger and despair—the ever present existence of *inequality.* By the mid 1960s, public support for nonviolent black protest was submerged by reactions to the violence in communities such as Watts and Detroit and the violent protests on college campuses to the war in Vietnam. After the mid 1960s, the movement for rights extended to other groups in American society, who felt that they, too, bore the burdens of inequality and oppression: American Indians, Spanish-speaking people, women, homosexuals, the aged, welfare clients, prisoners and released offenders, mental patients, students, and others.

During these years of protest, many people—social workers included—cast a critical eye on the profession's contribution to the perpetuation of inequality and racism. All professions were subject to similar scrutiny, but many believed that social work was an especially glaring example of malfeasance, because it represented the failure of what was supposed to be society's means of preventing poverty and discrimination. The greatest grievance against the pro-

---

* In the summer of 1964, the profession was especially shaken by the deaths of three young social workers in Philadelphia, Mississippi. James Chaney, Andrew Goodman, and Michael Schwerner, workers in a voter registration project, were brutally murdered. The Michael Schwerner Memorial Fund, Inc., organized by social worker in their memory, continued in this work (Kurzman, 1971).

fession was the clinical/therapeutic orientation, which was perceived to be society's way of blaming the victim, of putting the burden for social problems on the people who suffered from inequality, rather than eliminating the causes of inequality. The profession's response to this critique generally was to acknowledge its failures and reaffirm earlier commitments. In particular, attention was given to the social work function of advocacy, which spoke to the profession's responsibility to support clients' rights to dignified and humane treatment (Ad Hoc Committee on Advocacy, 1969). Increased social work resources were devoted to social action; and, with support from the economic opportunity programs, many social agencies devoted greater attention to community organization, development of consumer groups, support for increased citizen participation in policymaking, development of community care to replace institutional care, and other social change activities. These efforts expanded the profession's involvement in social welfare programs that were closer to the person-in-the-situation conception of practice described by Richmond than to a classical therapeutic approach.

The renewed interest in the advocacy function was accompanied by a new articulation of professionalism in social work. In this view, adherence to *professional* standards and ethics, as distinct from the concerns of an employing agency, is necessary if services provided are to be in a client's best interests. From the advocacy perspective, the job of the social worker is to help clients utilize the systems around them to their best advantage. Briar (1967, p. 32) expressed this view: "The advocate . . . function requires that caseworkers have much greater *professional* [emphasis added] autonomy and discretion than now prevail in many, if not most, social agencies. Ninety percent or more of all caseworkers practice in bureaucratic organizations, and the demands of such organizations have a tendency to encroach on professional autonomy. Every attempt by the agency to routinize some condition or aspect of professional practice amounts to a restriction of professional discretion, and for that reason probably should be resisted, in most instances, by practitioners." This increased attention to social reform and social change enhanced the profession's concern for the institution of social welfare, which, in the view of some, had been neglected too long by social workers (Gilbert and Specht, 1974).

Reform of the profession itself also was needed to counteract what many considered to be the elitism of the MSW as the sine qua non of professionalism. Social work became the spearhead of the "new careers" movement for paraprofessionals (Brager, 1965). The essential thought behind this movement is that the attributes of professionalism are not attained only through formal education. People learn from life experience with such problems as poverty and racism; some poor and disadvantaged people in the populations served have qualities that many professionals, because of their middle-class origins and life-styles, do not have. NASW gave formal recognition to the profession's rejection of elitism in 1971, when requirements for membership in the association were changed to allow full membership to BSWs; in addition, anyone doing social work with any kind of baccalaureate degree qualifies for associate membership.

Members of the profession were not of one mind about these changes. Some believed that the elements in the "new" social work represented *deprofessionalization* because they downgraded professional knowledge and skill. The new professionalism, in this view, encouraged professionals to be too political, freeing them to pursue their social and political interests regardless of the particular needs of a specific client (Specht, 1972). The concern expressed here is that the rights of clients are jeopardized when the ethical base of the profession is undermined (Gilbert and Specht, 1976).

Developments in civil rights pressed social work to move in new directions, and the explosion of social science knowledge in mid-century created several directions in which to move. Sociology, psychology, anthropology, political science, and economics are the primary theoretical disciplines useful in social work practice. Many universities began doctoral programs in social work and social welfare, increasing the profession's capacity for synthesizing theory for practice from the disciplines and generating its own theory for practice.

In the 1970s the course chosen in social work education was to allow "a thousand flowers to bloom." Essentially, the field moved in many directions at once (Pins, 1971). At a time of great ferment and strain in society, it was not likely that any single course of action could be approved by all. Schools of social work organized training in many ways. Some maintained the sturdy trinity of the 1940s;

some became generalist, training social workers to utilize all methods to solve problems. Other schools organized programs of training to focus on special problems and population groups (for example, the aged, community mental health, the black community, poverty). And some developed their programs by dividing the field into what appeared to be two distinctive streams: direct and indirect services, or a clinical track and a social change track.

Current Models of Social Work Practice

Do models make a difference? That is, does a particular conception of practice determine how a professional will deal with a problem? This is an important question for students, who invest a great deal in their education and who have every right to wonder whether discussion of models is of practical use or merely an academic exercise. And, if it is of practical use, they will want to know how to choose the best model. A thoughtful response to the question must be somewhat equivocal: models make *some* difference.

Currently, there are several models of social work practice. Each attempts to deal with the duality of social work in a different way. This duality refers to the two components of the profession's concern: providing direct services to people in need, and managing the institution of social welfare. The duality of the profession and how to deal with it has been a recurrent theme in the literature throughout the profession's history. Variations on this theme include the following: In 1905 Richmond (1917) wrote of the "wholesale" and "retail" methods of social reform; probably the best-known and most enduring variation was composed by Lee (1937) under the title of "cause" and "function"; Burns (1958) wrote about the distinction between "social work" and "social welfare"; Schwartz (1963) discussed the "service" and the "movement"; Richan (1972) identified different underlying language systems in social work; and Gilbert and Specht (1974), declaring the profession to be "incomplete," called for a more balanced and integrated approach to the profession's two sides, "social work" and "social welfare."

The following paragraph is the introduction to a case reported by a social worker at Mobilization for Youth (MFY), an agency organized to provide comprehensive social services to a community on the Lower East Side of New York City:

> Mrs. Smith came to an MFY Neighborhood Service Center to complain that there had been no gas, electricity, heat, or hot water in her apartment house for more than four weeks. She asked the agency for help. Mrs. Smith was twenty-three-years-old, Negro, and the mother of four children, three of whom had been born out of wedlock. At the time, she was unmarried and receiving Aid to Families with Dependent Children. She came to the center in desperation because she was unable to run her household without utilities. Her financial resources were exhausted [Purcell and Specht, 1965, p. 10].

How would different models of social work practice affect a worker's way of helping Mrs. Smith?

If the traditional model of practice were used, the outcome of Mrs. Smith's request for help would depend on which department she had gone to at MFY. Since she had come into the Neighborhood Service Center, which was staffed by caseworkers, the worker (largely through interaction with Mrs. Smith in a series of interviews) would try to help her use her resources to deal with her situation. An advocacy-oriented social caseworker would help Mrs. Smith deal with the institutions that were affecting her situation. Had Mrs. Smith turned up at one of the many group work agencies in the community, the worker probably would have sought to help her through the relevant social group of which she was a part—the tenants who lived in the same apartment house, all of whom were experiencing some of the same problems. And if Mrs. Smith had gone to one of the several community organization agencies on the Lower East Side, the workers there probably would have focused on the agencies and institutions that were part of this problem: the housing agencies, the health department, the welfare department, and so forth.

Why do social workers in different agencies respond so differently? First of all, the workers are not necessarily perceiving the problem differently; rather, there may be any number of problems operating in this situation. Mrs. Smith does need help. To determine what kind of help she needs will require some exploration. Perhaps this woman is in this situation because she is emotionally over-whelmed with her family responsibilities; therefore, intensive coun-seling might be indicated. Or interventions that focus on Mrs. Smith as an individual may be inappropriate. Possibly her problem is not unique; rather, she may be one member of a group of people in the same predicament because they share the same social-emotional problems. Perhaps they are vulnerable young women who are ex-ploited by men and might profit from an opportunity to explore their social-emotional experiences and provide strength to one an-other to change. Or perhaps the economics of housing and the regu-lations of the housing and welfare agencies may have forced Mrs. Smith into this situation. Perhaps the laws and/or the ways in which social agencies function ought to be changed. If that is so, Mrs. Smith and her fellow tenants ought not to be bothered with coun-seling, group work, or any other kind of intervention that stops short of institutional change.

Another reason why different social workers might respond differently to Mrs. Smith's problems is much simpler to state. Mrs. Smith may be searching for a particular *kind* of help. She may want some sort of therapeutic counseling so that she can change. Or she may want some help that enables her, along with her fellow tenants, to try to change some of the elements external to her situation. She may not be interested in changing herself or in being involved in changing other institutions. Perhaps she is interested only in bring-ing her *situation* to the attention of the agency, in the hope that some way can be found to make her life more bearable by changing laws and agency regulations. Thus, *what the client wants is variable.* Part of a social worker's job is to understand what the client wants, for we can help people do only what *they* want to do.

Finally, social welfare agencies are organized to offer differ-ent kinds of help to people with problems. Whether the agency is public or voluntary, it will have written in law or in the bylaws of the agency a "charge" that will direct and limit the services the pro-fessional can offer. Thus, one agency is charged to offer counseling services, another to offer group services, and still another to engage in social planning.

The strongest argument for the traditional approach is that social workers trained in one of these three specializations acquire an in-depth knowledge about one kind of practice that they can deliver with a high degree of skill. The major argument against this approach is that it is too narrow and tends to develop practitioners who are too clinical, in the sense that they are consumed by their interest in searching out knowledge about the refined details of a specialized form of practice and unable to understand the interacting and complex social forces that create social problems for people.

The generalist approach (sometimes called the "unitary" or "integrated" approach) is based on the view that most social problems involve a variety of social systems.* Whether articulated or not, all generalist approaches are based on social systems theory. With social systems theory, all kinds of social units are conceived of as *systems* subject to the *same* rules or behavior. Any system has an internal organization that comprises subsystems and is related to other systems in its environment. For example, an individual may be conceived of as a system made up of various physical and emotional subsystems. The individual is related to other individual systems and is a subsystem of larger systems such as the family, the social group, and the occupational group. A social group can be viewed as a system comprising individuals and subgroups who constitute its subsystems; it is a subsystem of a larger system such as an organization or the community. For example, the group of tenants mentioned above is a subsystem of the housing system in New York City, and the housing system is a subsystem of the entire ecopolitical system of New York City. Of course, there is more to systems theory than this brief summary statement suggests. It is a complex theory that developed in the physical sciences and later was applied to the social sciences (Bartlett, 1970; Goldstein, 1973; Pincus and Minahan, 1973). The interested reader may want to consult Churchman's (1968) *The Systems Approach* for a more detailed and nontechnical explanation or Emery's (1969) *Systems Theory Thinking* for some of the technical aspects.

* Generic practice had reference only to social casework. It established basic underlying principles for casework practice regardless of the functional area involved. The generalist approach establishes basic underlying principles for practice regardless of the size and composition of the client system; that is, regardless of whether the client is an individual, a family, an organization, or a community.

In the case of Mrs. Smith, the MFY workers used the generalist approach to the problem. As they stated it:

> Too often, the client system presenting the problem becomes the major target for intervention, and the intervention method is limited to the one most suitable for that client system. However, Mrs. Smith and the other tenants had a multitude of problems emanating from many sources, any one of which would have warranted the attention of a social agency. . . . MFY's approach to the problem was to obtain knowledge of the various social systems within which the social problem was located (that is, social systems assessment); knowledge of the various methods (including non-social work methods) appropriate for intervention in these different social systems; and knowledge of the resources available to the agency.

> The difficulties of the families in the building were intricately connected with other elements of the social system related to the housing problem. For example, seven different public agencies were involved in maintenance of building services. Later, other agencies were involved in relocating the tenants. There is no one agency in New York City that handles all housing problems. Therefore, tenants have little hope of getting help on their own. In order to redress a grievance relating to water supply (which was only one of the building's problems) it is necessary to know precisely which city department to contact. The following is only a partial listing:

> No water—Health Department
> Not enough water—Department of Water Supply
> No hot water—Buildings Department
> Water leaks—Buildings Department
> Large water leaks—Department of Water Supply
> Water overflowing from apartment above—Police
>   Department
> Water sewage in the cellar—Sanitation Department

[Purcell and Specht, 1965, p. 72].

Systems theory provides a good orienting perspective for social workers. However, once this dynamic perspective is adopted, systems theory does not provide specific enough guidelines for professional practice. At a high level of generalization, we can think of all organisms (for example, individuals, groups, organizations) as systems. But in practice, individual systems are considerably different from group systems, and each of these is different from organizational and political systems. More middle-range kinds of theories are necessary for day-to-day practice with each of these systems.

The generalist approach does not provide sufficient instruction about which parts of the person and the environment the worker should attend to first. This is a very important question for social workers, who usually work in agencies in which resources are limited. Also, the generalist approach, in attempting to cull common elements of all practice, ascends to conceptual levels that obscure real and important differences. For example, broadly speaking, it may be correct to say that all social workers require knowledge and skills in data collection and assessment. But the data collection skills of the social worker conducting a community-needs survey bear only faint resemblance to those of the caseworker attempting to assess the personal difficulties of individual clients. And though the MFY approach was generalist, the actual help that was given to Mrs. Smith, the other families, and the community was provided by a number of specialists—caseworkers, group workers, and community organizers (Purcell and Specht, 1965). Thus, the major utility of social systems theory, as stated earlier, is that it provided an orienting perspective for the professionals, leading them to achieve a higher degree of coordination in their efforts than otherwise would have been the case.

The problem and population-group approaches to practice are somewhat like the generalist approach, but they call for specialization along functional area lines. With this kind of approach, the attention of practitioners is focused on a specific problem, such as community mental health, or a specific population group, such as the aged; and practitioners' attempt to see the *whole* experience and the *entire* social environment in which these problems and population groups exist. Thus, in work with the aged, the social worker must be able to deal with the developmental problems of aging persons, have skill in utilizing therapeutic modes of working with individuals and groups, and use community organization methods to change institutional practices. This approach presents the segmentation of effort that occurs in methodological specializations; at the same time, it allows for an in-depth development of knowledge and skill in respect to the clients served. If this approach had been used in the case of Mrs. Smith, the "ideal" social work professional would be an expert on problems of housing: housing agencies; the economics of housing; the various groups confronting housing problems; the social-psychological aspects of relocation, redevelopment, and urban renewal; and so forth.

While we should not hold too strong a brief against this kind of specialization, neither is there sufficient basis for seeing it as a major organizing principle by which to educate students for the profession. One reservation is that most concerns of social workers are not bounded clearly by populations or problems. Aged people, minority groups, and children have many similar problems—income maintenance, housing, employment, and so forth; and these problems are not all that different for each group. Furthermore, an individual's social problems—such as housing, employment, and family relations—usually are not discrete. Populations that have any one of these problems frequently suffer from a host of associated problems.

Another shortcoming of this approach is that it locks students into a specialization too early in a professional career. Specializations in practice should be selected only after the student attains a broad understanding of the field of social work and social welfare. In addition, this is a questionable approach to career development even from the long-range view. Social problems and population groups are not static. As noted earlier, over the last twenty years social work and social welfare have changed in response to changes in the larger society. A good professional is one who questions given truths, tests new ideas, and has a demonstrated capacity to change and grow rather than one who has a fixed approach and a static view of society. For these reasons, we tend not to favor specializations that are too narrow.

Another model of social work practice—the model supported in this chapter—divides that practice into direct and indirect services. Direct services are the specific and concrete activities in which professionals engage to help those who are experiencing social problems. These activities include therapy, counseling, education, advocacy, information gathering, referral, and those aspects of community organization in which direct services are provided to community groups and organizations. Indirect services focus on the institution of social welfare. Included here are professional social work activities such as planning, policy analysis, program development, administration, and program evaluation. The social worker engaged in provision of indirect services usually does not deal directly with people in need but, rather, focuses on the institutional structure through which services are provided. If the social workers in the MFY example of Mrs. Smith had utilized the direct- and indirect-services approach, one or more of the workers in the agency probably would have been prepared to provide the services needed to work directly with Mrs. Smith and the other tenants. (These professionals would have a mastery of knowledge and skill dealing with the dynamics of interpersonal relationships.) And one or more of the workers would have had the knowledge and skill for indirect work, such as research on housing, analysis of the organizational and legislative arrangements that caused the problems, and planning policies and programs to prevent similar situations. (These practitioners would have knowledge and skill related to organizational and political systems and technical abilities for managing, manipulating, and analyzing large amounts of information.)

In summary, the traditional casework–group work–community organization approach prematurely splits interactional knowledge into three specializations and does not establish for the student a sufficient basis for development of technical knowledge and skill for planning, administration, and policy analysis. In contrast, the generalist approach and the problem and population-group approaches require that the practitioner be able to deal with direct- and indirect-service tasks equally well—which, in my view, demands too much of the practitioner. Systems theory, it seems to me, does not provide knowledge that is specific enough to do all these tasks. Moreover, the practitioner is likely to become a jack-of-all-trades and master of none. The direct- and indirect-services approach, I believe, avoids both of these pitfalls; further, it provides a logical organization of practice knowledge.

Generalist and Specialist Content
at Different Educational Levels

The various levels of competence in practice and the knowledge elements that should be learned at each of these levels are summarized in Table 1. On the vertical axis, three levels of competence are listed: (1) *orientation*—the level at which the student

Table 1.   Educational Content for Different Levels of
Competence in Social Work Practice

Competence Level	Types of Educational Content		
	Specific Content for Direct Services	General Content	Specific Content for Indirect Services
1. Orientation: Perspective on social work and social welfare		a. practice for direct and indirect services b. social welfare policies and programs	
2. Development of in-depth knowledge and skill	a. human growth and development b. social welfare policy c. direct-service methods (that is, counseling) d. research (application of)	knowledge about problems and population groups	a. human growth and development b. social welfare policy c. indirect-service methods (that is, social planning, administration) d. research (for program evaluation, needs assessment, policy analysis)
3. Synthesis: Development of knowledge for social work and social welfare		knowledge and skill for research, consultation, teaching and training	

acquires a perspective on the profession of social work and the
institution of social welfare; (2) *development of in-depth knowledge
and skill*—the level at which one acquires somewhat specialized and
focused knowledge for practice; (3) *synthesis*—the level at which
one develops and synthesizes new knowledge for practice. (These
levels of practice are not clearly associated with specific educational
degrees. Schools of social work in the United States vary consider-

ably regarding how much of this content is presented at the under-graduate, graduate, and doctoral levels of education. Most BSW programs would include the teaching of a good deal of material that we have allocated to second-level learning. At most schools, six years are needed to complete the BSW and MSW degrees. A few schools, however, have established five-year programs. It should be remem-bered, too, that there is no reason to assume that people acquire these different levels of proficiency through formal education only. Some persons work their way to higher levels of professional achieve-ment on the job and through independent study.)

The horizontal axis of Table 1 indicates the general content at each level of competence and the content specific to the direct and indirect services at each level. At the first level of competence, two bodies of *general* content should be covered: (a) an introduc-tion to social work practice and (b) an introduction to social welfare policies and programs. (By general content, we mean material that *all* social workers should master at the respective level of compe-tence.) Both of these bodies of content are the congruent elements that link the direct and indirect services of the profession, providing a unified foundation for professional identity. These elements are the institutional context of social welfare, social work's mission within that institution, shared professional values, and a perspec-tive on the broad range of functions carried out by social workers.

At the second level of competence, there are four bodies of *specific* content and one body of *general* content that social workers should master in preparation for work in the direct or indirect ser-vices. The *specific* content includes (a) human growth and develop-ment, (b) social welfare policy, (c) social work methods, and (d) research methods and techniques. One would expect to see differ-ences in the kinds of knowledge included in each of these areas in education for the direct and indirect services, respectively. For ex-ample, knowledge of human growth and development is most use-ful for direct-service practitioners when it illuminates the dynamics of interpersonal interaction. But for indirect-service workers this knowledge is most useful when the worker can apply it in the de-sign, implementation, and evaluation of programs. The sources of this knowledge for both kinds of workers are the same, but the way in which it is packaged and applied is different for each. The *gen-*

eral knowledge area for second-level competence is knowledge about problems and population groups (knowledge that *all* professionals who choose to work in these fields should have). These kindred targets of concern at this level of competence afford another congruent element that binds into one profession social workers in the direct and indirect services. (The four specific areas mentioned are required content areas for all MSW programs accredited by the Council on Social Work Education. "Problems and Population Groups" has not been defined as a separate content area in social work education. These kinds of courses are most likely to be given as electives in the social policy or human growth and development content areas.)

At the third level of competence, the knowledge requirements, for the most part, are *general*. Professionals who will be in the business of synthesizing and developing new knowledge require primarily the development of skills for teaching, consulting with other professionals, and doing research on all the bodies of knowledge described for the first and second levels of competence.

In an ideal model of education for social work practice, skills and knowledge would be organized into circumscribed areas that possess internal coherence and maintain a logical relationship to the whole. To a certain degree, the three-level model of competence outlined above captures these qualities. The first-level general orientation to social work practice and social welfare provides an internal coherence for all other training. These congruent elements cement the relationship of direct and indirect services to the whole of social work practice. This relationship is reinforced by the problem and population-group knowledge at the second level. But the model is not ideal. Conceptually, the congruent elements may contain too much water and not enough gravel to cement the model firmly. And while efforts are under way to define an orienting generic base for the direct and indirect services, the task of developing the elements of these practice specializations in detail is far from complete.

2

Toward Preparation
for Competence in
Social Work Education

Scott Briar

In January 1973 I wrote an editorial called "The Age of Account-ability" for *Social Work*. Soon after that editorial appeared, when-ever I attended professional meetings or conferences, some social workers invariably would give me undeserved and unwanted credit for inventing the issue of accountability and imposing it on social work. (Parenthetically, when I think of some of the undesirable things that have been done in the name of accountability, I some-times wish I did have the power to prevent or impede the progress of the accountability movement in social work.) In reality, of course, the accountability movement was under way long before I commented on it in that editorial, and the demand for it has in-creased in intensity and widened in scope. No area of social work and social welfare activity is immune. Experience since the 1976 presidential election clearly indicates that even an administration strongly committed to social services and social programs nonetheless will place a high priority on accountability, evaluation of effectiveness, and cost containment. As I suggested in my editorial, questions regarding what we do, how effective we are, and whether we cost too much are not easily resolved. But there have been some important changes regarding accountability in the past few years, and I would like to mention a few of them.

One of the most striking changes is in the attitude of the social work profession. The widespread resistance to accountability, especially evaluation of effectiveness, is passing. It has been replaced by an increasing acceptance of the importance of evaluation and research activities for the future development of the profession and recognition of the high priority that consequently must be assigned to such efforts in social work practice and education. This posture—by no means unanimous among social workers—has strong positive implications for the future strength and vitality of the profession. Second, higher education has begun to experience the demand for accountability in most serious ways. Social work programs also have been subjected to these expectations by the colleges and universities of which they are a part and by social work educators who recognize the need to address these issues in the education of their students. Third, disenchantment has set in regarding evaluative research—the mainstay of accountability—because some observers (for example, Weiss, 1972) believe it has failed to produce the answers promised by early advocates. This complaint is partially correct. What evaluation research could accomplish for social programs in a short period was oversold by some enthusiasts; a certain amount of disappointment, therefore, was to be expected. It is premature, however, to draw final conclusions about the utility of evaluation research. For one thing, relatively little evaluation research has been conducted. Yet, the most pessimistic, conservative conclusion that can be drawn regarding its value is a favorable one.

A major source of disillusionment for some has been the realization that evaluation research poses special methodological and conceptual problems. Evaluation is not simply a matter of applying traditional research methods to another problem; rather, it requires new and different methods and tools developed to deal with the special problems inherent in the evaluation task. To cite only one example, in many social services agencies intervention goals are individualized for each client. Consequently, traditional factorial research designs that seek to determine the effects of interventions on groups of clients are inappropriate and misleading, except in those special instances where clients can be grouped by common intervention objectives. (A good example of an appropriate use of a factorial design is Paul's, 1966, comparative analysis of alternative interventions for clients with the common problem of public-speaking anxiety.)

Significant progress toward finding better solutions to methodological problems has been made in several important areas. For example, the application of single-subject research designs, which permit rigorous experimental research on single cases, clearly is a response to the inadequacies of traditional factorial designs for evaluating the effectiveness of direct services. Furthermore, there is growing recognition of the need for *developmental research* (Thomas, 1975), partly in response to fundamental limitations in the evaluation research model. Evaluation research seeks to determine whether a specific program or intervention is, or rather *was,* effective. If the answer is negative—as frequently has been the case —that research has provided little or no information about what alternative interventions might be more effective. Developmental research, in contrast, seeks to discover and develop more effective intervention methods. Thus, whereas evaluation research asks whether a given intervention strategy was effective, developmental research asks what intervention strategy would be most effective. Developmental research is a familiar concept in other applied fields, such as engineering and space technology, where research programs are established to discover and develop needed tools and technologies. Application of this concept in our field, however, has not been attempted systematically until recently.

A particularly intractable problem in evaluation research is defining social work objectives in terms that can be measured without invalidating the meaning of these objectives by atomizing or otherwise distorting them in the process of measurement. Although this is called a measurement problem, it actually is a conceptual problem, because it basically entails explicating and describing the tangible, measurable manifestations that would be evident if a particular intervention objective were achieved. For example, if increased self-realization is the intervention objective, and if this objective is achieved, what changes will be evident in the client's behavior? This kind of specification requires a way of thinking about practice for which many social workers are unprepared. But these skills can be acquired, and even the most vague objectives can be expressed in measurable terms. (For an excellent discussion of the feasibility of preserving the validity and social significance of outcomes objectives while insisting on measurement of outcomes see Wolf, 1978.)

The task of defining and measuring objectives also is a central problem in the development of competency-based education. Assessment of competence in educational programs and practice represents an effort to be accountable by determining whether a practitioner or a student preparing to be a practitioner demonstrates the attributes necessary for effective practice. Competence assessment, therefore, is subject to many of the problems described earlier.

To determine whether a practitioner is competent—whether he or she possesses the attributes to be effective *and,* in fact, is effective—it obviously is necessary first to know what constitutes effective practice. Otherwise, how does one know whether the actions of a practitioner constitute effective—that is, competent—practice? Attempts to solve this problem by relying on the judgment of experienced practitioners clearly are not satisfactory, for how is it to be determined that these experienced practitioners are competent or recognize competence? Yet continued reliance on such judgments is understandable in the absence of feasible alternatives.

The conceptual problem of specifying the indicators of practice competence is particularly acute for educational programs that claim to be competency based. Such programs in social work usually take as their objective the preparation of competent practitioners. Thus, a central question for competency-based education in social work is "What is practice competence in specific, describable terms?" Until this question is answered, all others are secondary, including obviously important ones such as "How do we measure competence?" and "How do we help students acquire it?"

Do we know what practice competence is in social work? The answer depends, of course, on what we mean by "know." If we accept beliefs and assumptions as knowledge, then many social workers would insist categorically that we certainly do know what competence is, even if we cannot describe or measure it. But if we limit the meaning of knowing to practitioner actions that have an empirically demonstrated relationship to effectiveness in helping clients or working with communities, then the answer would have to be yes and no. For example, in regard to the reduction or elimination of acute anxiety reactions such as phobias, specific intervention procedures have been shown repeatedly to be significantly more effective than any known alternative. Consequently, every practitioner who is expected to help clients with such problems should know about these procedures and how to use them effectively. Moreover, it would be comparatively easy to test unambiguously whether a practitioner possesses this particular aspect of competence. By contrast, in the area of family therapy we have almost no empirically tested knowledge about which interventions are effective— with some exceptions, such as certain forms of parent effectiveness training. The list of empirically demonstrated aspects of competence, unfortunately, is shorter than the inventory of practice areas in which we do not have such knowledge.

What are we to do, then, if we cannot define practice competence objectively but want to take that as a central educational objective? First, where there is tested empirical knowledge about the necessary conditions for effectiveness in specific practice areas, there must be assurance that at appropriate levels students will acquire this knowledge and the skills to implement it. (This knowledge also must be made available to practitioners through continuing education.) Second, where tested knowledge is unavailable, we can continue to rely on professional judgments regarding what constitutes competent practice. A preferable alternative, however, is for the faculty and students of educational programs to participate actively in developing intervention methods of tested effectiveness. We have been trying to implement such an approach at the University of Washington School of Social Work.

One of the key components of practice competence within this developmental approach is the acquisition of the knowledge and skills necessary to empirically evaluate the effectiveness of one's practice. All the direct-service graduate students at the University of Washington, for example, receive intensive training in single-subject clinical research designs. They use these tools to conduct clinical research on at least some of their cases in the field and prepare reports of these studies in a form suitable for publication. As they learn how to determine which practices are effective or ineffective, they may make discoveries that are useful additions to the body of tested practice knowledge. In this way, the education of the student becomes in part a search for the answer to the question "What is competent practice?" Thus, the question and the educational effort become fused. The response of our students to this approach generally has been positive. I should add that our experience with this approach thus far has been primarily in the direct-services area of social work practice, principally because methodologies are available by which direct-service practitioners can rigorously evaluate their practice. We are in the process of trying to identify, develop, and teach comparable methodologies for the development of empirically based macropractice. (Rothman, 1974, has made a major contribution to the development of empirically based macropractice by extracting action principles from available research.)

We are moving on to the kinds of educational studies stimulated by competency-based education—studies that tend to concentrate on how students can best acquire this or that specific skill. We should push beyond those studies to ones conducted jointly by faculty and students and designed to determine the relative effectiveness of specific skills for practice. Such an approach not only will obtain the information needed for educational purposes but also can generate direct contributions to the knowledge base of the social work profession.

Finally, I would like to introduce another point that deserves more elaboration than can be given here. Lurking behind the question "What is competent social work practice?" is a more basic question, "What is social work?" I long have been puzzled by the paradox that, although social workers have difficulty defining a unique identity for their profession, they persistently have neglected an area of professional activity that social workers claimed many years ago, one we still could call our own if we attended to it. I refer to social diagnosis (or assessment) and social intervention. The tools needed to develop this emphasis are at hand, and some of the early efforts are fascinating and dramatic. If we do engage in faculty-student-conducted developmental research for practice, special priority should be given to the neglected area of social intervention.

3

Mastering
Specific Skills

Frank W. Clark
Charles R. Horejsi

As noted in Chapter One, the roots of professional social work in the United States are found in the activities of the private associations that were part of the Charity Organization Society movement. COS agencies developed in the latter part of the nineteenth century as a reaction and alternative to public poor relief programs. Early COS workers, all volunteers and often wealthy women, advocated a personalized approach to the problem of poverty. As the volunteers gained experience, they concluded that they needed formal training. In 1898 a six-week training course was established by the New York COS; by 1904 it was expanded to one year and offered by the New York School of Philanthropy. Subsequently, formal training of social workers shifted from agencies to universities. The university-based schools of social work emphasized generalizable social work knowledge, values, and skills, leaving to agencies the function of teaching those procedures that were peculiar to a particular agency setting. Thus, a distinction was created between university education and agency-based training. Universities focused on conceptual knowledge and broad humanistic values, while agencies taught agency policy and procedure. Consequently, the teaching of specific practice skills was ignored. Recent events and trends have called forth a reexamination of the place of skills in social work and thus in social work education.

Many state civil service merit systems and personnel departments have proposed that social work positions be declassified—that is, that educational requirements be reduced or eliminated. There are many reasons behind the move to declassify social work positions; certainly, financial expediency is paramount. While positions in areas other than social work also are proposed for declassification, social work positions frequently are selected because many personnel administrators, legislative committees, and ultimately the public do not see a clear distinction in the job-related performance of degreed and nondegreed social workers. Moreover, studies of effectiveness in the human services have not yielded persuasive evidence that these services alter people's lives. Thus, critics charge that social work is ineffective and the money spent on highly educated social workers cannot be justified when others with less education can perform as well. In a major address on the topic to social work educators, Briar (1973b, p. 17) remarked: "This charge is embarrassing because the profession cannot readily refute it. While it is true that some of the critics are using the question of effectiveness to mask other motives for attacking social programs, we lack credibility to make a countercharge if we cannot satisfactorily answer the ineffectiveness criticism. . . . Moreover, we owe it to our supporters and to our clients to know how effective we are and to demonstrate what we are doing to increase our effectiveness."

Levine (1974, p. 231) sees the centrality of skill in practice as one of the most serious issues facing professional social work. "I am convinced that the specific application of social work skill and knowledge, at the delivery point as well as at the policy level, can make a major difference to those seeking service." After citing examples of the harmful and inefficient consequences of nonskillful interviewing, planning, service, implementation, group work and so forth at service delivery, administrative, and policymaking levels, Levine concludes: "An understanding of the human condition, of growth, pain, of potential and limitation, a compassionate understanding of people and their attempts to negotiate a variety of interpersonal and social systems, the understanding of a professional help-ing relationship, and the ability to translate these into the effective delivery of a human service, these are in my view nonnegotiable, core elements of professional education for social work. The ability to verbalize, to feel, to advocate, to conceptualize this understanding is insufficient. The professional must be able to act it, to do it, to demonstrate it" (p. 238).

The profession is beginning to give increased attention to the relationship between specific skills and service outcome. These developments have obvious implications for social work education, which also must face the accountability issue. For social work education to prove its worth, those who have had the benefit of formal training must demonstrate a level of proficiency well above those who have had little or none. If social work education is to meet this challenge, it must place greater emphasis on the skill component.

The so-called competency approaches to education and cur-riculum building are one way of giving added attention to the skills. The basic elements of the competency-based education model (CBE) have been stated elsewhere (Armitage and Clark, 1975, p. 23): "(1) The ultimate purpose of the profession is practice. (2) The purpose of professional education is to effectively teach practice behaviors. (3) Practice behaviors can be specified as the operational objectives of social work education."

The competency- or performance-focused model of profes-sional education appeals to many educators because of its emphasis on measurable outcomes. Fortunately, this model appeared at a time when it was sorely needed. As Arkava and Brennen (1976, p. 4) noted in their review of quality control in social work educa-tion, "Evidence regarding the accomplishment of one of the primary objectives of social work education—that of preparing effective social work practitioners—has been lacking."

The press for accountability has begun to alter the way in which social work educators describe their programs. For example, a 1978 survey of degree programs in the United States and Canada by the faculty of social welfare at the University of Calgary indi-cated that almost 80 percent of the respondents characterized their programs as committed to and moving toward a competency-based curriculum (Knott, 1978). For most programs, this meant developing more explicitly stated objectives for educational experiences. Many of these objectives were described as "social work skills." Apparently, most educators and practitioners believe that social work skills exist, are teachable and learnable, and can be related to practice outcomes. They differ, however, in the way in which they think about skills, teach skills, and evaluate the skillfulness of students.

A cursory review of social work literature reveals that there have been several approaches to the definition of skills. A number of writers have described social work skills indirectly, by outlining roles and activities. For example, Teare and McPheeters (1970) identify twelve social work roles. Federico (1973, pp. 146–147) has summarized these roles as follows:

1. *Outreach worker*—reaching out into the community to identify need and follow up referrals to service contexts.

2. *Broker*—knowing services available and making sure those in need reach the appropriate services.

3. *Advocate*—helping specific clients obtain services when they might otherwise be rejected, and helping to expand services to cover more needy persons.

4. *Evaluation*—evaluating needs and resources, generating alternatives for meeting needs, and making decisions between alternatives.

5. *Teacher*—teaching facts and skills.

6. *Mobilizer*—helping to develop new services.

7. *Behavior changer*—changing specific parts of a client's behavior.

8. *Consultant*—working with other professionals to help them be more effective in providing services.

9. *Community planner*—helping community groups plan effectively for the community's social welfare needs.

10. *Care giver*—providing supportive services to those who cannot fully solve their problems and meet their own needs.

11. *Data manager*—collecting and analyzing data for decision-making purposes.

12. *Administrator*—performing the activities necessary to plan and implement a program of services.

The final report on the Florida Human Service Task Bank (Austin and Smith, 1975) describes five functions and eleven roles of human service, one hundred knowledge categories, and two hundred skill categories. The five functions and eleven roles are especially useful because they broaden the emphasis beyond one-to-one counseling or casework. The functions and roles are linkage (brokering, client advocating), mobilization (activating, systems advocating), counseling (counseling, consulting), treatment (rehabilitating, care giving), and administration (client programming, systems researching, administration).

Loewenberg (1977) has described core skills under five large categories: (1) interviewing, observing, and writing; (2) intervention activities (such as providing practical help; advice, information, and direction clarification; referral and linkage; emotional support; negotiating and bargaining; advocacy; setting limits); (3) engagement skills (such as structuring, focusing, bridging gaps, timing, judgment, activity, setting the tone, eye contact, facial gestures, body language, space); (4) assessment skills (such as collecting information; analyzing and interpreting information; making decisions about information; developing a contract; and preparing an assessment statement); (5) communication skills.

In their work on the task-centered model, Reid and Epstein (1972) identify numerous relevant skills. Epstein (1976) notes four types of skills needed to practice task-centered work: (1) problem identification, (2) selection and management of tasks, (3) formulation of treatment contract, and (4) measurement of results. More specific skills—such as enhancing client commitment, analyzing obstacles, modeling, rehearsal and guided practice, summarization, structuring, direction advice, enhancing awareness, and exploration—also are identified in the task-centered literature.

One of the most extensive and detailed studies of social work skill is being conducted by Shulman (1977), whose preliminary findings are available. This research focused on the effect of twenty-seven worker behaviors on building the helping relationship and helpfulness to the client. The worker behaviors are as follows:

1. Clarifying purpose
2. Clarifying role
3. Encouraging client feedback on purpose
4. Displaying belief in potential of the work
5. Holding to focus

6. Contact with systems people
7. Viewing systems people in new ways
8. Moving of general to specific
9. Connecting feelings to work
10. Reaching for between-session data
11. Pointing out the illusion of work
12. Reaching inside silences
13. Supporting client in taboo areas
14. Sharing personal thoughts and feelings
15. Understanding client feelings
16. Dealing with authority theme
17. Checking for artificial consensus
18. Putting client's feelings into words
19. Partializing client concerns
20. Supporting client strength
21. Identifying effective obstacles
22. Providing data
23. Worker displaying feelings openly
24. Pointing out endings early
25. Sharing worker's ending feelings
26. Asking for a review of learning
27. Reaching for ending feelings

Developments in the specification of social work skills have been uneven; more progress has been made in some areas than in others. For example, some of the most detailed descriptions and explanations of individual skills have been presented by social workers using behavioral approaches (Fischer, 1978; Fischer and Gochros, 1975; Gambrill, 1977; Rose, 1977; Sundel and Sundel, 1975; Thomas, 1974) and by workers in the field of child welfare (for example, Pike and others, 1977; Stein and Gambrill, 1976).

Just as there are different definitions of skills, there are apparent differences in underlying assumptions regarding the skill component of education or, more precisely, the relationship between skills, conceptual knowledge, and values.

Among many workers and educators, there is an assumption that skills and skillfulness flow directly from knowledge and values. It is assumed that skillfulness will follow automatically if one acquires an adequate knowledge base and holds a desired set of values. For those holding this view, the teaching of specific skills is of secondary importance. Primary emphasis is placed on grounding the student in foundation, practice knowledge, and professional values and providing socialization experiences that aid the student to internalize the professional role. Essentially, this is a cognitive approach to the issue of skill, in the sense that the basic social work tools are assumed to be primarily intellectual. Given the need to increase practice effectiveness, this assumption has been subjected to serious criticism.

While the social worker's professional judgment and the knowledge base on which he or she draws to form that judgment are important, it is the worker's behavior that directly affects the client. Fischer (1976, pp. 60–61) makes this distinction between theory and worker behavior when he observes:

> In the context of the worker's relationship with the client . . . "something" has to be done by the worker, or else he or she would be sitting passively, unengaged in therapeutic intervention. So the question is, what does the worker actually *do*?
>
> The worker obviously does not "do" theory. A theory, a complex set of ideas, observation, facts, etc., in itself cannot be applied to a person. There must be some way of translating the theory, or a principle of the theory, into action. The technique is that translation, that application in action. The technique or procedure of helping is merely the way the worker attempts to use some principles, or use the theory to make it "come alive" in application with clients. Without techniques, caseworkers could never accomplish their goals or even offer any services. Techniques are the expression, in action and in a precise form, of what the caseworker should actually *do* in a given situation and with a given client or problem. Techniques, in other words, form the core of the technology of social casework—the applied or practical methods of achieving practice objectives.

Fischer and others view skill as the proficiency with which the social worker engages in helping behavior. Skillfulness may be related to the worker's values and knowledge base, but skill does not naturally follow through or flow from a certain value orientation. Evidence for the belief that skill is separate from knowledge is shown by the high student demand for learning techniques and specific skills. Students typically complain, for example, that they are exposed to concepts and theory but are not taught how to actually practice. They perceive a difference between knowing and doing.

In an effort to be precise and train students to a high level of proficiency, some social work educators opt for an approach to skills that emphasizes technical competence. To help students achieve proficiency, the focus may be quite narrow—so narrow, in fact, that the student may not be able to generalize the skill across situations. Because of the narrowness of technical competence, curricula that stress the technical component often are designated subprofessional. The social worker must have more than technical competence; he must be able to generalize skills across many situations. Kaplan (1964) has humorously reflected the weakness of technical competence as the "law of the instrument," in which the availability of a hammer to a child creates a perceptual set where every situation encountered by a child requires hammering. Herein lies the problem of the technical competence approach to skills. If specific skills are not learned within the context of values and broad practice knowledge, they may be used inappropriately. It becomes a case of "have skill, will travel." The application of a skill may be appropriate in one situation but not in another.

Our need to respond to the challenge of accountability by increasing practice effectiveness requires greater attention to the skill component of social work education, but not by losing sight of the importance of a sound value and knowledge base. An approach that comes close to such a desired integration views skills as situationally appropriate performance competencies. Actual performance or worker behavior is emphasized but judged within the context of a particular practice situation. Educators defining skills as situationally appropriate performance competencies would require students to demonstrate their practice skills under at least simulated conditions during their formal educational program. The practicum is the ideal environment in which to require the student to demonstrate skill proficiency and proper application of skills to a given situation. Social work education may need to take another look, however, at the way practicum time is used for the teaching of specific practice skills. Korbelik and Epstein (1976) studied time and production variables in the social work practicum and concluded that explicitly structuring practicum experiences toward skill practice was necessary for students to master the objectives. Before practicum structuring, student groups spent only 2.5 hours per week in direct contact with clients and 10.5 hours per week total in the practicum. If these data are representative of other practica, similar structuring may be required to develop practice skills.

A limitation of the approach just described is that, even with a competency-focused classroom and rich practicum experience, the student's behavior can be observed only in a few practice situations. The educator, therefore, must assume that the appropriate application of skills is generalizable to a large number of other practice situations. This assumption is often held as an article of faith but seldom tested systematically. Ideally, proper evaluation of a person's skill would require observations over many and varied situations and for a considerable time, perhaps years. For most programs of education and training, this is not feasible. However, it does underscore the importance of keeping students in an educational program long enough to observe numerous applications of skills and performance in several practice situations.

Skills and Social Work Competence

Concepts of skill and competence appear to overlap. Like the concept of skill, there are different ways of viewing competence. Three distinct but interrelated types of competencies can be identified. The first type is *knowledge competency*—"what to do" when working with particular clients for given ends under specific circumstances. This set of competencies involves two subsets. The first is content; that is, the possession of information pertinent to social work. For example, human behavior, social environment, values, ethics, social policy, and human services organizations are areas of knowledge typically addressed in social work educational programs. The other subset of knowledge competencies deals with process, or the dynamics of professional practice.

The second set of competencies pertains to performance. *Performance competencies,* closely related to concepts of skill, are the action components of social work. They are ongoing practice behaviors as performed in the field setting. For example, performance competencies might include teaching a client money management, addressing the board of county commissioners, coaching a client in assertive skills, listening empathetically to a woman who has been physically abused, or consulting with a community group trying to determine the best course of action to stop a rezoning process. Performance of actual practice behavior also could take place in simulated settings—for example, through role playing.

The third major set of competencies relates to the actual consequences of worker performance. They can be termed *consequence competencies* and represent the most important level in the appraisal of social work practice. In order to appraise consequence competence, the evaluator must be able to determine, in terms of measurable criteria, whether clients were helped. The criteria can be stated as client change or maintenance (where change might represent deterioration of or erosion away from client goals, for example). At the minimum, consequence competencies must be defined in relation to the extent to which clients were enabled to reach desired goals. Beyond that, appraisal also must take into consideration total system effects of intervention and the undesired or unanticipated side effects. Since all intervention attempts entail risks, one must determine to what extent gains justified losses. Future evaluation of social work skills must utilize the broader perspective of consequential competency.

Efforts to evaluate the impact of practice performance and skills are extraordinarily difficult, given the variety of client systems, settings, theories, practice modes, and outcome goals. In his controversial book *The Effectiveness of Social Casework,* Fischer (1976) concludes that we should abandon the hope of seeking to validate large major areas of professional social work practice, such as social casework, because of the vagueness of terms like *casework.* Consequently, he advocates a reformulation of the issue; namely, "Are the methods used by caseworkers effective?"

Psychotherapy also has struggled to validate itself, with results remarkably similar to those in social work. In general, the suggested strategies for evaluating the effectiveness of therapeutic efforts require becoming more specific. For example, in concluding an examination of evaluation strategies, Paul (1967, p. 111) counsels that therapists begin to address "what treatment by *whom* is most effective for *this* individual with *that* specific problem, and under *which* set of circumstances." In another effort to evaluate therapeutic outcomes, Bergin (1971, p. 253) points out that "it is essential that the entire therapeutic enterprise be broken down into specific sets of measures and operations or, in other words, be dimensionalized. Otherwise there will continue to be little progress. What progress has occurred in recent years has come from the isolation of potent, specific variables from the broad milieu of events occurring in therapeutic practice." Certainly, social work practice is broader and more variable than more narrowly defined psychotherapeutic modalities. However, if the observation made by the writers cited above is valid for a more narrow field of practice, it may be equally applicable for social work. One dimension that may be critical to effective helping outcomes is social work skills. Fischer (1978) considers the social worker's use of structure, core interpersonal competencies, and certain behavioral techniques to be important skills in social casework, ones that now have sufficient empirical support regarding their impact on the client.

As can be seen from the above discussion, skills and competencies are similar in that they contain the dimensions of knowledge, performance, and consequences. Social work skills should not be construed as a narrow technological response to need; rather, they represent a holistic expression of the social worker's foundation, practice knowledge, values, and client understanding demonstrated through action. Skill is the operational definition of worker commitment to clients and their goals.

Selection of Skills to be Taught

Attempts to give greater emphasis to the teaching of practice skills logically must begin with the selection of the skills to be taught. This sounds like a relatively simple task, but it is not. In fact, the process is fraught with uncertainty and barriers to be overcome. Three basic approaches are used, but each has significant disadvantages. One approach employs expert opinion, since it is assumed that experts can identify the skills and other competencies to be taught. Although the use of expert opinion and practice wisdom enjoys widespread popularity in social work and other fields, Pottinger (1977, pp. 35–36) states that "the most popular yet inadequate technique for defining competence is the sole judgment of experts. This statement will arouse strong feelings among many educators and other professionals, but empirical evidence is overwhelming that the phenomena of selective perception, beliefs, and value systems contaminate objectivity so as to make expert judgments unacceptable. Even large groups of judges can be wrong; numbers are no protection against subjectivity." Social work has tended to use the expert-opinion approach because better alternatives were not available. Pottinger adds: "It is remarkable that . . . so little attention is given to competency identification methodology. The truth is that few educational test developers have seriously questioned the methods of using subjective expert opinions as the rock upon which tests are developed" (pp. 35–36).

In an effort to counteract potential bias inherent in the expert-opinion approach, panels of judges sometimes are employed to identify social work skills. This process can be very valuable, but the use of larger numbers of experts is no guarantee that error will be reduced. At best, error and bias will be randomized over a series of alternative choices selected by such experts.

Opinions expressed by experts often are reflections of their theoretical orientation. Thus, it is hardly surprising that theories or models of practice constitute the basis on which many educators identify skills to be taught. Conceptual models of practice may be useful because they allow one to build a structure of desirable practice that can be tested for its practical value. Conceptual models have the advantages of clarity, logic, internal consistency, and apparent practice relevance. There is great danger, however, in assuming that the model is an accurate representation of reality. The extent of correspondence between such schema and actual practice requirements may be unknown, leading to a situation analogous to Plato's allegorical cave, wherein the inhabitants were unaware that they observed shadowy representations of the world instead of the real thing. Conceptual models possess an eloquence and completeness that make them attractive; they meet our needs for creating order out of confusion. Like a good film, models may entertain, inform, and even educate, but they do not necessarily approximate practice conditions of various client systems in diverse settings.

The third major approach to identifying social work skills and competencies is the use of descriptions of activities in which social workers currently are engaged. The work by Teare in Chapter Ten of this volume illustrates the application of this approach to social work. Using a variation of the functional job analysis approach, he identifies twelve major practice dimensions of activities engaged in by human services workers in a large public service agency. His findings are useful because they suggest that workers must respond to organizational requirements with rather specific actions and activity. The problem with the approach is that current social work activities cannot automatically be assumed to result in benefits to clients. Secondly, new conceptualizations of practice may be needed. Third, skills considered relevant in one setting or agency may be less important in another. Moreover, one must find a way of determining which skills are job-level specific and important in all of social work practice regardless of the worker's specific job duties. Pottinger (1977, p. 36) recognizes this problem and notes two sets of techniques required in job analysis. The first technique is the analysis of the job into a set of activity or function categories. The second technique involves discriminating activities or functions that are broadly generalizable from one setting to another from those unique to specific settings. It is likely that the job analysis approach to skill development will be given added attention in the future, since it provides a valuable data base for selection and potentially can serve to distinguish the more important from the less important human services activities.

Experimental study may constitute a more valid means of identifying skills. Scientific experimentation allows one to isolate and identify the relative effectiveness of skills on specific criteria. When the criteria chosen relate to client benefits and costs, inferences regarding the consequential competence of the service may be drawn. While this chapter is not the place to begin a discussion of the use of scientific methods, clearly social work urgently needs to adopt an open posture toward the systematic collection of data bearing on the utility of social work skills. What is optimally needed from the viewpoint of rigorous science is the design of large-scale group experiments where confounding variables may be carefully controlled. Moreover, the demands of an *applied* scientific approach to the validation of practice behavior also must allow one to evaluate the way in which skills are used in situations where confounding variables cannot be eliminated because they constitute the normal practice milieu. How one optimizes skill consequences under varying circumstances may constitute a major metaskill in using other skills. Another metaskill may involve the manipulation of those confounding variables that can be used to enhance desired skill consequences such as client expectancy, client self-monitoring, and the effects of external evaluation of the worker.

Fischer (1976), among others, suggests that social workers may focus on the process of technique building and validation in their practice as an initial alternative to formal group experimental designs. Case study data accumulated over a number of clients and service episodes should provide a base of information on which to make initial judgments about the merits of specific social work skills. Controlled group experiments could further sort out skills on the basis of relative effectiveness. Fischer proposes four strategies for building research into practice: experimental investigation of single cases, objectified case studies, an "a priori model" in which clients and worker do not move from one stage of intervention unless certain criteria are met, and systematized recording. The key to identifying and validating social work skills from this perspective is systematic observation and recording of specifically defined practices and consequence criteria while noting the salient circumstances under which the skill is demonstrated. More rigorous research designs must include "(a) the formulation of a refutable hypothesis; (b) the precise specifications, in reliable and valid terms, of the independent variable (the treatment of input) and the dependent variable (means of measuring changes or output); and (c) the development of an experimental design that will reduce the likelihood of interpretive error" (Stuart, 1971, p. 1108).

Teaching Skills

In teaching social work skills, educators have been divided in their preference for teaching simple skills or integrated skills. Brammer (1973, p. 70) notes a similar distinction in interpersonal helping skills when he refers to "part and whole approaches." Employing the single-skill or part approach, one identifies a discrete performance; describes the skill in relation to client needs, other skills, and environmental contexts; and then teaches the skill as a performance through a variety of means, such as modeling, role playing, guided feedback, lecture, and discussion. When students learn the discrete skill, they encounter another. The key to the single-skill approach is that the skill must be simply described in behavioral terms. One then assumes that the skills can be used in different combinations according to the needs of the situation and altered to fit client needs and helper styles. The teaching and learning process is like that of stringing beads, one after the other, to make a necklace. It is assumed that the students can integrate the several discrete skills once they are part of the students' behavioral repertoire. Instructors may spend some time, of course, helping students with the integration process.

Numerous basic texts reflect this approach to skill development. In the areas of direct interpersonal helping, the work of Ivey and Gluckstern (1974, 1976) is well known. Illustratively, they define basic attending skills as attending behavior, open invitations to talk, minimal "encouragers," paraphrasing, reflection of feeling, summarization, and integration of skills (1974). One particularly noteworthy feature of the single-skill approach is the attention given to immediate specific feedback to students as they practice the skills. This feature appears to be instrumental in improving the skill.

Feedback may be behavioral and reflect thoughts and feelings as well. Kagan (1975), for example, has developed a feedback method of Interpersonal Process Recall to help students develop three general sets of skills: understanding overt and covert communication, identifying the personal impact of interpersonal communication, and appropriately sharing the understanding developed with clients. The process typically involves videotaping an interaction with the social worker and client and using a playback of the tape to stimulate a recall and discussion of thoughts and feelings experienced during the helping session. The student thereby is enabled to study inner processes, learn more about himself or herself, and improve interactions. A strength of the discrete-skills approach is that students definitely learn and are tested on the extent to which they have mastered a specific and clearly defined skill. If the skills taught bear some perceived relation to actual practice, students often find such learning exciting and relevant to their interests. Critics of this approach disdain the attention given to discrete skills and suggest that such an approach represents an oversimplification and unrealistic fragmentation of practice. Questions also are raised about the appropriateness of single-skill approaches for preparing students to engage in practice that is political, ever changing, and exceedingly complex. The single-skill approach should not be expected to be applicable automatically to the acquisition of skills that cannot be anticipated or specified. Within the boundaries discussed, however, single-skill approaches show a remarkable promise for social work. Students appear able to integrate the skills, particularly in structured field learning simulations or actual field settings.

Proponents of the integrated-skills approach stress the necessity for a holistic understanding and response to practice realities. With regard to interviewing skills, for example, students may study and perform the interview without giving great attention to discrete skills. They are then given feedback designed to improve their general performance. This approach tends to focus on practice role or worker functions rather than on specific discrete skills. For example, one can teach students the *role* of mediator without giving much attention to the many specific skills that can be used in the mediating role. The method rests on the implicit assumption that understanding the dimensionality of a function or role (for example, mediator, advocate, counselor, planner) is sufficient and will result in an adequate level of performance by the worker.

The integrated-skills approach has the advantage of economy in teaching time. Integrated skills can be explored fairly well within the constraints of the typical university schedule. A further advantage is that it allows the student to see more easily the skill's place in the entire social work enterprise. Therefore, those students who understand and can perform the skill reasonably well are able to advance more rapidly, with attention given only to those aspects of their performance that require significant remediation. At the same time, it is more difficult to provide a detailed critique of most aspects of student performance because of the holistic complexity observed by the instructor; there is much to see and comment on. Moreover, in many classes, the number of students allows the instructor to provide feedback only on the most obvious areas requiring further work. From a discrete-skills perspective, integrated skills do not reduce the performance into manageable units that would permit students to gain facility in evaluating their performance or ensure that each student has mastered every subskill sufficiently. Consequently, students may emerge from instruction with only a general understanding of a practice role and without possessing specific skills in their repertoire.

There also are practical issues to consider in teaching social work skills. First, skill development requires time and practice. For example, when the discrete-skills approach has been used in a course in basic interviewing skills at the University of Montana, the instructor has found that students can barely master a modest-sized skill in one academic quarter. A similar finding was reported by Larsen and Hepworth (1978) for a helping skills laboratory in another social work program, where only 30 percent of the students reached the minimally acceptable level of interpersonal skill functioning in the allotted time. Clearly, social work education must formulate sound methods for teaching social work skills more efficiently.

Paradoxically, the second issue stems from social work's increasing interest in specifying educational program objectives as "skills." As educators specify skills, the number of skills balloons in size, and comprehensive descriptions of skills may reach into the hundreds. For example, the University of Montana Competency Scales (Arkava and others, 1976) include seven areas of performance criteria containing 122 skill objectives. Subskill objectives for classes supporting the summative objectives increase the total. Selectivity in identifying and incorporating skill objectives must be employed. Design considerations in limiting the number of objectives have been discussed elsewhere (Armitage and Clark, 1975). Justifiably, skill development also must compete with foundation courses, electives, and other professional offerings.

Testing students for skill acquisition is a time-consuming task. Yet, if students are to demonstrate mastery of a skill to criterion, assessment and feedback are essential. These procedures easily can constitute most of the instructional time available in the usual three- or four-credit university course unless a balance is struck between other program objectives and skill objectives.

Adequate methods for testing specific social work skills also are in their formative stages and require continuing developmental work. The University of Montana social work program has developed a summative evaluation that correlates moderately with later job success (Arkava and Brennen, 1976). All BSW students are required to synthesize course content, including social work skills and practicum experiences, into a successful written and oral presentation of actual practice experience. Work samples, simulation approaches, and paper-and-pencil tests correlating with observed practice behavior are methods that are beginning to be used in testing skills. Again, we face not only conceptual issues in their development for social work but also considerations of method, time, and priority in the social work curriculum.

Another skill development issue facing social work educators is that skills do not stand apart from the people who demonstrate them. Some students are not ready to work productively on a given skill at a given time; others may need help in accommodating a skill to their unique life-style. Curricula of the future must become more individualized even as they strengthen their skill development potential. Competency-based education programs appear to offer much in this regard. Cultural and value differences among students also must be taken into account when skills become better specified. For example, to what extent should we talk about different communication skills being necessary in interpersonal helping with Native American or Chicano students? To what extent should we explicitly require students to demonstrate flexibility in their utilization of skills in different settings by actually testing this ability?

Social work skills are certainly more complex and elusive than most of us have assumed. The relationship between skills and helping outcomes has only begun to be investigated adequately. When the skill issues of practice become more clearly specified and when pertinent data are generated, social work will have made enormous strides toward the demonstration of competence.

4

Employing
Self-Corrective Methods

Harry Butler
Winifred Morphew Chambers

Social work practice cannot be judged competent unless it can be enacted in a purposeful, individual, and flexible manner to assist clients in reaching goals of importance. Social workers must develop and use information about clients to guide their work. What the social worker does varies according to the information generated about clients; such information forms the basis for the pattern of helping. When practice inherently produces information pertinent to client needs, helping has the potential of being self-corrective.

Presumably, all professional practice attempts to be self-corrective. This observation may not appear particularly noteworthy per se, but self-corrective practice becomes more significant when one reflects on the variability of competent service within professions, including social work. The thesis of this chapter is that a significant dimension of competent social work is the extent to which practitioners can learn to become more self-corrective. The methods employed to this end are largely cognitive and can be learned and taught.

In developing the elements of self-corrective practice, we examined logic and methods from the research literature. We sought to identify those factors that, if introduced in practice, would permit practitioners to learn from their efforts and correct their actions in light of those learnings. What follows is a description of those components of self-correction.

The following guidelines are neither exhaustive nor final, since they must be altered to fit the needs of practice. We hope that they will be built on to develop a richer and more comprehensive strategy for learning to practice.

The guidelines to be discussed in the following sections are (1) the use of knowledge to guide practice, (2) the assumption of responsibility for judgment and action, (3) the ability to gain objectives through improvisation, (4) the use of structure and constraints, (5) the assessment of short-term strategies by reference to long-term goals, (6) the pursuit of social justice, and (7) discipline.

Use of Knowledge to Guide Practice

By knowledge, we mean judgments and actions informed by the sound interpretation and integration of theory and published research with data generated in practice. In other words, data from specific cases are weighed in relation to data from classes of cases. While the best data are generated from specific cases in the context of practice, it would be misleading to suggest that practitioners bring to their practice no prior ideas and are shaped merely by client stimuli. In fact, it is impossible to enter any situation free of prior attitudes and ideas that shape what we attend to and how we interpret the situation. The proper use of knowledge involves bringing antecedent ideas, which shape our perceptions, and data from specific cases under the control of a methodology that minimizes bias and directs actions toward the true needs of clients.

Social workers try to reduce bias through self-awareness; that is, they assume that, if they are aware of their biases and the source of these biases, they will be able to control the noxious effects of bias on clients. However, although awareness of bias offers an opportunity for its control, it by no means assures it. Among other problems, the major weakness of self-awareness as a method of assuring valid practice is the absence of an inherent method by which awareness is shaped and checked by new ideas and new data from specific cases. While practitioners do continue to reflect on their cases, no method of correcting for new distortions is contained in the process by which practitioners seek to become self-aware.

Self-awareness, then, is only one component of the methodology by which we maximize the effects of knowledge in practice. Self-monitoring and self-observation also are needed to assure the validity and cogency of awareness in practice. Unlike self-awareness, self-monitoring and self-observation generate data independent of the private understandings and insights that practitioners develop about themselves and their work. Furthermore, data from observation and monitoring are collected in relation to all aspects of practice—assessment, action, and consequences—not just to the motives of the worker. Data collected from observation and monitoring are subject to assessment by colleagues whose independent judgments can prove corrective when self-awareness fails.

Self-observation involves methods by which practitioners can see their work as others see it. Although difficult to achieve, self-observation can have a salutary effect on the judgments of practitioners. The most common methods of self-observation include the use of videotaped recordings of one's work, observation and feedback from colleagues or supervisors, and observation and feedback from clients. A recently neglected but potent method of self-observation is recording one's work through writing. Justifying one's assessments, actions, and perceived consequences through the written word possesses powerful self-corrective features, since the method of writing itself requires the development of greater coherence and rationality than usually is present in one's work. Self-monitoring involves systematic collection of information and data related to all phases of practice, with particular focus on relating actions to consequences. Because data, no matter how rigorously collected, are sterile and must be interpreted, the combination of self-awareness, self-observation, and self-monitoring is necessary if we are to develop a practice that validly addresses the complexities and uncertainties of human need.

Responsibility for Judgment and Action

Theory and research are meaningful only if they help the practitioner make sounder judgments and take more valid actions.

Social workers must become capable of independent, responsible judgment on which they are willingly accountable for knowledge claims and the consequences of their chosen actions. Mature and competent practitioners aggressively engage in actions to remove or attenuate foreseeable possibilities that they are wrong or that their actions may be harmful. The risks of discretionary action may be reduced by disciplined use of theory, facts, and research as a framework for serious reflection and commitment to determining what is right. Argumentation (Perelman, 1963)—systematically thinking out available alternatives and probable consequences and then seeking criticism and suggestion from colleagues and other experts—is a preferred method of reducing error prior to action. The method of argumentation is effective, however, only if criticism and challenge truly are welcome. Responsible social workers not only are willing to live with the consequences of their actions; they systematically monitor the consequences of their actions and take the energy and time to follow through.

A variety of dynamics and influences can divert practitioners from their responsibility for the welfare of their clients. First, group norms and peer pressure are not necessarily self-correcting and can displace attention from practice to group needs (Janis, 1972). Second, more effective practice can be taken as criticism of the practice of others, leading to undue and injust criticism of those who seek to improve their practice. Third, bureaucratic procedures can become more important than practice itself, so that attention to service is displaced by attention to the needs of the organization in which practice occurs (Etzioni, 1964). Invariably, group and bureaucratic pressures support peace and harmony and militate against risks and conflict. Harmonious relationships in the workplace are desirable, but self-correcting practice demands confrontation and challenge through argumentation, peer evaluation, and methods of accountability. While the ideal would be organizational and peer pressure in favor of self-correcting practice, the improbability of this means that individual practitioners must safeguard the integrity of their practice by resisting inauthentic pressures to conform. Since undue conflict in any organization will tend to undermine service, judgments and actions to reconcile competing interests of the organization and clients are a proper focus of professional attention. No final solution to this dilemma is proposed; however, widespread acceptance of a methodology for a self-correcting practice would alleviate the problem, since disagreements would be resolvable on the basis of evidence and logic, not personality.

Use of Improvisation

Improvisation involves considerably more than flexibility, in that social workers must be able to develop alternatives or novel solutions in situations that are ambiguous, unstructured, and unpredictable (Butler and Bilorusky, 1975). Not to be confused with trial-and-error methods, improvisation involves sensitivity to subtle cues of change and novelty, so that previously unknown alternatives can be seen, assessed, and, if appropriate, tested. Improvisation is the inventive use of experimental methods in the action context of practice. Ordinarily, experiments are conducted under controlled conditions that are well planned and carefully constructed. Although practitioners may not have the luxury of postponing response or action, the logic of experimental design can inform and guide their extemporaneous judgments.

The use of improvisation requires that we be connoisseurs of action and evidence without the security of technology. Affect and intuition are strong components of improvisation; they probably are less mysterious than most believe, yet we have not developed methods for subjecting them to rational testing. We know little of the psychic processes by which novel ideas and intuitions arise, but we can develop rational methods of determining whether hunches are sound. Intuition can be a useful, if not essential, aspect of self-correcting practice if intuitions are treated as hypotheses to be tested in action. When a worker's feelings about one client remind the worker of another client, a reasonable hypothesis is that the known dynamics of one client are present in the circumstances of the other. Experiencing similar feelings when working with both clients does not prove that client circumstances are identical. The similarity of affect merely sensitizes the worker to explore possible similarities. Improvisation constitutes a method of case comparison by which novel solutions can be derived from synthesizing what is known from previous cases for use in a present case.

Improvisation, or the composition of practice in action, constitutes what has been called the art of social work practice. It is a vital aspect of what is meant by the conscious use of self. The emphasis placed on self-awareness is in part based on the recognized need for improvisation in practice. Various concepts from the literature—including transference, empathy, and redintegration—constitute attempts to bring order and control to this aspect of practice. The custom has been to expect practitioners to understand themselves in relation to the affect they tend to stimulate in various types of persons, so that these feelings can be used as an assessment instrument. While this aspect of practice has been given considerable attention, efforts to bring discipline to improvisation have been limited to developing worker self-understanding. The action implications that flow from improvised assessment have been subject to little testing that informs assessment and action by examining both in relation to consequences for clients. Far too many practitioners attribute self-evident validity to their intuitions and discount the intuitions of other practitioners. It would be more fruitful to subject intuitions to testing than to favor one's own and discount those of others with equal claims to validity.

Use of Structure and Constraints

A number of studies have contributed to professional concern over the degree to which social structure molds and restricts human development and expression. The tendency to view repression, or the restriction of expression, as a function of individual personality was challenged by studies demonstrating a tendency for individuals from various life roles to behave similarly to prison guards when placed in defined guard roles in prison simulations (Zimbardo, 1973). Milgram (1973) reported the tendency of many of his subjects to obey experimenters to the point of administering what they believed were punishing shocks to victims. Wasserman (1970) reported that professional social workers were confronted with an impossible situation when they attempted to carry out their professional mission in a department of public welfare. These and other studies make a compelling claim that the social structure of various situations is a strong determinant of the outcome. In fact, evidence from experiments with social structure can bring a more balanced view to the study of and intervention in human behavior that may have overemphasized the importance of individual personality as a determinant of behavior.

We have come to recognize that all social work practice involves working within, assembling, managing, and altering structures. Sound practice incorporates sensitivity to and purposeful use of structure, not only as a determinant of workers' behaviors but as an active force in the lives of their clients. The issue is not whether structuring is good or bad or, for that matter, whether social workers are able to adjust to the organizational policies and constraints of their work world. We propose that the responsible and actual exercise of social structuring can further the purposes of practice.

Social workers must be capable of acting purposefully without permitting structure to unduly shape their actions toward rebellion or acquiescence. Practice objectives must be set and achieved by using structure as a support or removing the restraints that structure provides. Social workers long have recognized the most obvious structures and their differential effects: group, family, and dyadic interviews. We are less advanced in our understanding of the differing effects on practice of authority, democracy, and client participation. While we may prefer one over the other, preference is not the same as understanding the contribution of each to the effectiveness of practice in various situations. Furthermore, some social workers function better in a context of a structure that orders their activity; others perform better when they are permitted greater discretion and latitude. The best social workers probably are able to work under structured and ambiguous situations. Since clients vary according to their needs for structure, and practice problems become attackable from diverse structural arrangements of action, it behooves social workers to become skilled in the creative use of various means of structuring their action in accordance with preferred consequences.

Short-Term Strategies and Long-Term Goals

When long-term goals are developed and understood, it is possible to develop and specify the preconditions for their achievement and then assess short-term strategies in relation to the specified preconditions. If a short-term objective would eliminate or undermine a precondition of the long-term goal, its achievement at best is risky and at worst destructive. A simple example is dropping out of school to seek employment because of immediate needs for income. If an education is a precondition for the achievement of economic security, meeting immediate needs can foreclose any possibility of achieving what ultimately is desired. Unless other compelling and confounding circumstances and dispositions are present, social workers in a case such as this would be wise to explore the means by which continued education would not be disrupted or prevented in meeting short-run financial needs.

The pressures of accountability, budget, and staffing tend to advance short-term solutions at the expense of long-term objectives. Accountability measures often are developed in respect to immediate achievements within a specified time frame. Budgets are allocated on a fiscal-year basis, and staff positions must be filled quickly if retention of the positions is to be assured. Open positions leave needs unmet and lower performance records, jeopardizing future budget allocations. To some extent, short-term goals are based on case responsibilities, while long-term objectives are based on population responsibilities. This is the paradox of competition between service and prevention responsibilities. Capitulation to pressures to shape and justify practice in terms of immediate objectives can undermine the mission of practice. Short-term accomplishments are more impressive to funding bodies. However, these bodies will not necessarily reject well-developed plans that forgo some short-term achievements in light of long-term objectives. Unfortunately, the relationship between immediate activity and long-range objectives is communicated too frequently in global and wishful terms. If preconditions for the achievement of long-term goals can be specified, short-term success in developing the preconditions may well impress funding bodies.

Most social welfare organizations are funded for population responsibilities and long-term social goals; the actual practice in many social agencies, however, is directed to case responsibilities addressed in terms of immediate needs. The pace and pressures of caseload responsibilities and the infatuation with the concept of crisis intervention attest to the bias that favors immediate objectives. Although the bias toward responding to immediate needs and the psychic rewards practitioners may accrue from this type of work are understandable, the limitation of resources available to the social welfare enterprise dictates a reexamination of current practice in terms of long-range objectives for populations. Case responsibilities should be approached with an eye toward establishing the preconditions for long-range case goals and avoiding short-run solutions incompatible with known preconditions. Furthermore, the selection of cases and the choice of alternative uses of time and resources should be examined in light of ultimate population responsibilities. We are proposing population and long-range responsibilities as a systematic control to be imposed on practice, so that data analyzed under this control can correct the myopia inherent in the perspectives of those responding to immediate needs.

Pursuit of Social Justice

The quest for social justice requires that we consider all whose interests may be at stake and discipline our efforts toward fairness. This question can be put as "What ought to be done, for whom, and at whose expense?" We always should carefully determine who loses or suffers if we act. Social workers cannot avoid responsibility for the justness of their actions by deferring decisions to their clients under the guise of self-determination. In addition, choosing specialized practice with individuals or a class of problems does not relieve us of considering the interests of those who are not part of our clientele.

A good example of the deception of individual cases is that of capital punishment. Courts treated each individual convicted of a capital offense uniquely, and each case was considered on its own merits. But when capital punishment was studied over many cases, it was found that few whites and many blacks were executed. Although the courts acted in good conscience on each case, an unknown and unintended systematic bias resulted in unequal treatment. Few social workers would admit bias across cases, but we cannot assure justice unless we study our judgments in individual cases in relation to patterns of judgments across many cases.

We have yet to come to grips with methods of determining what is just, but we cannot practice without tacitly assuming that we know justice when we see it. We have tended to rely on social work values, although a serious attempt to use these values to guide practice would be frustrating, since social work values are vague and contradictory. We are pledged to respect the values and cultural background of our clients and refrain from imposing our values. It is impossible to act without doing so, for acting or refraining from action cannot be neutral. If we act to prevent a threatened suicide, or if we decide that we cannot act, both choices are value choices. In the former, we may consider our responsibility to life to transcend our feelings about self-determination. In the latter, we may feel that a person has the right to a choice. In any event, we make a choice and we are responsible for it. If we are aware, if we have the power to act, and if we know how to act, we are not neutral.

Many social workers insist that values and questions of justice are matters of opinion and that one person's opinion is as good as anyone else's opinion. This is an impossible position to maintain; furthermore, it is not true. By refusing to admit that we make value judgments and that our actions have implications for justice, we fail to scrutinize our actions to learn which have more just consequences. Value opinions and actions derived from them can and should be viewed in relation to their consequences; in other words, value opinions also must come under the control of evidence.

Discipline

The only course we can follow if we wish our practice to come under the control of evidence while adjusting for bias and unintended consequences is to use systematic procedures to determine what ought to be done and assess the consequences of our interventions. Systematic procedures would include at least the following:

1. As part of the standard assessment strategy, value assumptions are identified that unwittingly may influence goals and objectives.

2. Arguments for alternative objectives are considered and compared in light of existing cases where various alternatives have occurred. The eventual choice emerges from a comparison of consequences in real situations, with one result being awareness of the value choice based on predicted consequences. Where actual cases cannot be found, the worker is aware of the greater risk that the objective may not be achievable, since we have no experience with its realization. Our search for unsuccessful cases should be as zealous as that for successful ones.

3. Objectives and interventive strategies are articulated carefully in concrete observable terms to permit ongoing examination and testing.

4. Action and its consequences are monitored continuously, so that action can be altered in light of emerging evidence.

5. Action strategies are selected because their success is well documented. When such documentation does not exist or is of a dubious validity, workers subject untried strategies to systematic inquiry; they formulate hypotheses, collect and record data, consider alternative explanations or interpretations of outcomes, and share results so that other practitioners can benefit from this experimentation.

An overlooked but critical aspect of practice using systematic procedures is the interpretation of data and experience. Evidence is more than data or information. Evidence includes data and its logical interpretation. If social reality were constructed from summations of observables, we would not need social workers. The social reality we seek to influence is one of perceived meanings, rendering our task one of making interpretations and translating meaning from complex cues and observations. The soundness of our work can be assured only if we make public our interpretive process, so that our reasoning can be checked by the reasoning of others. Therefore, documentation that includes data, information, observations, and our interpretations represents the evidence of our practice.

Implications

While the guidelines represent some but not all of the issues practitioners face in developing a self-correcting practice, the continued need for individual discretion and self-governance in practice demands an overall strategy of self-development for practitioners. Our traditions have included three predominant methods of stimulating, supporting, and certifying growth and development of individual practitioners: supervision, continuing education courses inside or outside agencies, and psychotherapy. It is not our intent to discount these methods; we do hope to cast doubt on the cogency of these methods in their predominant and traditional use. Snyder (1971), through his concept of the "hidden curriculum," has sensitized us to the power of the structural arrangements of learning to affect the learner. The traditional methods of professional development can be characterized by their essential emphasis on social workers receiving learning from teachers, workshop leaders, supervisors, and therapists. Although active learning is not necessarily discouraged, it is not required by the usual structure. Teachers, supervisors, and therapists are challenged to generate or support aggressive activity in the face of a structure that favors passivity.

Self-development and quality control involve multiple efforts and activities. The evidence-action relationship is inherently a superior learning and development process because it informs practice more directly than others, and a self-generated overall program of learning and development should be employed whose hidden curriculum channels active and heuristic habits. Both ideas are based on the assumption that continued learning has its greatest effect when the learning thoughts and actions are challenged by contradictions from the empirical and theoretical worlds. The evidence-action unity challenges the worker from a specific context. The program of learning challenges the workers in respect to their overall careers.

Mills (1959, pp. 52–53) suggests in his guides to intellectual craftsmanship an approach that can be tailored to the interests of social work. He proposes nine guidelines.

1. Do not separate work from life, because each can be used to enrich and inform the other.
2. Keep a file on personal, professional, and intellectual experiences to promote organization, the preservation of experience, and the discipline of writing.

3. Continuously review one's thoughts and experiences instead of waiting for external pressures such as requests for reports.
4. Learn to read and select reading relevant for one's file (or practice).
5. Develop a system of notes that includes tentative ideas for testing one's interest stimulated by reading or experience.
6. Develop a sense of playfulness toward one's phrases, ideas, and words; accompany it with a fierce drive to make sense out of the world.
7. Try to view one's situation, world, or problems by imagining the view others (members of other disciplines, historical figures, former teachers, and so forth) might take toward it.
8. In the preliminary stages of a speculation, do not be afraid to think in terms of imaginative extremes.
9. Do not hesitate to express ideas in the simplest possible language.

At any one point, it should be possible for any social worker to submit documentation of his or her self-development for review, since self-development activities generate evidence of process and substance. We are convinced that good habits of self-development that generate evidence are superior to the typical means by which we assess professional competence through standardized tests.

5

Alternative Approaches Based on Moral Reasoning

Sonia Leib Abels
Paul Abels

Like the other authors in this volume, we are committed to the improvement of social work education and practice and share the desire for a standard of excellence. Within this spirit of ethical science, we have attempted to assess the contribution that competency-based education (CBE) could make to our profession. To do this, we have explored the theoretical underpinning of CBE, examined its development and use in other professions, and tried to draw some inference that might help us in future curriculum decisions. In the process of this exploration, we have used comparative analysis (an approach based on grounded theory—a set of hypotheses generated from comparative experiences and tested in current practice). We also viewed the CBE material against an alternative structure, moral reasoning as developed by Kohlberg (1969).

At this point, we shall summarize briefly the basics of a CBE program. Clark (1976, p. 28) states that to qualify as CBE a curriculum must contain (1) clear statements of the competencies to be demonstrated, (2) a system for assessing student performance that has a direct relationship to each competency statement, and (3) a learning environment explicitly organized to help students acquire competencies. Most CBE programs are goal or outcome focused; teaching and learning are defined in performance terms, and outcomes are stated as behavioral objectives.

Although we started with an attitude favorable to the use of CBE, our findings have led us to believe that CBE will not accomplish comprehensively the task of making the profession more competent; in fact, our data suggest that CBE may be dysfunctional—turning us away from the important issues of determining what should be the theoretical and methodological structures for social work.

Model Reasoning and Logical Reasoning

Initially, we assumed that competencies based on comparative analysis, in the framework of Kohlberg's moral reasoning, would be a more appropriate foundation for social work education than either "model reasoning" or "logical reasoning," which are the current social work CBE frameworks utilized by the University of Montana and the University of Georgia. In model reasoning, the student is judged competent if he is able to reason and demonstrate that reasoning in practice within the parameters of a particular model; in logical reasoning, the student is judged competent if he is able to make logical connections between theory and practice. We believe that neither model reasoning nor logical reasoning is the best standard for social work education. At this point, our profession has not come to terms with what should be the foundation of practice.

Model reasoning is related to abstract conceptions that no longer are guided by the discrete and specific aspects of reality. Models are positions of certainty, often preventing practitioners from discovery or awareness of the variables that do not fall within the model's predictive aspects. Life's complexities often are unpredictable. No one practice model at this point is able to account for all the variables present in most practice situations. Models are artificial theories of action. What makes them artificial is not that they are necessarily untrue but that the abstractions tend to simplify the very complexity of the situation, offering generalization that may or may not be present in the particular situations. In a sense, abstractions are several steps removed from the actual experience and unable to provide the richness of the reality.

Social workers continually are confronted with ambiguities that the simple ordering of reality through abstract generalization does not resolve. Models tend to be self-sealing. The rules and laws often lead the practitioner to act in ways that induce or confirm behavior that supports the model's assumptions. In professional practice, one does not and cannot predict all the relevant variables. In models the variables are predetermined in a way that is impossible in social relations.

There are many practice models, some of which are represented by schools or departments of social work, such as the psychoanalytic orientation at Smith School and the learning theory orientation at Michigan. There also is model variance among faculty within departments and schools of social work, suggesting that no one model has won the approval of the members of the social work profession. "None of the various abstract frameworks that attempt to define or communicate the unity and identity of social work have succeeded in winning general acceptance" (Richmond and Butler, 1977, p. 17). Those frameworks could not serve as a foundation for CBE, for to have a variant set of competencies across social work in effect would mean that there are no agreed-on social work competencies.

Logical reasoning is the dominant construction of the Georgia CBE (Jarrett, Kilpatrick, and Pollane, 1977). In a sense, its approach is an eclectic one, utilizing logical reasoning as the basis for evaluation of student competency. But logical reasoning is not necessarily sound reasoning. An argument may be logical in its systematic connection but may not necessarily reflect reality. Moreover, logical reasoning may not necessarily be ethical reasoning. Logic is essential in all scientific reasoning. However, logical reasoning based on a priori construction may not reflect in Dewey's terms the "practical character of reality."

In the Georgia program, students in the field are asked to tie their reasoning to conceptual theories (Jarrett, Kilpatrick, and

Pollane, 1977, p. 11). One example of the competencies identified in the field experience is as follows: "Specify, using some explicit conceptual framework, the intended results of the particular intervention and the acceptable range of outcomes and explore the possible unintended consequences involved in the chosen intervention prior to its implementation." This is a logical prescription, for students are asked first to select the premises and then to argue from them and predict their consequences. However, as the discussion on models suggested, many of the premises in social work have low validity. Therefore, although certain conclusions may validly follow from an accepted premise, they may not necessarily be true, since the premise itself may be invalid.

Grounded Theory and Moral Reasoning

Kohlberg's (1969) theory of moral reasoning has received considerable attention from social work educators. Lewis (1972), in an article on moral development and social justice, attempted to integrate Kohlberg's (1969) theory of moral reasoning with Rawls' (1971) theory of social justice and set its implications for social work. Richmond, Butler, and S. Abels (1975) used Kohlberg's theory of moral development as the framework for their articulation of empirical reasoning. P. Abels (1977) discussed its use in supervision and staff development. There is consanguinity between social work and Kohlberg's theory because the profession has a powerful set of moral commitments. Kohlberg's structure could improve the quality of social work education, for it prepares students to utilize moral reasoning in their reflective processes as well as to utilize the methodology to improve the moral reasoning of funding and allocation agencies, boards of directors, legislators, and service users.

In Kohlberg's view, the essential ingredient of moral development is not social pressure, the superego, or habit but rather a certain mode of reasoning and judgment. All forms of reasoning are products of particular cognitive structures. In his studies, six stages in the development of moral reasoning are identified within three levels: preconventional, conventional, and postconventional (Kohlberg, 1969, pp. 375–377).

Stage 1. The value of human life is undifferentiated from the value of property, and right is obedience to power and avoidance of punishment.

Stage 2. The differentiation between persons and property is made.

Stage 3. The intrinsic value of human life—based on social sharing, community, and love—is differentiated from the merely instrumental value of particular persons.

Stage 4. The value of the human being as a categorical member of a moral order is differentiated from a person's personal significance to those who know him or her, yet the value of human beings still is seen as coming from the sanction of the group.

Stage 5. A further differentiation is made between the value of human life and the value of the social order. Right is based on recognizing individual rights in a society with agreed-on rules, a social contract.

Stage 6. The value of human life is differentiated from the general will; the right to live is seen as a right that must be upheld despite the exigencies of society. At the sixth level, persons reason at higher stages and use more universal principles of social justice—principles such as reciprocity, equality, and human dignity. They achieve a greater scope of consistency across their actions and are motivated in ways that are more likely to be valid over a greater range of situations.

We view the characteristics of six-stage reasoning as desirable for social work, for one might have greater confidence in practitioners and policymakers who reason at the sixth level. We believe that this level would be benefited, however, if comparative analysis were used in the reasoning process (DeMarco and Richmond, 1975); for comparative reasoning enables us to determine empirically whether a principle is really universal: whether it can be applied in all situations and whether reasoners of comparable ability agree to its validity given a common set of premises from which to reason.

The central difference between present practice models and the one we have proposed is that ours focuses on how to think about practice, while the present models in social work, which can be considered content models, prescribe what to do in practice. As yet, the field has not documented the value of using comparative analysis in social work. Obviously, we have a strong hunch that a grounded approach coupled with public documentation would lead to more effective practice. We also know that Kohlberg's theory is not fully validated, since we do not know whether moral reasoning is related to moral actions. Additionally, one concern is that moral reasoning could become an evaluation structure if we were to reduce the concept to a narrow view that those who reasoned at low levels would not be considered competent. Although we believe that comparative reasoning would contribute to the development of the profession, translating the methodology into competency tests would not solve the problem of making our profession more competent.

Inquiry into Other Professions

One of the benefits of employing comparative methodology is that it permits use of research of other professions involved in competency-based education and gives access to data not necessarily related to the social work profession. The findings from other professions may lend support to one's research and/or raise questions about its reliability. Five professional education groups that recently have written of their concerns related to defining and evaluating CBE serve as a basis for our comparative analysis.

The medical profession has invested a good deal of its resources in defining and evaluating competency. One report (Linn, Arostequi, and Zappa, 1973, p. 169) on competency states: "Grades reportedly have had little predictive validity; neither has our [medicine's] system of credentiality. Although student behaviors seem important, those which specifically predict success in practice have not been identified. Furthermore, there is still a question concerning how these behaviors can best be measured and by whom."

Examining competency by the use of patient management problems (cases) often is subject to debate; present data as to their concurrent validity are ambiguous, ill defined, and difficult to interpret, and evidence of their predictive validity needs to be collected. "Good performance on a patient management problem will not predict real-life performance" (Finkel and Norman, 1973, p. 176). Utilizing direct observation of pediatric students and comparing their results with overall long-term evaluations of the students, Finkel and Norman (1973, p. 179) noted that "single evaluations correlated very poorly with long-term evaluations."

The nursing literature reveals somewhat the same type of analysis. After surveying the field comprehensively, Wooley (1977, p. 21) declared: "There is no valid [or] reliable method of grading students in the clinical area in baccalaureate education." Research on educational techniques indicated that modules were not significantly more successful than other tutorial methods and that the independent study approach was no more effective than small-group teaching with a supportive teacher.

A project to initiate competency-based learning (CBL) in graduate courses in organizational behavior was initiated at Case Western Reserve University in 1975. Although it is too early to assess results, certain factors have emerged. The task of delineating detailed behavior descriptions can be overwhelming, and "one rapidly loses sight of the organic wholeness of effective competent professional work. It isn't the individual minute-by-minute acts that produce the effect; it's their organization into significant gestalts" (Wolfe, 1976, p. 86). In reaction to a concern for the fragmentation of practice through overspecification, participants began to evaluate using more general criteria. Issues developed over new faculty roles and autonomy. Compromises that were made to resolve issues were seldom satisfactory (Wolfe, 1976, p. 100). Additionally, students were under increased stress, compared with earlier organizational behavior programs.

Teachers of prospective business professionals found that reaction to rising educational costs has resulted in a desire for accountability, leading to measurement of "the product by statements of competency and objectives" (Sheehan and Brown, 1977, p. 211). One program attempted to limit classes to fifteen students, so that individualized instruction and time would be enhanced, but the class sizes soon increased to about thirty. No grades were given, and individual statements were made about the students' progress in each competency area. Student transcripts then listed the competencies demonstrated in each course. "Consequently, a student's transcript may be from twenty to forty pages in length" (Sheehan and Brown, 1977, p. 214). The self-pacing concept also had limitations, since students who failed to complete course work within six months were not likely to finish at all.

The University of Houston evolved a major list of sixteen competencies required of its business school students (Sheehan and Brown, 1977). Each competency, however, has a number of subparts, so that the number of items to be evaluated is increased. Because of the number of items, plus the different levels of student competencies, "the tracking of students as they progress through the program systematically building toward competence can be a nightmare" (Sheehan and Brown, 1977, p. 225). In addition, "the faculty member may find [that] his/her course content needs to be brought into line with the goals and objectives of the entire competency-based system. This can be disruptive to most faculty and may border on infringement of academic freedom" (Sheehan and Brown, 1977, p. 227).

Social work educators and researchers have a long history of attempting to assess the competence of students and practitioners. The results of their efforts, however, have been negligible. The University of Chicago attempted to assess skills in casework through a list of sixty-four performance items. The instrument's major limitations were related to inconsistent, disparate levels of specificity in each task definition and few clear guidelines to discriminate between acceptable and unacceptable responses (Arkava and Brennen, 1976, p. 11). Cummins (1976, p. 8) notes low correlations of .28 when comparing the Tulane assessment score with field instructor ratings. Other methods of judging also have proved inconclusive. In discussing simulation experiments, Cummins notes, "These data are not particularly encouraging and leave us with the conclusion that the validity of stimulated assessment situations needs to be demonstrated" (p. 59).

In a self-assessment of their CBE program, the Montana group acknowledged the difficulties encountered in assessment procedures: "The experience of conducting the program has made its many shortcomings all too obvious . . . ; [they] appear to be both a function of our selection of criteria for social work practice competence and a function of our choice of a work sample methodology for obtaining a measure of that competence" (Cummins, 1976, pp. 90–91).

Another crucial issue is dealt with by Brennen (1976, p. 130): "Perhaps the most questionable aspect of the work sample approach is that it places a severe limitation on the content of the exam. In other words, one is constrained to test primarily on what the student has actually been exposed to in the practicum. This approach works very well with dental hygienists, all of whom are required to scrape teeth and can be examined readily on this module of learning."

CBE's greatest impact has been on the education profession. "Rarely if ever has any movement swept through teacher education so rapidly and captured the attention of so many in so short of a time" (Quirk, 1975, p. 316). There have been countless articles on CBE and its variants. These have mushroomed because of the efforts to make CBE training compulsory for the education of teachers. There is general agreement, even among its supporters, that CBE is a concept that has not been initiated fully in a nearly pure form in any curriculum, has not yet been tested, and is fraught with problems administratively, politically, and evidentially. In a recent survey of five undergraduate institutions using CBE, Jarrett (1977) examined six areas of concern, including faculty and staff satisfaction and curriculum and administrative problems. However, he did not ask about the effectiveness of the program. This is fairly typical of most reports on CBE. They are descriptive and analytical when discussing attempts to initiate the program, resistance to it, formulation of competencies, training of faculty, scheduling, and so forth; however, none deals evaluatively with the program outcomes over any period.

A substantive report, *The Power of Competency-Based Education* (Rosner, 1972), advocates the establishment of national, government-subsidized training programs in CBE. Criticisms attached to the report, however, note that at Michigan State 2,700 modules were developed as competency requirements for elementary education. The report concludes that "competency-based training and performance-based certification are new and virtually untested concepts" (p. 309).

A number of states have made CBE compulsory. In some, competency examinations have been established for high school graduates. There is a strong push for establishing CBE throughout the United States, but these programs have been opposed rigorously by several groups. The reasons for the opposition range from self-serving perspectives and alternative views to the dangers of loss of academic freedom. In Texas a law establishing CBE as the only approach to be used in teacher training was challenged, and the challenge was upheld. At present, it is one of a number of options. The argument regarding academic freedom was the critical variable. In Arizona a similar law was defeated in a state election. There has been concern, however, that funds still will go to programs similar to those using a CBE model. The influence of the CBE programs has been enhanced by the willingness of the federal government and some state legislatures to support their initiation.

The supporters of CBE maintain that current educational programs have been a dismal failure and point to nationally poor reading scores and minority failures in schools. Pettigrew (1974, p. 76) states, "When minority pupil behaviors are unsystematically changed in the classroom, as in traditional school settings, they are not involved in a competency-based program of education." Supporters further contend that we too often are more concerned with the admissions criteria of the student than with the outcomes of the educational process. CBE, they say, would individualize the student, who could proceed at his or her own pace, and use faculty members for personal developmental needs.

Critics of CBE maintain that teachers are being blamed for the failures of society, poor student learning, parental neglect, insufficient funding, and political maneuvering. It is now the teachers' fault that students do poorly in school. Statements such as "faculty learning is perceived to be a product of the classroom environment rather than a product of postulated incompetencies and incapacities of a faulty pupil" (Pettigrew, 1974, p. 75) tend to make scapegoats of teachers. Critics also point out the dangers in an educational system where everyone has to learn the same things in the same way. This, they say, promotes control of education and ensures that the status quo will prevail, limiting creativity once the initial creative thrust of the new approach has subsided. Critics and supporters agree on the extreme tentativeness of any list of competencies, but there is a lack of agreement as to what makes competent professional teachers; the list varies from program to program as well as from the philosophical mode of one instructor to that of the next.

Results of Comparative Analysis

We have examined five professional disciplines and one area of multidisciplinary study interested in attempting to evaluate their students' competence: medicine, nursing, business, social work, education, and organizational behavior. Of these, four attempted to establish competency-based education. What does our analysis show?

1. There is universal concern among these professions regarding producing competent practitioners as well as finding ways in which this competence can be measured. None has found a method it considers valid.

2. All the groups have had extreme difficulties in establishing the competencies to be measured, even though there is general agreement on some basic items. All refer to long lists of items, disputes over items, and a lack of specificity. In all cases, decisions were made by consensus.

3. All groups found it difficult to make the jump from effective student learning in the classroom to effective novice practice.

4. Each expresses near failure in attempts to measure competency because of measurement validity; that is, the use of either judges, simulations, or pencil-and-paper tests has proved invalid. There is a groping for any method that will offer a solution. One study suggests establishing a panel of judges comprised of the student, his supervisor, and a faculty member. Such a panel would be comparable to that used to judge an Olympic swimming meet.

5. Those involved in CBE have commented that it requires a great deal of time, faculty training, and development of new faculty roles.

6. Personal political issues developed and impinged on what properly should be educational issues.

7. Research on CBE is lacking. There is no evidence that it does a better job than, or even as good a job as, more traditional approaches.

8. To permit measurement, it has been necessary to narrow and limit the definitions of what professionals do.

9. None of the current CBE programs has been established in a manner that maintains the totality of the approach in all its projected benefits.

10. Although the self-pacing idea seems to help individualize the learning experience, time limits have been set because student interest lags if the time drags on.

11. None of the programs has been in existence long enough to assess its success. There is a positive feeling that faculty members work together, students like the approach, and agencies seem to believe it is a feasible educational technique. No control methods have been instituted, and critical evaluations by supporters or others have not yet been made.

12. In some programs, CBE has created increased stress for the student, and it has been noted that there is pressure to learn for the test.

13. Three of the professions have low status and are "women's" professions. Business and organizational development are not low in status but have struggled with their professional image. In that sense, business, nursing, organizational behavior, teaching, and social work have had to work hard to gain professional recognition.

Admitted difficulties and program results seem to indicate that competency-based education in social work has not provided clear advantages over other approaches and is not viable with our current and near-future levels of knowledge. Evidence from other professions indicates that they, too, have been unable to mount adequate CBE programs. Why, then, do efforts continue to establish CBE as an alternative in education for the professions? Why are professionals who are working for a more scientific, effective approach to education so willing to expound the benefits of CBE programs without scientifically oriented inquiry?

First, we must admit that in social work education the motives are clear and not suspect. The goal is to train more effective practitioners, not to sell a particular approach for political reasons (for example, teacher education in Texas and Arizona). One is impressed by the amount of painstaking work in which the authors and prime movers of the Montana and Georgia programs became involved. We not only are impressed but exhilarated that faculty would work so well together, attempt new things, and be as self-critical as their reports suggest. However, we must look beyond their work to the subtle influences in our society that must have affected them as well as others in their determination to look to CBE as an alternative form of professional social work education.

The task for all of us is the development of a "scientific" approach to professional education. But *scientific* in the minds of many educators means utilizing behavioral objectives, an outgrowth of behavior management and/or scientific management approaches. Callahan (1962) traces the line from Taylor's Scientific Management (SM) to the current efficiency experts, SM's discreditation in management, and its movement into education. This led in turn to the growth of the profession of "education administration" and the strong influence of trained administrators on educational policies and programs in recent years. The reasons for the popularity of these scientific management processes seem simple, obvious, and related to the concepts of science and management (therefore business and therefore success and prestige). State the objectives in behavioral terms, organize the program to meet the objectives, evaluate, and then onward to success. It sounds simple, but the complications set in when one must decide the following: (1) What are the objectives, are they valid, and who sets them? (2) Can all objectives be observed equally well? (3) Should the teacher/worker control the objectives? (4) Should all social workers have the same objectives? (5) Is it true that we should not be concerned about the values underlying an objective? (6) Will specifying the objectives so that they can be measured reduce them to worthlessness? (7) Will enough specific objectives lead to the whole of social work, or is the whole greater than its parts?

Finally, in our profession what evidence indicates that setting educational behavioral objectives leads to improved learning? How universal are the results when translated to practice? Do the students then practice with a behavioral objective frame of reference? Stevens (1976, p. 39), investigating the effectiveness of the behavioral objectives approach, states: "Whatever the claims made for behavioral objectives, however, the empirical evidence for lauding their use is sketchy at best. . . . The inconclusiveness of research on behavioral objectives at this point would seem to argue for restraint in attempting to make them a matter of public policy."

Mager's (1962a, 1962b) theory of education, which serves as a basis for all CBE programs, "is essentially a managerial theory, and indeed is identical with the idea of behavior management reinforcement theory" (Gardner, 1977, p. 390). As an educational idea, it appeared on the American scene early in "this century in the guise of the efficiency movement. . . . It has reappeared in the current emphasis upon competency-based instruction" (Gardner, 1977, p. 390). Thus, we see that a weakly established educational formulation, behavioral objectives, served as a basis for a weakly validated educational methodology, competency-based education.

Although CBE programs generally claim to be based on concepts of systems theory, the concept tends to be reductionist rather than holistic, for two reasons: (1) the number of competencies (tasks) that can be examined and evaluated must be limited and (2) to meet the requirements of specificity in behavioral objectives, tasks have to be partialized and delimited to their most simple forms. According to Gardner (1977, p. 381), "the movement toward operational clarity required us to progressively delimit the scope of the objective. The method may be stated formally as the decomposing of a complex whole behavior into smaller, simpler, more manageable parts." Our own initial interest in evolving further the base of CBE is an example of the seductive appeal of such a simple idea. On the surface it seemed solid. On reflection, its shortcomings become clearer and the dangers worrisome. Perhaps our marginal commitment to CBE permitted a more critical comparative view.

It is important that we be clear about the direction social work must take and the skills and knowledge necessary to reach that goal. We have a legitimate responsibility to attempt to devise methods of assessing whether these goals have been achieved. However, when we are required to state these objectives in terms that reduce the complexities to a list of observable techniques, we no longer are involved in professional education but in training programs. Competency-based education will tend to narrow our profession's perspectives on helping rather than keep it the more open profession it has worked hard to become. It was not too long ago that the doctrines of Freud enveloped 99 percent of social work education's orientation. We need practitioners who can think beyond the pattern of restricted, agreed-on competencies. In fact, it may be that the novel, nontraditional responses permit helping to occur in some situations. Strean (1977) recently examined the paradox of the beginning social work student who is able to help clients when more experienced workers fail. He suggests that often it is their lack of knowledge and experience that permits a more accurate and effective response. Our additional suggestion is that it, indeed, may be a more creative response but one that may be trained out of people over time. Until we can discover the evidence related to what it is that works in the helping situation, CBE's contribution can be valuable in those defined areas where it is clear which skills are needed. For instance, conducting research or surveys, reporting accurately, making referrals, locating supportive services, and writing proposals are tasks that can be defined, objectified, partialized, and simplified. They are applicable to the type of CBE that the initiators of the approach had in mind when they spoke of the child's inability to read, do mathematics, or write. And these are the types of tasks in which the variables are more limited and able to be controlled by the educator.

Social work is not a simple profession; it probably is one of the most complex in the range of professions. The reason, of course, is that an extraordinary number of variables must be dealt with in any work with people. Weizenbaum (1977, p. 38), an expert on computer science, notes his choice of mathematics over human relations work because of the simplicity of the former and the complexity of the latter.

As we draw to a conclusion, there is one further point we must examine. Does CBE support the social work profession's commitment to social justice? Does it seem to demand this commitment from students? We think not. It is neutral and passionless because concepts such as commitment to social justice are difficult behavioral objectives to measure. For the benefits of a "competency fix," we may be forced into a values "cop-out" and a mechanical approach to helping. If we can write behavioral objectives and reach them, we are told, we will be competent and will have resolved the demands for accountability. Too often we are told to be accountable to funding sources or to the client. In fact, our accountability goes beyond any one group. Our accountability is to the betterment of the social life of the community.

We are suggesting another approach to social work education that, in our view, melds into the central thrust of the research orientation proposed by many social work educators. Like other approaches, it is in the exploratory stage, with one major difference: experienced practitioners use comparative analysis as their reasoning framework. The utilization of grounded theory permits a development of knowledge from the expanded experience of practitioners. The efforts of professionals to raise the levels of their reasoning ability, as set forth by Kohlberg, provide an escalation of the professional thought process and, perhaps, more competent actions. Our emphasis on learned experience as exemplified by traditional field learning is a model that other professionals are initiating in their curricula. Field experiences are a primary source of grounded practice. We can enhance our use of the field experience by attempting to structure more of the theoretical component (for example, increased moral reasoning and comparative approaches) to avoid the error of students' learning only what the experience has to teach without being able to put those experiences into a broader perspective. The foundation for future professional competence seems to be the capacity to learn how to learn. This, it seems to us, would be one major contribution to the field that a grounded approach to education could make.

6

Using a Social Competence Framework for Both Client and Practitioner

Claude F. Wiegand

Competence in the practice of social work has foundations in the larger domain of human social functioning. The capabilities of a helping person appear to be as much the product of life experience as they are of professional education. Hence, the elements of performance found in the social worker have analogs in the social competencies of the client. Understandings about the one provide insights about the other. Crane (1974) identified basic elements of practitioner performance and aligned them with the six components of interpersonal competence described by Foote and Cottrell (1955) in their family research project.

The first part of this chapter is devoted to a description of a framework of competence constructed from the six components of competence supplied by Crane (1974) and Foote and Cottrell

(1955). Each component of competence is further delineated by stages or levels of development supplied by numerous researchers on human development. The remainder of the chapter deals with implications of the framework for social work education and practice on topics such as professional entrance requirements, the recognition and integration of experiental learning in professional education, learning methodologies for academic degrees and continuing education, and, finally, the generalist-specialist dichotomy.

Before we describe the framework of competence, a definition of the term *competence* might be in order. Competence often is used as a synonym for ability. According to Foote and Cottrell (1955, p. 36), "it means a satisfactory degree of ability for performing certain implied kinds of tasks." The term *social competence* is used because the ability pertains to interpersonal relations and skills involved in controlling the outcome of episodes of interaction. Siporin (1975) combines White's (1963) conception of competence with the Foote and Cottrell version and defines it "as a capacity to interact with one's environment, to have influence on the environment, and to interact cooperatively with others so as to achieve life tasks and goals" (1975, p. 365).

In light of the above definitions, a fuller definition of competence begins to emerge. *Competence is the capacity of a person to engage his full range of abilities appropriately in interaction with and by influencing his environment and the people in it in such a way as to achieve life tasks and goals fairly.* The term *cooperatively* used in Siporin's definition has been replaced here with the word *fairly.* Not all interaction among people needs to be cooperative as long as it is fair. Pincus and Minahan (1973, p. 81) identify three types of relationships in social interaction; namely, collaborative, bargaining, and conflictual.

Framework of Social Competence

There appear to be six distinctive components or categories of competence basic in the gamut of abilities manifested in social workers and clients alike. This was noted in a study completed by Crane (1974) involving 261 students in field placements from the University of British Columbia School of Social Work and 31 students in field placements from the Calgary School of Social Welfare. His aim was to identify major factors or components in social work practice performance and to explore their relationship to characteristics of the students on admission to an MSW program. A factor analysis of a general seventy-item Q-sort of the 292 students revealed that more than half of the variance in items was accounted for by four factors: confident, goal-directed performance or morale (21 percent); effective performance of discretionary tasks (13 percent); analytical skills (10 percent); and assertiveness on social and professional issues (7 percent). Separate Q-sorts of thirty items each were used with students in casework ($N = 205$), group work ($N = 26$), and community organization ($N = 17$). The latter two sample groups were too small to permit the use of multivariate data reduction procedures. Three factors accounted for more than half of the variance in casework performance: development and management of treatment relationship with individuals (34 percent), skills in family casework (14 percent), and problem exploration and assessment (5 percent). Crane noted the resemblance of the factors he had identified to the following components of interpersonal competence identified by Foote and Cottrell (1955) in a family research project (Crane's factors are those in parentheses): health (confident, goal-directed performance or morale), intelligence (analytical skills), autonomy (assertiveness on social and professional issues), empathy (development and management of treatment relationships), judgment (problem exploration and assessment as well as skills in family casework), and creativity (effective performance of discretionary tasks and part of the morale factor). These components and factors will be discussed in the sections to follow.

The health dimension provided by Foote and Cottrell (1955) includes more than the absence of disease. Rather, it signifies "the progressive maximization—within organic limits—of the ability of the organism to exercise all of its physiological functions and to achieve its maximum of sensory acuity, strength, energy, coordination, dexterity, endurance, recuperative power, and immunity" (p. 52). The "maximization—within organic limits"—allows for the recognition of the competence potential of physically and mentally handicapped persons (Wolfensberger, 1972). As a factor influencing coping ability, health can be regarded as a consequent as well as an antecedent in the human condition. Rest, hygiene, diet, recreation, and exercise become important considerations related to fatigue, for example, as one of many conditions affecting interpersonal episodes.

Among the indicators contributing to the morale dimension of the health-morale component, "the strongest are the ability to maintain hope in the face of frustrations and setbacks and to cope with everyday work difficulties with no sign of disorganization or immobilization" (Crane, 1974, p. 85). A confident, goal-directed orientation appeared to be a good predictor of performance among the students in the Crane study. This area of consideration relates to the much-discussed topics among social work clients, students, and practitioners—alienation, disillusionment, and cynicism. Physical, psychological, and environmental factors affect personal motivation levels related to quality of service and living. Various instruments have been developed to measure these variables. Heimler (1975) has developed an approach that combines an assessment technique with a method of counseling based on his theory of human social functioning. Jones and Pfeiffer (1973) assess the motivation level and direction of individuals, on the job and elsewhere, by using measurement instruments based on Maslow's (1954, 1968), hierarchy-of-needs scale.

Of various alternatives that might be used as a scale to differentiate levels of development in this component of competence, Maslow's hierarchy of needs lends itself well to the framework of social competence being proposed. Maslow identifies five levels of needs: basic physiological needs (hunger, sex, and thirst), safety needs (security, protection, limits), social needs (love, belongingness), esteem needs (self-esteem, esteem of others), and—the highest level—self-actualization (peak levels of self-fulfillment). If a person's level of need is fixed on basic physiological needs, such as wondering where the next meal will come from, it becomes exceedingly difficult to discuss with that person his responsibilities for meeting the emotional needs of his family. However, if an employee's highest level of need peaks in the area of social and esteem needs, the employee probably will be able to assume a fair amount of responsibility on the job.

The realization of these individual needs suggests another

aspect of this dimension of competence—a dimension that White (1966, p. 395) calls "expansion of caring." He refers to Adler as the source of this concept, the meaning of which can be found in phrases such as "sense of human solidarity" and "fellowship in human community." In an attempt to bring together all the elements described above, I suggest that the term *self-realization* be used to describe what we started out calling the health-morale component. In the proposed framework of social competence, *self-realization* is developed by ensuring *adequate opportunity* as a basic right through the instrumental principle of *caring provision*.

The intelligence component includes the "scope of perception of relationships amongst events; the capacity to abstract and symbolize experience, to manipulate the symbols into meaningful generalizations, and to be articulate in communication; skill in mobilizing the resources of environment and experience in the services of a variety of goals" (Foote and Cottrell, 1955, p. 53).

Going beyond the much-studied subject of measures of intelligence, our "future shock" generation of educators should be concerned with creating relevant antecedent conditions in maximizing the intelligence component for use in ever changing sets of conditions. A universalist education seems to call as much for the development of basic reasoning, analytical skills, and evaluative skills as it does for the acquisition of information and ideas, which are being constantly replaced or developed. Various authors contribute theory about cognitive development that provides distinguishable stages in intellectual development (Bloom and others, 1956; Piaget, 1948). These stages generally include movement from concrete memorization, through recognition of relationships among variables, to cognitive processes that construct combinations of relationships as well as create new combinations and, finally, apply concepts or principles to new settings and evaluate the outcomes.

Crane (1974, p. 104) found that intelligence was the only variable that was discriminated to an important degree by the variables of the student's college record and rated academic potential. Our experiences at the Regina School of Social Work in Saskatchewan, where a rather open admissions policy has been in effect, do not entirely support the direct relationship between intelligence, in the way it is traditionally defined, and rated academic potential. One of our colleagues at Regina recently presented a position paper on experiential learning (Stange, 1977) that identifies differential perceptions of social work educational goals that have evolved historically. Emphasis on any one of three learning models may provide differing opportunities for students of varying academic potentials with respect to the development of intelligence components: an apprenticeship model, which derives from agency task-factoring; a socialization model, which focuses on competency criteria of an emerging profession; and a developmental model, which implies generalist approaches based on assessment of client/consumer needs. The Regina School of Social Work has emphasized the developmental model but includes elements of the other two models as well. The developmental model lends itself particularly well to a wide range of learning methodologies that engage students in learning. Furthermore, such approaches help to develop cognitive capacities irrespective of the level at which students function at the outset. Experiential learning techniques are utilized along with the more traditional methods. The effect of this approach is that concrete examples in the students' experiences underpin the cognitive processes even as they move to higher levels of abstraction.

Considered as a competency, intelligence requires that an individual's right to *freedom of thought* not only be acknowledged in terms of what a person thinks but also with respect to how that individual thinks. In social work, the instrumental principle of *acceptance* is intended to ensure such freedom.

Empathy, according to Foote and Cottrell (1955, p. 54), refers to the "ability correctly to interpret the attitudes and intentions of others, to perceive situations from others' standpoint, and thus to anticipate and predict their behavior. This type of social sensitivity rests on what we call the empathic responses. Empathic responses are basic to 'taking the role of the other' and hence to social interaction and the communicative processes upon which rests social integration." Other more recent and popular researchers in the field of communications have developed the concept of empathy to a rather high degree (Carkhuff, 1969; Rogers, 1961). Rogers (p. 284) says: "To sense the client's private world as if it were your own, but without losing the 'as if' quality—this is empathy."

Ten variables describing the development and management

of treatment relationships had high factor loadings in the Crane study (1974, p. 82). He found relationship skills to be the most heavily weighted component in casework performance (p. 53). Items that failed to discriminate at a statistically significant level in the Crane study are worth noting. Students with high scores in dominance—a trait that Cattell (1962, p. 11) associates with being extrapunitive, opinionated, and authoritarian—may have difficulty accommodating the needs of the client, genuinely accepting the client's limitations, respecting the client's need to defend himself, being tentative and open to change in diagnostic judgment, and helping the client focus on a part of the problem (Crane, 1974, p. 61).

While many different systems of communication are used in establishing empathic relationships with clients, I use and teach Ivey and Authier's (1978) microcounseling approach to facilitate helping relationships. Three reasons support the recommendation of the microcounseling approach for competency-based education. First, it emphasizes behavioral forms of communication that translate desirable qualities (warmth, empathy, genuineness, and so forth) into sight and sound messages. Videotape recordings and measurement instruments are used to confirm the development of these skills. Second, it focuses on the meaning and direction of the client's principal concern, which maximizes the openness of the communication relationship and increases the pertinency of material used in problem solving. Third, the skills taught can be used by counselors and therapists of differing persuasions.

In the framework of social competence, this component is listed as *communication,* with the instrumental principle described as *openness.* Openness is aimed at enhancing the client's right to *freedom of expression.*

According to Foote and Cottrell (1955, p. 55), autonomy refers to "the clarity of the individual's conception of self (identity); the extent to which he maintains a stable set of internal standards by which he acts; the degree to which he is self-directed and self-controlled in his actions; his confidence in and reliance upon himself; the degree of self-respect he maintains; and the capacity for recognizing real threats to self and of mobilizing realistic defenses when so threatened. That is, autonomy is taken to be genuine self-government, construed as an ability, not a state of affairs. A narrower definition, close to operational, is ease in giving and receiving evaluations of self and others."

Crane's (1974, p. 112) factor corresponding to autonomy relates to the student's assertiveness on social and professional issues. Top scorers in this factor "were less likely to have learned about social work from 'academic' sources and more likely to have been influenced in career choice by work experience, more likely to have reported spare time activities concerned with civil rights or similar groups . . . and more likely to have grown up in a small town or rural area." The last factor, however, accounted for 1 percent of the total discrimination.

Autonomy, in my estimation, is one of the most important characteristics of the professional helping person. Based on the primary value of freedom, self-determination is a cardinal principle to be observed in the helping relationship. Fromm (1941, pp. 136–206) identified mechanisms of escape that prevent people from assuming autonomy. More recently, Freire (1970, 1973) has taught a humanizing pedagogy of the oppressed, in which people in cultures of silence achieve autonomy through a process of consciousness raising. Through communication and dialogue, people move from magical consciousness (other determined), through naïve consciousness (intellectual awareness), to critical consciousness (responsible action) in the conduct of their lives in community.

Stages of development for the autonomy component are derived from the literature on ego development. Chickering (1976) has provided an excellent summary of the research on this and many of the other stages and levels of development referred to in this chapter. Levels of autonomy, extracted from five sources and categorized by Chickering (1976, p. 67), include the following: amoral, fearful-dependent, opportunistic, conforming to persons, conforming to rule, and principled autonomous. Loevinger, Wessler, and Redmore's (1970, pp. 3–6) version of these levels identifies *autonomous* and *integrated* under the last-mentioned category.

Another interesting accommodation of these categories can be found in a paradigm developed by Jackson (1973) at the University of Massachusetts. He calls it Black Identity Development Theory. I have been able to adapt the theory to all majority-minority dichotomies in which autonomy is at issue—for example, male-female, teacher-students, parent-offspring, rich-poor, leader-follower, employer-employee. Also, whole groups of people and social movements often are noted to move through stages of the Jackson paradigm. The majority and minority sides of each dichotomy move through stages related to their respective roles, generally called active acceptance, passive acceptance, active resistance, redirection, and internalization. An example of how the two sides of the dichotomy might look at the stage called internalization follows: The minority persons are proud of their culture and identity in or out of a majority setting; they feel free to eliminate all that promotes oppression. The majority persons respect minorities by being sensitive to the differences among them; there is no felt need to compensate for past oppression. This stage corresponds to Loevinger's (1970) autonomous-integrated level of ego development. In the framework of social competence, this component is rightfully described as *autonomy,* which requires *freedom of choice* as a right. The social work principle of *self-determination* is intended to recognize and promote freedom of choice.

"Judgment refers here to the ability which develops slowly in human beings to estimate and evaluate the meaning and consequences to one's self of alternative lines of conduct. It means the ability to adjudicate among values, or to make correct decisions; . . . it is an acquired critical ability differing in degree among individuals" (Foote and Cottrell, 1955, p. 56). In Crane's (1974, pp. 62–69) study, judgment is represented by the categories of family casework skills and problem assessment, both of which have high loadings on Q-sort items related to judgment. The predictors in the family casework skill area point to such requirements as a clear sense of direction, a feeling of confidence in what one is doing, and a belief in the usefulness of available resources. In the problem assessment area, the factor loads support a need for exercising judgment as to what information is relevant, taking the initiative in exploring the problem with clients, and, in the process, helping the client to partialize the problem.

Foote and Cottrell (1955) point out that in their day studies were focusing on the outcome of judgment—ethics, logic, or abstractions of contingencies and relative utilities. In contrast, the work of Kohlberg (1975) has focused on the choosers, their identities, and the conditions under which their critical abilities develop. Over a period of twenty years, Kohlberg carried out validation research on the Dewey-Piaget levels of moral reasoning. These separate longitudinal studies of widely dispersed groups (in Chicago and in Turkey and eight other countries) have produced some excellent definitions and understanding of moral stages of judgment that have significance in the work of anyone who relates to people in community. A second development related to judgment has been in the field of values clarification (axiology), which is being developed by people such as Simon, Howe, and Kirschenbaum (1972).

Kohlberg's (1975) six stages of development represent progressive degrees of concern for justice; movement is usually forward except in extreme trauma, development is one step at a time, and thinking at a higher stage includes or comprehends within it lower-stage thinking. At each higher stage, the conception of justice is reorganized. A summary of Kohlberg's (1975, p. 49) six stages (the sixth stage is based on Rawls, 1971) of development in moral judgment follows:

Stage 1: The punishment-and-obedience orientation. Justice is punishing the bad in terms of "an eye for an eye and a tooth for a tooth."

Stage 2: The instrumental-relativist orientation. Goods and favors are to be exchanged in an equal manner ("you scratch my back, and I'll scratch yours"), not out of loyalty, gratitude, or justice.

Stage 3: The interpersonal concordance or "good boy–nice girl" orientation. Good behavior is what pleases others or is approved by them.

Stage 4: The "law-and-order" orientation. Right behavior consists of doing one's duty, respecting authority, and maintaining the given social order for its own sake.

Stage 5: The social-contract legalistic orientation. It is recognized that all rules and laws flow from justice, from a social contract between governors and the governed, designed to protect the equal rights of all.

Stage 6: The universalist-ethical-principle orientation. Personally chosen moral principles also are principles of justice—the principles any member of a society would choose for that society if the person did not know what his or her position was to be in the society and in which he or she might be the last advantaged.

The educational process for moral development suggested by Kohlberg (1975, p. 52) is the cognitive-developmental theory. In it "morality is a natural product of a universal human tendency toward empathy or role taking, toward putting oneself in the shoes of other conscious beings." Reconstructions of tendencies to role-take and the reorganization of conceptions of justice occur in two ways. First, through discussion and communication such as is used in value clarification exercises, individuals can be faced with moral dilemmas that challenge them to move to a level one step above the current one perceived as unsatisfactory. A second and perhaps more important way of stimulating moral growth is to be found in the total moral environment or atmosphere in which we live—in our homes, schools, and the broader society. In these places, opportunities for role taking must be provided to allow individuals to take the point of view of others. Varying levels of moral development pervade these environments that influence and shape us.

Social work, with a code of ethics and principles of practice pitched at a stage-6 level of moral development, has a contribution to make to society by creating a moral climate for living. In the Netherlands, *agogy* is a term used to describe a generalist approach to human helping that emphasizes autonomy and judgment. Education of the young "places emphasis on harmonious character or personality formation, on a training for social competence, on the guided development of emotional and moral life, on building an inner-directedness and life-orientation, on guided growth toward human adulthood with its requirements for participation in societal and cultural life" (Ten Have, 1973, p. 41).

Judgment, in the social competence framework, is a component of human competence that generates and demands the *right of equality,* equality used in the sense of fair treatment. In social work practice, the principle of being *nonjudgmental* promotes these attitudes.

Creativity is defined by Foote and Cottrell (1955, p. 57) as "any demonstrated capacity for innovations in behavior or real reconstruction of any aspect of this social environment. It involves the ability to develop fresh perspectives from which to view all accepted routines and to make novel combinations of ideas and objects and so define new goals, endowing old ones with fresh meaning, and inventing means for their realization. . . . Among other things it seems to involve curiosity, self-confidence, something of the venturesomeness and risk-taking tendencies of the explorer, a flexible mind with the kind of freedom which permits the orientation of spontaneous play."

The creativity area of competence is researched by Crane (1974) under the rubric of effective performance of discretionary tasks. This emphasis was chosen in the belief that the ability to meet the demands for discretionary tasks may be a critical determinant of the student's overall development. The 13 percent of total variance explained by this factor is fairly high. Crane (1974) reports that Goodwin's (1972) study of sixteen widely ranging professions places social work students near the top of the group on factors of trust, venturesomeness, tendermindedness, and imaginativeness and near the bottom on role adherence and preference for experimentation. This pattern is associated with traits of sociability, boldness, readiness to try new things, rule evasion, expedience, confidence in one's beliefs, group dependence, and trust in others (Crane, 1974, p. 97).

Stages in the process of creativity are identified by Alamshah (1967, p. 312) as preparation, incubation, illumination, and verification. These correspond rather closely to the stages of Bloom's (1956) cognitive domain. Interestingly, Alamshah stresses the significance of the relationship between the creativity process and what he calls the minimal conditions for creativity. These conditions include motivation, self-limitation (selectivity), receptivity (openness), and competence. The condition of competence involves mastery of those tools required for creative activity in any of the modes of creativity, including creative art, creative intelligence, and creative living. This writing concerns itself primarily with creative living, the tools of which appear to be attributes and skills founded in the six components of competence.

Another point worth noting in Alamshah's article pertains to the condition of self-limitation or selectivity: "the adoption of an adequate valuing system and the development of the kind of character that will help us meet the demands of the environment and our creative projects" (1967, p. 313). Chickering (1976, pp. 83–85) refers to this adoption and development process as clarifying purposes or developing interests. He uses Allport's phrase in saying that the pursuit of major goals "configurates a life." Creativity, then, is not an activity that merely reconstructs life, ideas, or objects out of what comes from the environment (second causes). "The creative act is a free and independent force, immanently inherent only in a person, a personality. Only something arising in original substance and possessing the power to increase power in the world can be true creativity. . . . Creativity is an original act of personalities in the world" (Berdyaev, 1955, p. 135). "Original substance" is of the order of first causes. It involves the interaction of an individual, guided by primary and secondary value principles, with events and alternatives in one's environment. In the face of many forms of determinism (economic, psychic, historical, and technological), the human personality can become fragmented and plagued with ano-mie. Free, creative, principled persons are energized and directed by purposeful ends, not by means that cause other-directedness. Von Bertalanffy (1955, p. 243) calls this kind of self-directness "per-spectivism," as distinguished from reductionism.

In the social competence framework, we have identified caring provision, acceptance, openness, self-determination, and non-judgmental as secondary (instrumental) principles that ensure the basic human rights (abstract values) identified respectively as ade-quate opportunity, freedom of thought, freedom of expression, free-dom of choice, and equality (fair treatment). These rights have their foundations in the general requirements for human function-ing (the components of competence): self-realization, intelligence, communication, autonomy, and judgment. To the five spheres of competence in the framework, the final sphere now can be added. It is *creativity*. Since creativity involves a principled configuring of one's life, the term chosen to describe the right that arises from the need to create is the *pursuit of happiness*.

Interrelationships of the Components of Competence

The components of the framework of social competence represent internal dimensions of the domain of human competence.

In the definition of competence given earlier, the phrase "capacity of a person to engage his full range of abilities" suggests a capacity arising out of the synergistic effects of the components in combination. In everything a person does, all these components operate in concert. This is somewhat exemplified in Kirschenbaum's (1976, pp. 101–103) description of factors essential in the valuing process. These include *thinking* (in terms of the following dimensions: levels or types of thinking, moral reasoning, and divergent thinking), *feeling* (cherishing a value, self-image, awareness, discharging feeling), *choosing or decision making* (goal setting, information gathering, selecting alternatives, considering consequences, choosing fully), *communication* (sending and receiving messages, empathy, conflict resolution), and *acting* (repeatedly on beliefs, consistently toward goals, skillfully). The self-realization component is not included here, but all five of the other components of competence are included. This exercise of starting with a focus on one component, in this case judgment, to ascertain related skills would no doubt turn out the same way with each other component. What begins to suggest itself is that all the components of competency essentially affect the others. For example, persons faced with danger (safety need within health-morale factor) temporarily may revert to lower levels of judgment (in Kohlberg's, 1975, stages) and autonomy in the ego stages. Minority persons operating at the passive acceptance stage (Jackson, 1973) tend to make judgments at the third level of orientation of Kohlberg's scale (good boy–nice girl stage). The same person would tend to manifest minimal creativity and communication skills. Freire (1973) reports that much higher levels of creativity and literacy follow consciousness-raising experiences.

What is important about being able to recognize the general level at which a person is operating in a given situation is that the practitioner can "begin where the client is at," as we say in social work. Beginning where a reward-punishment-oriented person is at may require the use of a behavioral model of helping. However, knowing the other levels and dimensions of the framework of competence aids also in knowing where the client might go. Kohlberg's (1975) work indicates that any individual can progress only one level at a time. These phenomena of structural growth patterns have been identified by Boulding (1953). One of his principles of structural growth is the "carpenter principle." The analogy is of a carpenter who constantly is making adjustments within the dimensions of a structure due to the variability of the materials used in construction. However, the adjustments within dimensions occur in relation to a plan or blueprint. He says, "What we have here is essentially a homeostatic process, the divergence which excites action being the divergence at any time between the actual condition of the structure and the 'planned' condition" (p. 337). He then calls for interdisciplinary research that will generate a general theory of growth: "The sort of general theory which I have in mind, however, is a generalization from aspects of experience which include more than mere abstract quantity and which are common to many or even all the 'universes of discourses' which constitute the various sciences. Growth is one such aspect; organization is another; interaction is another" (p. 340).

Another way in which the carpenter principle applies is to observe the general patterns of competence in human behavior and to observe patterns that appear to be more situationally specific. In this respect, we have used the term *culture specific* to identify the unique role situation in which an individual operationalizes a generic set of competencies. Cultural, environmental, or social specificity may be influenced by one's ethnic, racial, religious, class, rural-urban, professional, parent-child, male-female, work-context, or stage-of-life development. One of our confreres at the Regina School of Social Work extension in La Ronge, Saskatchewan, has developed some interesting material on culture-specific living patterns of people in the northern areas of Saskatchewan, reflecting varying manifestations of competence in life-styles related to forager, agricultural, and industrial patterns of survival (Collier, 1977). Competent practice will vary as a function of the cultural patterns of community settings. Also in this regard, one must relate a person's competencies to the interactional influences occurring between the individual and the environment. An agency or a whole society within its policies and programs also evidences levels of development that may enhance or limit the range of possibilities for an individual. Selznick (1977, p. 36) defines a normative system as "a living reality, a cluster of problem-solving individuals and groups, and its elements are subject to change as new circumstances and new opportunities alter the relation between the system and its master ideal." So, while one may be able to come up with a master ideal, any plan of action must be derived not entirely from a master ideal but from a realistic awareness of where people and institutions are at in a given problem-solving instance.

Implications of the Framework

Crane's (1974) research has provided us with a list of admissions characteristics that are major determinants of student performance. Maslany and Wiegand (1974) reported the results of the reliability of an admissions procedure used at the Regina School of Social Work. High reliabilities were obtained among the raters, using criteria similar to those Crane (1974) has identified. However, there is a real challenge in validating these admissions criteria. If we compare them with student academic performance, this will tell us only which criteria are indicators of performance in our academic programs. There are similar problems connected with using criteria based on agency expectations or client needs. A survey of 109 practitioners by students in one of my classes indicated that workers saw the primary operational criteria coming from the agency ideally, but secondarily, and from clients. An alternative for testing criteria might be found in the attempt to measure growth levels of human development and generic helping skills suggested by the framework of social competence. This means that data collected from practice settings would focus more on *how* a worker functions than on *what* the worker does.

Other concerns around admissions include the need to have a clear determination of the state of the student's skills, knowledge, values, and qualities as a baseline for negotiating learning goals and counseling relationships. Faculty members and the student also need to know whether the resources and learning approaches are adequate to engage and develop a student at the level at which he or she is functioning.

I have reviewed the prior learning credits of more than 250 students. Out of 128 required for a Bachelor of Social Work degree, twenty prior learning credits can be granted. The instrument for assessing prior learning was based on material generated by the

Canadian Association of Social Workers (1969) and the Committee on the Study of Competence (1968). An extensive evaluation of
the procedure has led to revisions. Sixteen credits now are available;
eight can be awarded on the basis of subject equivalency evaluations, and eight can be granted for prior experiential learning.
The instrument for measuring the latter has been reduced to fewer
categories of competence with anchored scales. Recognition of
prior learning in this way is a statement to students about the importance a school places on experiential learning.

Cooperative learning programs create a similar effect. At the
Regina School of Social Work, a small number of second-year
undergraduate students are admitted to the Faculty of Social Work
and asked to "stop out" for one year of noncredit, paid social work
experience before continuing with their studies. In this way, the
experience of gaining self-confidence as well as forming career
goals usually is promoted. These students also are eligible for the
experiential learning credits. Those other students with experience
who take studies while being employed find a reciprocal effect
occurring between classroom learning and work experience, thus
strengthening maturity and autonomy.

The point being made here is that competency-based learning can be recognized and developed in all the parts of the social
work education and practicum continuum. Another example of a
description of how this is done can be found in the Council on
Social Work Education monograph edited by Arkava and Brennen
(1976).

If students are expected to develop and continue to develop
the components of competence in their quest for helping skills, the
learning opportunities and methodologies must be broadened to
include all the dimensions of cognitive and affective learning. The
development of a taxonomy of educational objectives by Bloom and
others included the cognitive (1956) and the affective (1964)
domains. Bloom observed that while many teachers spoke of the
necessity of affective learning, very few of them did much about
implementing this conviction in their classes, mainly because it was
easier to evaluate cognitive outcome. One writer (Samoff, 1971)
has described how the structuring of social work learning content
can hinder or facilitate affective learning. She draws heavily on a

framework developed by Ausubel (1968), based on the Bloom taxonomy. To some of the traditional organizing principles in curriculum, such as continuity, sequence, and integration, Samoff adds a fourth principle in organizing affective/cognitive content; namely, development. "Developmental learning unites the logical structure of the curriculum with the psychological needs and interests of the learner, and facilitates movement from the big idea to small and focused parts of the big idea" (Samoff, 1971, p. 261). Samoff's principle of developmental learning from general understanding to focused analysis is best understood by following through the steps of Ausubel's (1968, p. 270) framework.

Social work educators have succeeded in varying degrees in the effort to implement the affective and cognitive domains in what often is called the confluent model of education. Williams (1972) has developed a learning package to improve the creative-learning potential of students. He has identified a wide range of learning modes to help students develop the cognitive and affective domains of learning. By combining traditional and experiential learning inputs with these modes of learning, an instructor can provide varied opportunities to meet the broad range of needs presented by student groups. Students will unlearn old behaviors and devise and practice new ones. However, in all of this, both the instructor and the student need to appreciate that age, maturity, and other factors have a bearing on the readiness of the learner to proceed to new levels of professional and personal development.

Becoming a generalist requires something more than being able to work with a wide range of clientele, and more than being able to involve all significant systems in the plan of change, and more than being versatile in the use of a broad range of practice models and approaches. Similarly, becoming a specialist requires something more than acquiring great expertise in working with a particular type of client, and more than working with an agency that specializes in particular problem areas, and more than becoming skillful in the use of certain models or techniques of social work practice. The McPheeters and Ryan (1971, p. 22) definition of a generalist is helpful in this regard. They say a generalist is "the person who plays whatever roles and does whatever activities are necessary for the person or family when the person or family needs them. His concern is the person in need—not specific tasks or techniques or professional prerogatives. He is an aide to the individual or family—not an aide to an agency or to a profession." The same description should be applicable to a specialist in many respects. When agency policy limits services to special areas of helping, the "necessary activity" of the specialist would be to assist the client in obtaining the required service where it is available.

What becomes more significant in the blurring of these roles relates to McPheeters and Ryan's sentence "His concern is the person in need" (1971, p. 22). The framework of competence in this chapter identifies a pattern of needs in clients that, when identified, requires an individualized response from the practitioner. The capacity of a worker to respond in this individualized way requires the breadth of a generalist as well as aspects of a specialist's insight. And more than this, the practitioner must recognize to what extent his or her levels and limitations of competence can realistically meet these needs. The rights of a client to have needs dealt with in a particular way are suggested in value dimensions of the framework here proposed. For example, if an individual person's difficulty arises from trauma caused by poor interaction within the family group, it would be irresponsible for the worker to continue using only a particular technique of individual counseling.

These remarks suggest that a competent social worker will be able to utilize all the categories of models identified by Lathrope (1969, pp. 46–48); namely, the normative, expository, research, and practitioner models. The normative model provides a description of general problem-solving and planning processes in which generic skills of data collection, problem assessment, goal formulation, task completion, evaluation, and so on, are used. The use of social work methods becomes more specific when client needs suggest a certain theory or model base appropriate for intervention. These are the expository models, such as crisis intervention or the task-centered approach, which are intended for rapid scanning. The research model enables the worker to identify, compare, hypothesize, and draw certain conclusions regarding the development of planned change. As this plan is operationalized with the client, we see the practitioner model unfold.

It becomes quite obvious that the processes just described

are the work of an artist as well as a scientist. One of Michelangelo's biographers pictured the artist scientifically studying the potentials of a block of marble. When his artisan hands went to work with the chisel, Michelangelo was described as having freed the sculpted form from the marble. There is a comparable balance of the scientist and artist found in the social worker who recognizes the potential of the client and enables that person to achieve that potential. Social work educators have a similar challenge in their students. Rogers (1972, p. 230) sums it up well in the following statement:

> The goal . . . is to assist students to become individuals who are able to take self-initiated action and to be responsible for those actions; who are capable of intelligent choice and self-direction; who are critical learners, able to evaluate the contributions made by others; who have acquired knowledge relevant to the solution of problems; who, even more importantly, are able to adapt flexibly and intelligently to new problem situations; who have internalized an adaptive mode of approach to problems, utilizing all pertinent experience freely and creatively; who are able to cooperate effectively with others in these various activities; who work, not for approval of others, but in terms of their own socialized purposes.

7

Developing a New Curriculum for Social Work Education

Betty L. Baer

ᚼᚼᚼᚼᚼᚼᚼᚼᚼᚼᚼᚼᚼᚼᚼᚼᚼᚼᚼᚼᚼᚼᚼᚼᚼᚼᚼ

The Undergraduate Social Work Curriculum Development Project was funded to West Virginia University as a "nationally significant" project with 426 child welfare funds for the overall purpose of "improving" and "strengthening" curricula at the baccalaureate level of professional practice. As is known, the availability of federal funds specifically earmarked for baccalaureate development provided the impetus for the rapid growth and development of such programs throughout the late 1960s and into the 1970s. By the mid 1970s staff members of the Social and Rehabilitation Service no longer were as concerned with increasing the numbers of programs; the focus had shifted to the quality of programs. Were the programs delivering to the service structure practitioners with the needed skills? This concern emerged along with an economic retrenchment that heightened anxiety about the job opportunities for all graduates of baccalaureate-level social work programs. In addition, the

1970s saw increased awareness regarding accountability issues. A large investment in development had been made; the federal structure was anxious to invest part of its resources in stabilization, improvement, and refinement of curricula at the baccalaureate level.

Much work in this direction was under way with the creation of standards for the accreditation of baccalaureate programs in 1973, followed by the implementation of accreditation by the Council on Social Work Education (CSWE) in 1974. By the time the Curriculum Project was funded in June 1975, more than two hundred baccalaureate social work programs had been reviewed by the Commission on Accreditation. Of these, 135 received initial accreditation. The turndown rate was about 30 percent.

While the project was funded to improve baccalaureate curricula, how this would or could be done was left to the project's staff. Accordingly, and following consultation with the staff of the Council on Social Work Education, it was determined that the project must focus on the objectives for entry-level practice in social work. From the objectives, an attempt would be made to define further the basic knowledge and skill necessary to achieve the identified objectives. While the accreditation standards specify that educational objectives, or anticipated outcomes, of the educational program must be explicated, a specific definition was the prerogative of each education program. The standards provide some minimal direction: Students should have "a breadth of learning opportunities designed to familiarize [them] with a variety of interventive modes" (Council on Social Work Education, 1974b).

A project-conducted analysis of all accredited programs as well as those denied accreditation indicates considerable variance from one program to another in specifying educational objectives. In other words, outcomes when specified vary greatly in substance from one program to another. A similar situation exists with curriculum content. Given the variance in the specification of outcomes, it naturally follows that there would be variance in the emphasis given to content areas. As long as this situation exists, there cannot be assurance to the practice community, including employing agencies, that all baccalaureate entry-level professional practitioners share a common body of skills. Moreover, there can be no assurance to the next level of social work education—namely, graduate education—that all graduates of baccalaureate programs bring with them a common knowledge and skill base on which advanced education can be built. For these reasons, the determination was made that attempting to further explicate the objectives and basic content for all baccalaureate programs would be the way to improve and strengthen baccalaureate-based education.

The events of the time also contributed to the decision to pursue the further definition of the basics for entry-level practice. In 1975 the CSWE House of Delegates had determined that "immediate attention" must be given by the appropriate CSWE bodies to further explication of the core content of professional social work education (Council on Social Work Education, 1975). The National Association of Social Workers also had emphasized the need for the fundamentals, as they chose to call the base,* to be specified fully, so that the essential content taught in one city is as consistent as possible with that taught in other programs (National Association of Social Workers, 1975).

By the time the project was funded in June 1975, the new CSWE Commission on Educational Planning had been appointed. The structure of that commission included the appointment of a subcommittee on base to pursue the mandate of the House of Delegates. An interesting phenomenon resulted. The Council on Social Work Education had the mandate and the structure, while the School of Social Work at West Virginia University had the essential resources through the special grant award to carry out the task.

Finally, before turning to a discussion of the way in which the West Virginia project carried out its work, I want to note what is obvious to anyone familiar with the events described above. The issue of base was, and perhaps still is, about as controversial an issue as any ever confronting social work education. Indeed, since the inception of social work education, the debate around the existence or nonexistence of a common base has surfaced repeatedly. The most recent debate, brought about by the report of the BSWE Task

* The definition of base used in the project is as follows: "There is basic curriculum content that can be identified and that should be mastered by all graduates of accredited baccalaureate programs prior to entering professional practice in social work. . . . The basics include the professional core, as well as content relevant for practice from supporting disciplines."

Force on Structure and Quality, resulted in bitter controversy throughout 1974 and much of 1975. I mention this only to indicate that this was the environment in which the West Virginia project was funded in June 1975. Because of these events, the project always recognized that it accepted responsibility for working with a curriculum area that had and has enormous political overtones. This fact certainly was taken into account when our curriculum development strategy was selected.

Selection of a Strategy

In selecting an approach that would accomplish project objectives, staff reviewed approaches utilized by several other curriculum studies (Bisno, 1959; Glick, 1972; Hollis and Taylor, 1951; McPheeters and Ryan, 1971; Madison, 1960; Teare and McPheeters, 1970). All these studies dealt in some way with social work education at the baccalaureate level. Indeed, several of them had purposes very similar to those of the present project in that they aimed to define objectives and content for educational programs at the baccalaureate level.

The review of these earlier approaches suggested that objectives and curriculum content could be defined through (1) beginning with what workers actually do, such as "task analysis"; (2) examining current curricula and discussing them with educators, so that educators become major definers of objectives and content; and (3) including some mix of educators and practitioners in dialogue, with educators generally occupying major decision-making roles. In most instances, these earlier curriculum development efforts engaged individuals regarded as experts, but the institutions in which social work education is imbedded were largely disregarded. In this sense, earlier curriculum planning and development activities appeared removed from the mainstream and the politics of social work education.

Whenever curriculum development of any magnitude is undertaken, many different vested interests will necessarily be involved. This is not viewed as negative but simply as a reality. Yet, unless a consensus is reached regarding what an entry-level professional practitioner in social work should be prepared to do and what practice competency he or she should have, forward movement and implementation seem unlikely. A similar situation exists in the debate about what ought to constitute general education in the nation's colleges and universities. As Lockwood (1977, p. 32) notes, until a consensus on the basic purpose of general education is achieved, any prescribed curriculum is bound to be "artificial." It seems that this would apply to social work.

For these reasons, the decision was made that our curriculum development project could not carry out its goals by gathering a few experts to work in isolation in the mountains of West Virginia. To do so, it was felt, might result in another batch of materials collecting dust on a shelf. Rather, the project had to develop a strategy that would aim for a consensus around critical areas but would not compromise the ultimate purpose of the project's work.

With this background in mind, I turn to the identification of some principles that rather consistently have guided the activity of the project.

1. The project always should keep clearly and firmly in mind the scope of its charge. That is, the project was funded exclusively for the purpose of improving and strengthening baccalaureate or entry-level practice in social work. Other issues, such as what should be the content of advanced education or should basic content be taught on more than one level of social work education, are beyond the charge of this project and consistently should be rejected as topics for deliberation. The project can contribute best to the whole of social work education by carrying out its charge as effectively as possible.

2. The charge to the project—that is, to further explicate objectives and basic content for the entry-level practice in social work—mandates the inclusion of all major systems involved. The issue and how it is resolved will affect, in addition to social work educators, the organized profession, the institution of social work education, practitioners and employing agencies, students, and consumer groups. Since all are affected, all should be involved to the maximum extent feasible and possible.

3. Specific educational objectives for the preparation of the first-level practitioner and basic curriculum content can be developed only if there is greater clarity and agreement as to what the first-level practitioner should be prepared to do. The project, there-

fore, must strive for clarity and consensus in this area among the major groups and individuals involved.

4. The project should function in a climate of openness, inviting contributions, suggestions, and critiques at all stages, so that there is an ongoing process of feedback and modification.

5. Practitioners, either as individuals or as representatives of organizations, should be involved as full partners in the endeavor, with neither educators nor practitioners dominating the other but with the recognition that roles, interests, and contribution appropriately may differ.

6. Curriculum content should flow from the anticipated practice outcomes rather than from any preconceived notions regarding past and current curriculum content.

7. The project should recognize that it simply is another step in an ongoing, long-term process to further define the basics for first-level social work practice. In this sense, participants in the activity of the project should view the project's work as contributing to this process rather than being final or definitive.

Structure of the Project

The Project Task Force, formed during the early months of the first grant period, comprised social work educators and social work practitioners, including two who were appointed by the National Association of Social Workers as liaisons between that organization and the project. Other individuals represented the American Public Welfare Association. The task force held three formal meetings as a body during the period 1975–1977. However, individual members of the task force participated in and assisted with the coordination and planning of all workshops. Other nonproject meetings and conferences allowed ongoing, frequent contact between task force and project members. The task force, through its discussions of practice and curriculum issues, provided substantial input to project documents. It also reviewed and critiqued drafts of all documents, making suggestions for revisions. It is fair to say, I think, that through this process the members of the task force became interested not only in project outcomes; they became equally interested in what happened to those outcomes.

Throughout the life of the project, a select group of educators served as consultants; they intensively discussed issues, drafted position statements in many areas, and gave special counsel and assistance. Other social work educators, including representatives of major ethnic and minority groups, provided consultation to the project on an ad hoc basis.

In order to ensure consistent direction and maintain momentum, the project director was relieved of other assignments in the West Virginia University School of Social Work and was assigned on a full-time basis to the project. During the second year of the project, a second full-time project associate was employed. In addition to initiating and coordinating project activities, project staff did extensive research and wrote the final draft of the project report. The staff maintained ongoing formal and informal contacts with the profession and did the preparation necessary to relate project activities to contemporary trends in higher education.

During both years of the project's work, consultation was secured from the Council on Social Work Education through subcontract. Select staff people employed by the council were assigned to the project and provided the consultation service. The purposes of this special arrangement with the council were (1) to assure that, as the project materials developed, any areas of inconsistency with current CSWE policy would be identified; (2) to secure ongoing access to and linkage with the appropriate CSWE bodies, specifically the Commissions on Minorities, Women, and Educational Planning (the subcommittee on base of the Commission on Educational Planning was invited to participate at meetings of the project task force for review of project materials as they developed); (3) to secure and utilize data available at the council as well as the special expertise of the consultants assigned to the project by the council. An analysis of current baccalaureate programs was made by the council consultant using accreditation data. In addition, the consultants as well as the executive director of the council participated in project planning meetings and the development of project documents.

Project Activities and Outcomes

Early in the life of the project, work was begun on the development of a series of "assumptions," which have undergone numerous revisions and modifications throughout the life of the project. These assumptions aim to articulate the point of view that would form the basis both pragmatically and philosophically for the subsequent curriculum development activities. Certain of the assumptions could be, and were, readily accepted because action and/ or consensus had been achieved in large measure within social work education and the profession. For example, there was ready consensus that BSWs frequently would be employed by large organizations and needed to be better prepared to function more effectively within them. Other assumptions, however (such as a definition of social work), achieved some degree of acceptance only after lengthy discussion and debate. Clearly, however, the project could not carry out its mission unless it took a position on specific issues related to the nature of social work practice and education. These positions are stated in the assumptions.

Five special workshops were held during the first year of the project for purposes of identifying issues and concerns for practitioners and their relevance for curriculum planning and development, securing reactions from educators and practitioners to the project and determining its initial positions, and sensitizing project staff and curriculum consultants to practice needs and issues as well as educator concerns as they were perceived by participants in the workshops. The workshops were as follows: (1) The project cosponsored a workshop with a group of public welfare personnel selected by the American Public Welfare Association and representing the range of levels of practice within the public welfare agency. (2) The project cosponsored a workshop to which persons selected by the National Association of Social Workers and representing the professional association were invited. (3) The project sponsored a workshop to which a range of individuals representing national voluntary and federal agencies, many of whom were in personnel utilization as well as planning and policymaking positions, were invited. (4) The project cosponsored a workshop with a group of educators selected by the Council on Social Work Education and including persons chairing and/or serving on commissions of the council. (5) With the Association of Baccalaureate Program Directors, the project sponsored a workshop to which two BSW practitioners from each of the ten HEW regions were invited. In selecting this group, all of whom were graduates of CSWE-accredited programs, the sponsors tried to involve individuals who represented a broad range of practice settings.

From these workshops emerged certain consistent themes that were thought to have strong significance for curriculum planning. These were developed in a paper entitled "Practice Perspectives on Undergraduate Curriculum Development." In most instances participants represented themselves, not the whole of practice. However, most of the positions held and issues raised also were confirmed and supported by the recent CSWE (1974a) Task Force report on practice and education.

The workshops also served to identify some areas that, in the judgment of project staff, needed further and more specific elaboration. These areas, for which special papers were commissioned, include bureaucratic functioning as a social work skill, professional values and professional ethics in social work education, social work in governmental agencies, and the importance of the educational milieu. A fifth area, dealing with preparation for practice with human diversity, also was deemed critical by the project. However, an appropriate paper could not be developed given time and other limited resources. The papers, as commissioned, were not intended to be definitive. Rather, it was hoped that they would raise issues and begin a process of rethinking the area and its treatment in social work education.

Finally, the workshops were a mechanism for making a wide range of educators and practitioners aware of the work of the project. They helped create a network of people who were interested in the project's work and who increasingly became concerned that the issues addressed would be resolved at some level. These people helped build an audience for the project's findings. They also mobilized pressure from both education and practice for changes consistent with those suggested by the project.

No other area created as much frustration and difficulty for the project as did the development of its definition of appropriate entry-level professional practice activities. For the first several months of the project, efforts were made to develop objectives and curriculum content for first-level practice in social work without the specific delineation of what the first-level practitioner might be expected to do. "Laundry lists" began to emerge. Following the second meeting of the task force in September 1976, project staff members were urged to attempt to define with as much clarity as possible the activities deemed appropriate for the entry-level practitioner. It was argued that specification of these activities was necessary given the goals of the project so that curriculum content could be developed from anticipated practice outcomes.

The project developed a statement of "Objectives, Functions, and Activities for Baccalaureate Practice in Social Work" by drawing on a variety of materials and activities: the Florida Task Bank, a comprehensive study that examined tasks being carried out by a range of workers in public agencies; other task analyses available to the project; the work of the Chicago Community Fund, a study of job descriptions for workers in a range of private agencies; the Syracuse University Veterans Administration Project; the work of the Southern Regional Education Board in defining a "core of competence" for the baccalaureate social worker; contributions from practitioners in the project-sponsored workshops held during its first year; the project's advisory task force; the literature in the field; and a broad range of educators with whom the project had contact.

Throughout the development of material, project staff engaged in testing its contents with groups of educators and practitioners. Finally, the material was submitted for formal review to several groups: selected educators representing official bodies of the Council on Social Work Education, including the Commissions on Accreditation, Educational Policy and Planning, Minorities, and Women, as well as educators selected for their acknowledged expertise in curriculum conceptualization; the National Association of Social Workers' Task Force on the Baccalaureate Social Worker in the Profession; official representatives of the National Association of Social Workers; and individuals representing practice in the public agency. From the point of view of project staff, these groups served as panels to review the materials and flag activities that substantial numbers of the participants considered inappropriate for the entry-level worker. In addition, areas of omission were noted. Following revisions, the material was submitted to the Project Advisory Task Force for final review. The involvement of various groups in the critique and revision process helped achieve gradual consensus. People increasingly felt that the project materials represented them and their points of view; thus, they became committed to these materials.

The "Objectives, Functions, and Activities" material was utilized to develop a statement of ten basic competencies (listed below) that would guide the educational preparation of the entry-level professional social worker. Presumably, these would be utilized as a guide to individual programs in formulating their unique educational objectives.

1. Identify and assess situations where the relationship between people and social institutions needs to be initiated, enhanced, restored, protected, or terminated.
2. Develop and implement a plan for improving the well-being of people based on problem assessment and the exploration of obtainable goals and available options.
3. Enhance the problem-solving, coping, and developmental capacities of people.
4. Link people with systems that provide them with resources, services, and opportunities.
5. Intervene effectively on behalf of populations most vulnerable and discriminated against.
6. Promote the effective and humane operation of the systems that provide people with services, resources, and opportunities.
7. Actively participate with others in creating new, modified, or improved service, resource, or opportunity systems that are more equitable, just, and responsive to consumers of services; work with others to eliminate unjust systems.
8. Evaluate the extent to which the objectives of the intervention plan were achieved.
9. Continually evaluate one's professional growth and development through assessment of practice behaviors and skills.
10. Contribute to the improvement of service delivery by adding to the knowledge base of the profession as appropriate and supporting and upholding the standards and ethics of the profession.

The project decided to adopt a competency approach from which knowledge, values, and skills would be explicated. The approach is described by Houston (1974, p. 7) as follows: "From these two perceived needs—accountability and personalization—has come the movement referred to as competency-based education. . . . Advocates of [competency-based education] refer to the way in which the learner demonstrates knowledge and skills. . . . The emphasis on performance reminds us that knowledge alone is inadequate; knowledge must be employed in overt action."

An important aspect of competency-based learning is the evaluation of competency mastery. This is one of the approach's important contributions to social work education; it provides a mechanism for ensuring that the graduate of a social work education program has attained the competencies specified by that program. At this point in the project's progress, it is premature to develop evaluative tools, but the project recognizes this as an important priority for the future.

Defining educational outcomes in terms of competencies has a number of advantages for baccalaureate-level professional social work education.

1. *Increased acceptance and recognition for baccalaureate degree holders within the profession.* The ability to identify in a reasonably precise way the specific practice abilities of baccalaureate entry-level professional practitioners will clarify appropriate roles for them in the profession. This will help reduce conflict and anxiety generated by lack of clarity among the various practice levels in social work, especially between the baccalaureate and master's levels. The ways in which all levels can work together to provide quality services that relate to but do not overlap each other can more readily be identified as specific competencies, since each is enumerated. This in turn can help the profession resist professionally unsound declassification efforts as well as financially motivated substitutions of professionals with lower levels of training in positions needing more highly trained persons. Focusing on competency at the baccalaureate level, then, may assist the whole profession to more clearly articulate its objectives and find the most effective ways of achieving them.

2. *Compatibility with the current societal environment in which higher education exists.* Davies (1973, p. 4) has summarized this environment as follows: "Education and training represent the largest single national expenditure, and many economists and

politicians now believe that it is doubtful if society can any longer afford the high costs and low productivity associated with education. In the past, we have, to a very large extent, been concerned with teaching rather than the ends of education. The last decade, however, has witnessed an increasing concern with and emphasis upon the achievement of educational goals and objectives."

The increasing demand for accountability requires that all higher education, including social work, be more concerned with whether education is effectively doing what it says it is doing. This includes baccalaureate professional social work education that claims to educate effective practitioners. Unless it can demonstrate that its graduates are competent in the performance of their professional tasks, the basis for professional autonomy will be eroded seriously.

3. *Educating an increasingly diverse student population.* Given social work's historic and continuing commitment to persons from different socioeconomic, ethnic, racial, and life-style backgrounds, the curriculum must incorporate content on difference and permit students with diverse knowledge and learning background to use their knowledge and build on it. The curriculum also should be amenable to flexible structural patterns, since many students have to work while they study. In a society characterized by rapid occupational shifts and the reentry of older students into programs of study after raising families or when retraining becomes necessary, the curriculum should be adaptable to adult learners with a rich life-experience background. It must also enable the student seeking a second degree to proceed, with minimal waste of his or her previous learning experiences, to master that content. These learning experiences generally include a variety of activities: readings, films, role play, observation, research activities, community involvement, and so forth. This background allows students flexibility in learning opportunities rather than limiting them to one educational activity —one that for them may be ineffective. The student also is allowed to proceed at his or her pace, studying until competency is attained. This eliminates a time-limited educational experience that may be inadequate for competency attainment. Moreover, it allows the student with competency in a content area to move on to areas in which learning is needed. These characteristics of a competency ap-

proach allow students to make maximum use of their learning abilities and existing competencies regardless of their prior educational background and life circumstances.

4. *Effective communication.* In a practice profession like social work, it is important that educators and practitioners communicate effectively. This is necessary if practitioners are to have ongoing input into social work education and if they, as potential employers of graduates, are to have realistic expectations when hiring baccalaureate social workers. Effective communication is facilitated by educational outcomes stated in terms of practice competencies.

5. *Identification of knowledge and skills supporting competencies essential for entry-level practice in social work.* Project staff developed knowledge and skill elements from each of the competencies. Obviously, there was overlap, since practically all the competencies include some similar knowledge and skill components. To eliminate overlap, the components were categorized for presentation purposes. We did not attempt to secure consensus on the knowledge and skills essential to achieve the basic competencies, because we are not certain what content is essential to achieve competence (however one defines it) in any of the competency areas. The project has elaborated content that most educators, I am certain, would agree is critical. However, if the emphasis is on practice competence, some content areas or different mixes of content areas might be equally effective in attaining the specified competency.

Planning for Implementation

As has been noted at various points in this chapter, the project sought to involve a wide range of relevant groups in its work, thus enabling the project to obtain the widest possible input and allow for the open and thorough discussion of views about important issues from which consensus could emerge. However, another purpose was to make as many relevant groups as possible aware of the project and generate support for project findings within these groups. Experience has shown that such efforts to plan for implementation from the beginning are necessary if project results are to be used rather than stored.

The project also has planned for implementation in another way. A series of regional workshops was held to help educators and practitioners understand, interpret, and implement project findings. Papers were commissioned from educators and practitioners to help faculty address issues related to curriculum and program structure. Specific resources and suggestions were developed in these papers that would be helpful to educators and practitioners involved in baccalaureate social work education. At the workshops, the papers were discussed and feedback was obtained. The papers were revised and will be published in book form (Baer and Federico, 1978), thereby becoming a readily available and enduring resource for those concerned with baccalaureate social work education.

8

Incorporating Objective Outcome Measures into Competency Training

Martin Bloom

Competency training for social work students should include the ability to measure the process and the outcome of practice with clients in field settings; yet to my knowledge such skills are nowhere taught as a significant part of competence training (Arkava and Brennen, 1976; Chommie and Hudson, 1974). We have taught students how to conduct themselves as helping professionals, and these efforts are laudable (Ahrons, 1977; Armitage and Clark, 1975; Danish and Hauer, 1973; Duehn and Mayadas, 1977; Egan, 1975; Ivey, 1971; Ivey and Gluckstern, 1974, 1976; Jarrett, Kilpatrick, and Pollane, 1977; Marshall, Charping, and Bell, 1977; Mayadas and Duehn, 1974). But it is as if we have run a long

Note: This paper was supported, in part, by HEW Grant No. 1 T32 AA07130-01, National Institute on Alcohol Abuse and Alcoholism; and NIMH Grant No. 1 T21 MH 14980-01 (Social Work Education Branch, Division of Manpower and Training Programs).

111

race in excellent form and have *almost* arrived at the end of the course when we stop, sit down, and wonder why others are passing us by. We do not teach the skills by which students, their clients, or future employers can determine whether a given strategy should be continued as is, modified, or discontinued; we are not training students to be able to discover whether the outcomes of all these fine efforts are successful.

A review completed in 1974 of the literature on research in educating social work students found overwhelming interest in process measures, in contrast to outcome measures (Bloom, 1976a). Underlying this empirical state of affairs is an orientation toward social work education that can be reconstructed as follows: The ultimate goal of social work practice is to help clients function in more socially effective ways (compare to Armitage and Clark, 1975; Kadushin and Kelling, 1973; Meyer, 1976; Tropp, 1976). However, some social work educators admit that effective social functioning for different types of client systems is too vague a concept; that it is difficult to specify the underlying causes of the manifest problems and to attach meaningful numbers to relevant behaviors, feelings, or ideas; and that many factors are operating that would likely contaminate any research design dealing with clients, even if it were ethical to impose such extra constraints on them.

Noting the prohibitive difficulties in dealing directly with ultimate objectives of practice, Kadushin and Kelling (1973, pp. 9–10) suggest that attention be given to a more feasible task: measuring when a worker "expresses the professionally prescribed attitudes, follows the professionally prescribed processes, manifests the professionally prescribed behavior, attitudes, and values, and displays a familiarity with the requisite professional knowledge" because this worker is more likely to help the client "effect a greater amount of therapeutic change" than a worker who does not follow such a procedure.

I doubt whether any social work educator seriously would question Kadushin and Kelling's reasoning. But I also doubt whether these authors would make these same assumptions today, because the last few years have seen a proliferation of theorizing and research concerning more feasible ways of enabling the average student to generate measures of process and outcome in natural field settings (Bloom, 1975; Fox and Rappaport, 1972; Hersen and

Barlow, 1976; Ho, 1976; Howe, 1974; Kiresuk and Sherman, 1968; Rose, Cayner, and Edleson, 1977). I call attention to three aspects of this literature. First, it deals with individual-, group-, and community-level client systems; second, by and large the methods are not attached to any given theory and can be employed by social workers and others using a broad range of theoretical guidelines, as long as the specificity and objectivity of the procedures are accepted; third, all are relatively simple procedures intended for average practitioners, which also means that they make a number of statistical and design assumptions in providing approximate information (Bloom, 1978; Gottman and Leiblum, 1974).

Given this flurry of activity, one might assume that schools of social work would have rushed to adopt various procedures by which to measure the outcome of practice, as well as the process of practice insofar as this information provided corrective feedback to that process. However, this has not been the case. There probably are many reasons for this resistance, some reflecting the profession's historic antipathy toward research (compare to Kirk, Osmalov, and Fischer, 1976; Rosenblatt, 1968). But I want to consider a new and paradoxical situation—the role of competency-based education as an unintended impediment to the very scientific practice it seeks to attain.

Congruent with developments in outcome measures, there was a magnificent efflorescence in various forms of competency-based education. In an age of accountability (Briar, 1973a), it clearly was the time to rediscover an old and honored concept in social work (compare to Clark, 1976; Jarrett, Kilpatrick, and Pollane, 1977). Definitions of the term *competency* became challenging as two aspects emerged. One, an internal aspect, involved personal traits and specific items of learning indicating ability. The second, an external aspect, referred to performance relative to some criterion demonstrating that one's ability led to some desired result. Parallel to the task of defining the nature of competency is the task of educating for competency. My reading of the literature suggests that the internal or ability approach to competence has been dominated by educators who use microteaching, in which a complex process is broken into elements that are taught to criterion. The result is what Clark (1976, p. 26) calls a method-centered approach. In contrast, the performance approach to competence has been associated with a measurement orientation; Clark labels this the objective-centered approach (p. 26).

However, the paradoxical upshot of these developments is that the very specification of the abilities involved in competence—the knowledge, skills, and attitudes as the means of practice—has made it easier for class and field teachers to focus, with even greater clarity of educational purpose, on the processes of practice while assuming that practice will more or less inevitably lead to desired outcomes. And, as has happened so often before, the performance aspect of practice is given short shrift. This results in a one-sided education rather than the thorough integration of practice methods, concomitant evaluation, and effective information retrieval that represent the sine qua non of scientific practice (Bloom, 1975). We teach perfect eye contact, but no vision; we produce workers with excellent posture, but with no objective standing among helping professionals; we generate ample reflection of feeling and accurate paraphrasing, but without the sense of the total mission of social work, which, whatever else it does, must include concern for positive client outcomes.

The essential question, as I see it, is to combine training for competence in ability with training for competence in performance (compare to Arkava and others, 1976; Clark, 1976; Glick, 1974; Short, 1977). I believe that these two types of training can be done simultaneously (Bloom, 1976b; Bloom and Gordon, 1976), in part by the microteaching approach. This approach, however, may not train students to deal with unknown problems that call for skills and knowledge not yet developed and involve client goals perhaps not currently sanctioned. Where is a competency-based program for innovation? What are the microteaching steps to creativity in problem solving and risk taking (compare to Bloom, 1976a)? What small learning modules are appropriate for educating students about the diversity of needs and potentialities of ethnic minorities, women, various age groups, and so forth?

New Directions: Single-System Design

Single-system designs evaluate the *outcome* of practice and therefore employ objective measurement systems that impinge on the *strategy of practice* itself. Thus, both ends and means of practice are included directly in these evaluative designs. How does such a research orientation affect practice?

Practice usually moves through a sequence of steps: (1) defining the problems and strengths of the clients, (2) generating alternative conceptualizations of these events, (3) deciding on the optimal plan to be implemented, (4) evaluating concurrently, (5) providing corrective feedback as the client moves toward goal attainment (Bloom, 1975). Each of these practice steps is influenced by training for competency in single-system designs.

1. *Definitions of problems/strengths.* Evaluation requires that the events under study are known and clearly described. Researchers have found that operational definitions of concepts fulfill this requirement; a given concept is defined by the set of operations that measures the referent of that concept. When translated in the practitioner context, a given concept may be defined by the set of operations that influences the referent of that concept in a desired direction, which becomes known through measurement. This modification of the *researcher's operational definition* into what may be called a *practitioner's impact definition* has immense implications for the conduct of practice. For one, impact definitions make clear that the client's language—"I just feel lousy and blue" —is not useful information to either the client or the practitioner, because it does not carry specific implications for how to bring about change. In a similar vein, the clinical concept of "depression" may describe a set of problems without implications for action. A new common language is needed that can be shared by client and practitioner. One way to develop a common vocabulary would be to reconstruct the history of events prior to social work contact by taking a social history in the client's language. Describing the chain of social and internal events that preceded or led to the client's specific problems, as well as those that followed up on the client's problems, will help the client and the practitioner identify causal antecedents and consequences that may be addressed by joint action. This method of history taking also allows the practitioner to use information from the scientific literature with the clinical concepts that seem appropriate. When professionals and clients can work cooperatively on the basis of shared information to bring about change, the probability of success will be enhanced.

Elsewhere, I have described a Cartesian coordinate diagram

in which the vertical axis represents the event to be defined (Bloom, 1975). The intervals on this axis represent units of the event to be measured. One concept, such as depression, may require a number of graphs that represent the various phases of that experience: moodiness, listlessness, inability to sleep the whole night, and so forth. For each, there would be some agreement about the scale of units, what constitutes more or how much more. These two steps—specifying the distinctive components of the problem and moving from nominal to ordinal or interval measures for each—are the basis for a common language between worker and client, particularly when both are involved in its construction. On the horizontal axis of the diagram, representing appropriate time units, the client can record how much of what component was occurring in a given period. This operational type of definition focuses the worker's attention on the active ingredients of the case; by monitoring changes before and after intervention, the worker can assess whether the strategy of practice is leading in the right direction with appropriate speed.

2. *Alternative conceptualizations.* Single-system designs are theory free, as long as the theory permits its concepts to be operationalized. A number of implications may follow when the components of a client's situation are clearly describable. First, specific actions can be taken to determine whether the event is affected. The term *practice hypothesis* (Bloom, 1975) might be used as the connecting link between methods-oriented competency and the performance-centered approach. The practice hypothesis represents the sum of worker decisions and actions to effect client change in the desired direction: "If I do X, the client likely will do Y." What goes into the "doing" part of the hypothesis is the focus of present microteaching approaches; what occurs by way of client reaction is part of the performance focus. A series of such client reactions represents measurement feedback of the process of helping; when compared with desired goals of practice, such measurement becomes the evaluation of outcome. Moreover, the set of practice hypotheses becomes an individualized theory about client dynamics. Classes of X-type actions become predictable for their Y-type reactions. The value of the practitioner's conceptual mapping appears empirically in the client's demonstrable improvements over past

performances. This form of grounded theory does not cast off general theories of personality and behavior; indeed, the worker likely would continue to draw on these broader theories to isolate patterns of behavior to be tested as practice hypotheses. In practice, alternative conceptualization means a sequential focusing and sharpening of whatever theory the worker was most comfortable using.

3. *Optimal plan.* The term *optimal* suggests a balance between risks and benefits. By use of single-system designs that specify the components of the problem and assist workers in generating individualized theories about the cases, workers also may learn what the odds are in following one or another plan. A times-series approach may enable one to determine how long it will take before an intervention will produce some desired outcome (compare to Bloom and Block, 1977). If there is no way of demonstrating whether a given strategy works or does not work, this information should weaken its claim as an alternative plan. Furthermore, by monitoring data as one's plan is in progress, one may find that some modifications or major changes are necessary to assist a client's attainment of his or her goals.

4. *Concurrent evaluation.* Concurrent evaluation by the client may become another form of intervention (see, for example, Evans, 1976). Counting events—that is, looking carefully and closely at what we do—may be a simple and effective means of self-monitoring and self-control. The client implicitly, if not explicitly, assesses how the case is transpiring. Single-system designs offer the potential of examining this phenomenon directly. Counting and related acts involve the clients continuously and meaningfully in their treatment; indeed, it is these acts that constitute the awareness of improvement (or deterioration).

5. *Corrective feedback.* Corrective feedback resulting from the data collection and analysis is vitally important and, again, creates new pressures on competent practice. For the client, knowledge of results may act, as has been found in laboratory studies, to improve performance and maintain persistence. For the worker, such feedback becomes an acid test of the fruitfulness of the theory and its translation into practice. An objective series of data points provides an individualized norm against which to compare new behaviors. Each data point represents an opportunity to make a

fine-tuned adjustment, while the overall pattern presents the big picture.

Let me review briefly the characteristics of single-system designs ($N = 1$). Using a time-series format, in which data are collected for some period before a planned intervention is to take place, the worker arranges for these same observations to be made during the intervention period, so that some form of comparison can be made between the earlier and the later periods. The basic question is, "Could the events that occurred after intervention have happened by chance, or are they unlikely—meaning that there was some probable cause?" Since the worker planned certain events to occur, by checking "alternative causal explanations" (Campbell and Stanley, 1963), the inference of worker causality is appropriate. By analyzing the pattern of outcome, the worker can determine whether the observed events were desired—that is, whether the client's goals have been satisfied by the given occurrence or whether they were undesired—and respond accordingly (Bloom, 1975). Sometimes the comparison between the preintervention and intervention periods is made by visual inspections of the measurement graph (Ayllon and Azrin, 1968), by observer ratings and scaled judgments (Kiresuk and Sherman, 1968), by table values (Bloom, 1975), or by computer analyses (Gottman and Leiblum, 1974).

In this chapter, I will extend some themes developed elsewhere (Bloom and Block, 1977); these themes depend on certain basic characteristics of time-series analysis. I assume that behaviors are the result of the fields of personal and environmental forces acting on an individual (compare to Lewin, 1951). People tend to exhibit consistent patterns in their behavior; by observing one set of events over time, we may sample the patterned behavior from those fields of forces. Using personality theories, workers can make hypotheses about the dominant forces in those fields and create plans to influence them selectively. Implementation of these plans can be monitored continually to check whether the practice hypotheses are fruitful; that is, whether changes that conform to theoretical predictions begin to emerge in the set of observed events. (For specific details on use of this approach, see Bloom, 1975.)

The time-series approach has been used with a variety of

social work and clinical situations involving worker-client contact over extended periods. However, there are many variations on this typical therapeutic situation. One class of special problems involves the situation where the worker has only one or two contacts with a client, such as in a crisis center, traveler's aid, and various telephone information services. Several colleagues and I recently completed a project at the St. Louis branch of the American Red Cross that services military families (Bloom, Butch, and Walker, 1978). Since frequently there is only one direct service contact with the client, how is the worker to evaluate effectiveness?

We label this type of situation $N = 1$, $T = 1$, meaning that a single client (system) is involved in a one-time contact. In analyzing the agency's closed cases, we discovered two major types of $N = 1$, $T = 1$ cases. The first involves a reconstruction of events based on information from the one contact. For example, a parent comes to the Red Cross for help because his son, who is in the army in Germany, has not written for a month, unlike his usual pattern for the previous six months. Follow-up information from a telephone call or from memos from the agency to which the case was referred may supply postintervention data. For example, the soldier in this case was in a serious automobile accident, and no one had informed the parent until the Red Cross message arrived. This soldier was aided in communicating with his parent and eventually reestablished his weekly writing pattern.

The second type of case calls for arbitrary goals to be determined and uses no baseline data. For example, a soldier's father has had a serious operation and is entering a terminal phase. The soldier might request a compassionate reassignment through the Red Cross. If the worker is able to document the facts in the situation well enough and the soldier receives his reassignment, the desires of the client are fully met. This type of case has an all-or-nothing character, but it still permits summary evaluation of how many components of a given case were resolved successfully and how many successes were obtained by some sample of clients. The result is a form of agency "batting average" for percentage of successes.

The system in single-system designs may include any number of persons, so that groups as groups may be evaluated. However, a worker often is as interested in the progress of individual members of the group as in the movement of the group itself. In another research project, a colleague and I are engaged in an extension of the single-system design to include pairs and groups as well as individuals. Conceptually, the possible comparisons among these combinations are important. How is the progress of a therapeutic group related to the progress of its constituent members and the small cliques existing within the larger group? Let me give an example of a comparison of one person to his group or any component to any larger component.

A group of retarded young men share a structured group-living situation, two men to an apartment in a four-apartment complex (including accommodations for the houseparents). A complex behavior modification program has been instituted to develop and maintain physical and personal functioning skills; a new program is being developed for more effective interpersonal functioning essential to maintain these men in the community. To make the necessary objective measurements, we are analyzing house council meetings in which the residents plan for social programs and apartment-related matters. Videotapings are made of these sessions, so that interpersonal behaviors of individuals and pairs can be observed in relation to overall group projects. Each individual has a prescribed training program to fit his needs; for example, one person is very nonassertive, and others tend to take advantage of him. If progress is made in this person's training, what effects will there be on the overall goals of the group? If the group plans an extensive social outing, how will this affect the nonassertive individual? By having time-series analyses of each individual and grouping, we may be able to tease out some of these relationships, about which there is only speculation.

A final example of the extension of the single-system design is that of the client seen over long periods (compare to Risley and Wolf, 1972), metaphorically indicated by the infinity sign: $N = 1$, $T = \infty$. I do not refer to psychoanalytic sessions that may last five or ten years, but to life periods. The scope of this investigation concerns *preventive* efforts rather than *interventive* or *rehabilitative* ones; it concerns promoting the strengths of individuals and groups over their lifetimes and obviating predicted problems facing them at certain critical stages of life. Thus, the demands placed on the evaluation system—to know whether our preventive efforts have any effect—are considerably different from those in the conventional interventive situation.

Actuarial knowledge of similar populations at risk is the basis of prediction for this type of analysis: How far does the individual deviate from the ranges of acceptable performance in given areas? If an individual has unusual deviations in one area, does this necessarily predict problems for other areas in the future? For example, if a child falls two grades behind her age-mates, there is a statistical likelihood that she will become a high school dropout, with all the predictable sequelae of that event for her lifetime. As other events emerge—such as poor reading level, few contacts with peers, and extensive outside employment—the prediction of dropout becomes stronger. For some of these factors, we have in effect years of advance notice regarding dropout. What is lacking is a scale of observation to bring these specific events into perspective as the basis of preventive action.

A time-series design that reflects long-term events might be one vehicle to bring about fuller utilization of these available data. There clearly are a number of difficulties with using a conventional time-series analysis for life-span development when there are qualitatively distinct stages within the quantitative time line. However, these stages or critical milestones can be used as normal developmental challenges for which certain personal and environmental resources are needed. The preventive issue is whether these resources will be available to the individual or group and, if not, what action can be taken in the present to compensate for predicted problems. The evaluative question is how to determine whether in fact actions taken in the present are related to future outcomes. Conventional research wisdom suggests that control group designs would enable us to test this prediction, but it is becoming increasingly difficult and unethical to maintain no-treatment control groups over long periods. Therefore, a new use of single-system designs emerges as sequences of developmental challenges are monitored for their adequate resolution. This opens a new path of clinical evaluation. Thus, use of single-system designs promises a sharper look at the longitudinal problems of preventive social work, even with the individual client. Competent practice methods are integrated with competent measures of effective process and successful outcome along the milestones to long-range preventive goals.

Summary

A number of procedures concerning the objective measurement of client outcomes—the ultimate measure of professional impact—are available to the average social work student in most field settings. Some of these use a variation of time-series designs in which any conceptualized problem or goal may be measured objectively before, during, and after intervention or prevention. These measurement procedures are not a part of competency training in schools of social work. Why?

Among possible reasons, I have called attention to one paradoxical explanation. The very fact of our becoming good in one area may have interfered with our becoming better in another. Being able to teach the more familiar practice methods with greater rigor made teaching the less familiar evaluation methods less interesting. Obviously, this need not be so. The single-system design, among its other uses, might be one method by which we can integrate practice with the logical outcome of that practice through measurement. As my several illustrative case studies pointed out, there still is much to be done in perfecting measures of process and outcome for workers in different settings, and it is true that we have yet to resolve how to teach creative practice through the competency approach.

9

Confusion in Applying
the Concept
of Competence

David E. Cummins

In an article entitled "Accurate Empathy: Confusion of a Construct," Rappaport and Chinsky (1972) question the existence of a phenomenon long held essential to the helping process. Their concern about the viability of empathic understanding as a construct and necessary condition for therapeutic change is based on data from a number of studies. A central issue raised by these investigators is that empathy may be little more than a style of therapist verbalization that is relatively independent of what the client is feeling or attempting to communicate. They note that client perceptions of accurate empathy frequently are unrelated to therapist self-ratings and trained raters' evaluations of empathy. They also report that ratings of therapist protocols with and without client statements yield similar empathy scores. Further, they cite evidence that empathy ratings are related to the number of words spoken by the therapist. Their misgivings concerning whether empathy is a matter of substance or style are echoed by Kagan (1972b, p. 44), who notes: "I wonder, too, if judges are not unnecessarily influenced by what might be thought of as an empathic vocabulary, in which, for instance, 'lust' is rated higher than 'like' and 'hate' carries a more empathic loading than 'anger.' "

A second concern of Rappaport and Chinsky is that empathy is an abstract, complex phenomenon lacking discriminant validity. They point out that empathy ratings generally are strongly correlated with ratings of genuineness and warmth and appear to be highly correlated with a global "good" therapist quality as rated by trained judges. An independent factor-analytic study by Muehlberg, Pierce, and Drasgow (1969, p. 95) reached a similar conclusion; namely, that "a single major factor accounted for practically all of the observed correlations among the obtained facilitative conditions."

Rappaport and Chinsky go on to question the relationship of measures of accurate empathy to therapeutic outcome; that discussion, however, is of less relevance to our purposes than are their points about style and lack of discriminant validity. The title of this chapter, which was suggested by that of the Rappaport and Chinsky paper, was chosen because I found some interesting parallels between problems in the specification of accurate empathy and those in the specification of social work competence.

If empathy is more a matter of style than of substance, can the same be said about competence in the profession of social work? That there are a number of styles of social work practice hardly can be debated. The appendix of *Social Treatment* by Whittaker (1974) lists twenty-one approaches to interpersonal helping, including such diverse traditions as behavior therapy, existential psychotherapy, psychodrama, and social group work. And Whittaker does not even consider activities aimed at institutional and social change. Attempts to tease out a common core to the diverse forms of social work intervention appear to leave us with little more than the statement that social workers are problem solvers; yet there is nothing unique to social work about the problem-solving processes of assessment, planning, execution, and evaluation. The difficulty of determining the essence of social work practice is captured nicely by Gordon's (1962) inquiry about precisely what kind of situation would prompt the question "Is there a social worker in the house?"

This chapter will not attempt to provide a definitive statement concerning the nature of social work practice, nor will it attempt to determine what are and are not legitimate social work concerns. In general, I agree with D. M. Austin (1977) that social work practice is marked by pragmatism and situational specificity and at present is based on organized practitioner wisdom rather than a body of scientific knowledge.

Whatever social work practice is, it is a complex phenomenon. As such, social work competence, like accurate empathy, is vulnerable to being assessed more as a matter of style than one of substance; hence, measures thereof should be examined with particular caution. Rappaport and Chinsky's observations concerning attempts to measure accurate empathy suggest by analogy that judgmental measures of social work competence tend to be global, rather than specific, and are subject to consensual drift and stylistic debates. What is the evidence for these conjectures?

While data concerning the competence of practicing social work professionals are difficult to come by, evaluations of the field performance of social work students have been subjected to considerable study. In general, field work supervisors are required to assess student competence with regard to knowledge, values, and practice skills, often along a multitude of supposedly discrete dimensions such as diagnosis, execution, and evaluation. Yet, as studies of fieldwork ratings indicate, supervisor judgments of competence, although elicited along discrete dimensions, tend to be highly interrelated and dominated by global good/bad evaluations. In other words, breakdowns of practice performance—whether into knowledge, value, and skill components; into the processes of assessment, planning, execution, and evaluation; or into intellectual and relationship skills—demonstrate little or no discriminant validity. Instead, global ratings predominate, as was demonstrated by Gordon and Schutz (1962) in the Field Instruction Research Project at Washington University. That investigation found that field instructor ratings of thirty-three performance items were dominated by a single factor. The report notes: "Either students, during their first year of field instruction, tend to come along well or not so well on the whole range of field behavior, or they are perceived by the field instructor as coming along well or not so well on the whole range" (p. 59).

The fact that judgment of field work competence is marked

by unidimensionality is not necessarily a problem, provided the judgments are consistent and meaningful and not merely a function of the stylistic allegiances of the individuals doing the evaluating. Unfortunately, available data are not very reassuring.

In evaluating the Wisconsin 3-2 Program, Kadushin and Kelling (1973) report interjudge reliabilities of .44 and .39 when they obtained overall judgments of tape recordings and typescripts of student interviews. With regard to the issue of style, it is interesting to note the following observation made by the authors: "There were ideological problems, particularly toward the end of the project, when, because of changes in course content at the school, some taped interviews were behavioral modification oriented. The approach clashed with the more traditional therapeutic approaches to which raters were committed. Raters had difficulty keeping ideological disagreement with the approach separate from an assessment of adequacy of skills manifested" (p. 66). Kadushin and Kelling also indicate that raters had difficulty keeping ratings of discrete components clear and separate. Thus, within a single attempt to evaluate student interviews, the issues of style and global judgment proved to be troublesome.

In a study of the competency of clinical psychology graduate students, Kelley and Fiske (1951) reached similar conclusions about the validity of judgmental ratings. They obtained a "fairly satisfactory degree of agreement among raters with the same general orientation but a much less satisfactory degree of agreement among raters representing different points of view" (p. 126). Kelley and Fiske furthermore found ratings dominated by a single overall factor.

The Wisconsin study also examined relationships among judgments of clinical skills made by field supervisors, clients, and peers. One would expect that these evaluations of competence from different sources would bear some relationship to each other. Consider, however, the following matrix of correlations provided by Kadushin and Kelling (p. 156).

| | Evaluation of Student Competence | | |
	Supervisor	Client	Peer
Supervisor	1	.272	−.265
Client		1	−.056
Peer			1

These data are alarming because they indicate that there is little or no agreement concerning the fieldwork competence of the students. But perhaps these results should not be surprising when we recall the Rappaport and Chinsky observation that clients and therapists showed little agreement about levels of empathy in a therapeutic encounter.

The Washington University study cited earlier reports the following correlations between successive fieldwork evaluations of MSW students (p. 60): first and second semester, .45; second and third semester, .22; third and fourth semester, .71. The first and third correlations represent relationships between evaluations provided by the same field instructor. The middle correlation represents the degree of agreement among field instructors with regard to the same students and is appreciably lower than the other two. The results suggest that the evaluations of fieldwork competence are largely idiosyncratic to the evaluator.

The above findings do little to inspire confidence in the measurability of social work competence. At least with regard to judgmental measures, we seem saddled with two disconcerting trends. First, no matter how we try to identify separable components of skill, we usually end up with unidimensional evaluations; that is, an individual is either competent or not competent across the range of measured performances. Second, evaluations tend to be peculiar to the evaluator, with little evidence that they can be replicated independently. Thus, the evidence for the robustness of the global construct of social work competence is slim indeed. Instead of a stable, well-defined entity, we seem to have an elusive phenomenon on our hands.

A way out of this dilemma, of course, is to avoid judgmental measures of competence. One clear alternative is to employ objective measures of client improvement or goal attainment as an indicator of the competence of the practitioner involved. This, unfortunately, is easier said than done. Although there is no dearth of proposals for ways to evaluate the outcome of an intervention attempt (see Chapter Eight), the problems inherent in devising quantifiable yet meaningful indicators of client progress are considerable. In all too many clinical situations, the measurability of a phenomenon is directly proportional to its triviality. Contracted objectives and prespecified schemes for quantification of complex human behavior have a way of appearing, in retrospect, just plain naïve. Perhaps the most naïve assumption of all is that the measurement techniques employed are nonreactive; that is, they do not contaminate the phenomenon being measured. In addition to all these problems, practitioner competence or lack thereof is only one of many factors influencing client outcome. So, while it would be convenient to assume that social workers have at their disposal an armamentarium of well-defined methodologies for objectively assessing their own effectiveness—or the effectiveness of their colleagues, for that matter—I am inclined to agree with the contention of Butler and Richmond (1977) that existing measurement methods generally are inadequate and ill suited to deal with the complexity of most clinical situations.

Another alternative to judgmental measures of competence is that of reducing clinical skills to their rudimentary components. Ivey (1971) has proposed a technique that attempts "to break what has previously been considered extremely complex behaviors into an increasing number of discrete, identifiable behaviors" (p. 34). His approach is attractive from an educational standpoint. Yet paraphrasing is not social work. Furthermore, as Ivey moves students up his hierarchy to training in skills of self-expression and interpretation, we become enmeshed in the same dilemma of diffuseness and stylistic evaluation cited by Rappaport and Chinsky.

Whatever the appeal of micro or behavioral approaches to the evaluation of competence, there remains an obligation for the proponents of such programs to demonstrate that mastering rudimentary skills will generalize to performance in more complex settings. Furthermore, in the transition from elementary to complex performances, they need to show that their methodology for assessing performance can deal with the increased complexity. In my judgment, the counting methodology typically employed rarely survives the transition, and we are left with no recourse but to rely once again on subjective evaluation of complex performances.

Does it follow, then, that there is no adequate procedure for reliably measuring social work competence? Perhaps we should resign ourselves to reliance on the global assessments of experienced practitioners, understanding that we must counteract stylistic biases by seeking evaluators who represent a number of theoretical orientations. After all, another domain of complex performances—namely, competitive gymnastics—is measured this way. Moreover, there are techniques that can be employed to minimize the bias inherent in subjective judgment.

First of all, the concept of social work competence in the abstract should be abandoned forthwith. From the point of view of measurement, the proclivity—particularly pronounced among social work educators—for making sweeping generalizations about what social workers do does not serve us well. And the same can be said about notions concerning the generalist practitioner. Social work practice is conditioned strongly by critical contextual variables, including agency sanction, cultural setting, and relative emphasis on individual or social change. While it is difficult to say what social workers do in general, it is considerably less difficult to say what a particular social worker in a specific setting does. An analysis of the job duties of a particular worker can identify a variety of specific activities and, in so doing, lay the groundwork for evaluation of practice competence.

In Chapter Ten, Teare describes a project that seeks to characterize job profiles of human services personnel in terms of their involvement in a predetermined set of job tasks. Investigations such as this are essential if we are to determine on the basis of data rather than impression what social workers do. My preference in job analysis is to identify representative procedures rather than tasks, the only difference being that a procedure generally defines a more complex performance than the task statements espoused by Fine and Wiley (1971). Examples of procedures might be an analysis of a family setting in support of a proposed adoptive or foster placement or a plan for soliciting community support for a halfway house or group home. A procedure should be a relatively self-contained, meaningful episode of clinical practice. An essential characteristic of a procedure is that it can and should be documented, with the resulting documentation available for evaluation on its own merits.

The evaluation of clinical procedures moves assessment from concern with worker attributes to a focus on worker products. The worker can explicate clinical decision making within the context of the particular case and compare and contrast its characteristics with those of other relevant experiences. Butler and Richmond (1977) have proposed a similar approach, one that calls for comparative documentation of clinical intervention followed by public scrutiny of each other's work by researchers and practitioners with similar concerns.

While assessment of competence through the evaluation of practice documentation does not avoid the liabilities of subjective judgment, it does help to avoid the trap of overconcern with the personality attributes of workers. Furthermore, it provides a procedure for anchoring judgments of competence to specific samples of practice.

Perhaps the day will come when judgmental procedures can be replaced by objective techniques without doing violence to the complexities of social work practice. But at the moment practitioner wisdom remains the primary means for guiding social work practice; we must therefore learn how to harness that wisdom most effectively. The central premise of this chapter is that judgmental measures of competence can be useful if they address themselves to what a worker accomplishes and avoid preoccupation with the worker's personality. We especially need to maintain some humility in the exercise of our wisdom in evaluating the competence of others, seeking the independent judgment of as many practitioners as is feasible. The use of documented procedures as a basis for assessment facilitates such independent evaluation.

It would be nice to conclude on an optimistic note, but the available evidence would have it otherwise. The problems involved in assessing competence in social work practice are not likely to yield to catchwords and pseudotechnology. We should remain cautious and skeptical, but not paralyzed, as we seek to refine our techniques. We are dealing with imprecise measures of complex phenomena; hence, we need to anchor our survey points as strongly as possible and triangulate our observations. Above all, we must avoid the promiscuous use of the phrase *social work competence* until we have a better idea of what we mean by it.

10

A Task Analysis
for Public Welfare
Practice and
Educational Implications

Robert J. Teare

During the past fifteen years, considerable discussion within the social work profession has centered on the nature of practice and the most appropriate ways of dividing the labor among various levels of practitioners. To be sure, this preoccupation has pervaded most fields within the human services (for example, education, mental health, corrections, rehabilitation). In social work, however, the concern has been particularly great due to a number of forces operating on the profession: the emergence of undergraduate training programs, changes in basic social service programs and policies, "turf" disputes within the human services, and challenges to the nature and value of credentials. This mix of philosophical and pragmatic issues, combined with the relative newness of social work as a profession, has caused manpower planning during the past decade to become a curious endeavor indeed.

The field has not been lacking in the formulation of practice models and frameworks. The enduring quality of the writings of Richmond (1917), Perlman (1957), Ross (1955), and others has served to lay the methodological foundations for the field. For comprehensive descriptions of both traditional and recent practice frameworks, the reader is referred to Federico (1973, especially chapters 8 and 9) and Klenk and Ryan (1974). Important contributions to these basic frameworks have been made by Briar (1967) and Specht (1968). A number of alternative practice perspectives, resulting from the focus on undergraduate education, have emerged from the writings of Bisno (1969), Dolgoff (1971), and Teare and McPheeters (1970). In addition to these theoretical formulations, recent research efforts have begun to focus on the development of "banks" of data about tasks performed within the social welfare setting. Of significance among these is the work of Austin and Smith (1975) and Fine and Wiley (1971).

Diverse as these approaches have been, they do have several things in common. Many of these frameworks were formulated as remedies to a less-than-satisfactory existing state of affairs. Thus, at the time they were proposed, they were depictions of what *ought to be* rather than what *was*. Second, these formulations have been largely theoretical in nature and therefore lack specificity. Although they may identify ends (or objectives), they are not very descriptive of the tasks or activities used to achieve these ends. Finally, there is a real need for an empirical foundation for the practice area. Data must be collected to determine whether tasks or roles exist or can be implemented in practice settings and whether the rationales proposed for grouping tasks and organizing practice into job dimensions are meaningful and feasible.

The data to be described below will depict social work activity. This depiction, however, is a blend of theory and empiricism. It is designed to bridge a gap that exists between practice theory and job design. In a sense, it represents an attempt to "validate" elements of the practice models proposed by Austin, Bisno, Dolgoff, and Teare and McPheeters. As will be seen, generalization may be somewhat limited by the nature of the methodology and the setting in which the data were gathered. Despite these limitations, the material contributes a certain amount of structure and sheds a little light on the organization of contemporary practice within a public welfare setting. It also enhances our understanding of the generalist/specialist dimensions possible in such settings.

Background of the Research

Before I discuss methodology, some descriptive comments about the sponsoring agency are in order.* The data were collected in a state public welfare agency in the southeastern United States. The agency is a free-standing (nonumbrella) public welfare department and is designated as the Title XX agency for the state in which it is located. The department administers twenty-eight service programs to its clients. In addition to direct service provision, the department provides an increasing number of services through interagency agreements and contracts with vendors in the public and private sectors. The agency supplements (through state funds) the federalized public assistance programs and directly administers the AFDC payments. The department has a rapidly growing food assistance (food stamp) program, carries out screening for Medicaid, and has a Work Incentive Program.

Almost four thousand people are employed by the agency, which was serving approximately 76,000 clients in 1977. The programs of the department are supervised by the state office and directly administered by the counties; a departmental office is located in each county. All employees are state employees and, with the exception of the commissioner, are covered under the state merit system. All jobs in the department are classified; until recently, employees were selected from a register of incumbents compiled by means of state civil service examination.

As with much applied research, data were collected with an eye toward addressing a number of problems and concerns. Most of these were related to personnel matters, which fell into four general areas:

* I would like to express my gratitude to Waldo Spencer, the personnel specialist with the supporting agency, for his collaboration in data collection and analysis. Without his many contributions throughout the course of the study, much of this research would not have been possible.

1. The degree of correspondence or "fit" between job titles and descriptions in the department's existing classification system and the actual work performed.
2. Insight into worker attitudes toward work content and attributes, conditions of work (for example, salary, supervision), and the department itself.
3. The development of a framework for grouping existing tasks and jobs into a meaningful whole that would provide for major "streams" of practice as well as career progressions.
4. The arrangement of this framework into an ordered hierarchy on which salary schedules could be based.

As can be seen, this is a broad scope of work and has been going on for several years. Some questions fall into sensitive areas, and data remain proprietary to the agency. This chapter will discuss the findings and the methodology developed to generate them.

Methodology

Given the nature of the questions to be answered, it was obvious that the collection of information about job activities would be a central task. Of the many approaches possible, a structured self-report questionnaire was selected. To ensure a wide range of content, a variety of sources were used as inputs to the questionnaire: existing agency job descriptions, a limited sample of desk audits, task and role statements from the Southern Regional Education Board (Teare and McPheeters, 1970), representative task statements from the Florida Task Bank (Austin and Smith, 1975), and samples of tasks from the National Task Bank (Fine and Wiley, 1971).

This material was synthesized in a self-report questionnaire called the Job Analysis Survey (JAS).* The questionnaire has four parts. Part I contains limited demographic information about the respondent (job held, education level, time in position). Part II, the most important section, contains the seventy-seven task statements by means of which the respondent describes his or her job.

* Further information about the JAS can be obtained from the author at the School of Social Work, P.O. Box 1935, University, Alabama 35486.

These tasks are grouped arbitrarily into eight categories. The category labels and some examples from each are presented in Table 1.

Table 1.   Item Content of the JAS

I. Direct Clinical (examples)   (28 items)
   Try to locate people who might need services or financial assistance by means of home visits, telephone calls, or talks with clients.
   Take clients to specific places (using agency or personal car) to link client with service or treatment resource.
   Talk with clients about problems in order to help adjustment or promote "responsible" behavior.
   Teach client about hygiene, personal grooming, or care of clothing.
   Bathe, shave, and/or wash client in order to increase personal comfort or improve personal appearance.

II. Indirect Clinical (examples)   (8 items)
    Use telephone or other methods to arrange for or find transportation for client.
    Explain social or service programs to lay people (in office meetings, speeches, television interviews) in order to inform them of the programs.

III. Programming and Directing Work (Self) (examples)   (5 items)
     Review file and records of client prior to an interview, recertification, or visit in order to plan a course of action.
     Interview client or relative, using available information to carry out intake with the client.

IV. Programming and Directing Work (Others) (examples)   (7 items)
    Rate worker's (subordinate's) performance, using performance-rating form and dictating narrative when necessary.
    Review case records in order to assign (reassign) cases to unit or staff members.

V. Development (Self) (examples)   (2 items)
   Review administrative literature (manuals, letters, memos) in order to become familiar with (or review) agency policies and procedures.

VI. Development (Others) (examples)   (5 items)
    Teach group of workers, in classroom or other setting,

Table 1. (continued)

according to a training plan, in order to increase knowledge (or skills) of staff.

VII. Information Processing (examples)   (7 items)
Record or dictate client information (case narratives, forms) in order to update records, provide case status data, or document services provided.
Fill out requisitions or vouchers to order supplies.

VIII. Managing Work Units (examples)   (15 items)
Use standard form or methods (for example, work sampling, time study) in order to provide data for reimbursement, analysis, or other uses.
Write policy or procedural statements (occasionally with others) in order to develop/provide standard operating procedures.
Prepare or review budgets or financial (expenditure) statements for your unit (department) in order to determine or control financial status.
Keep track of the distribution and use of supplies (food stamps or any tangible goods) in order to ensure an adequate supply for use.

As the reader can see, the tasks are quite diverse in content. Care was taken to phrase all tasks at an optimum level of abstraction, and jargon and traditional labels were avoided whenever possible. The number of items in each category was not based on any preconceived rationale. Respondents were asked to indicate—by using a five-point Likert scale—how often, if at all, they carried out each task. The frequency designations on this scale follow the wording suggested by Schriessheim and Schriessheim (1974).

Part III of the JAS was designed to determine how much time workers spent in various types of activities. Accordingly, respondents were asked to indicate the percentage of time spent in each of the eight categories in Part II. They were to use a typical month as a frame of reference.

The last part of the JAS contained an attitude survey. Respondents were questioned about their feelings about their jobs. Conceptually, the survey was based on the work of Hackman and Oldham (1975, 1976) for assessing the satisfaction potential in jobs. This section includes information about the characteristics of the respondent's job, his or her satisfaction with various aspects of the work situation, and indications of the type of job preferred. (Since data from this section of the JAS will not be presented here, it will not be discussed further.)

Various versions of the JAS were pretested, modified, and refined. All items were written in machine-processable format, and an instruction booklet was prepared. The final version of the instrument, including a standardized briefing to respondents, can be administered to groups as large as fifty. The average time to complete this questionnaire is one and a half hours.

Given the objectives of the study, the sampling plan had to cover the entire range of job classes in the social worker series and reflect the salient characteristics of the different counties as well as the state (central) office. Consequently, a stratified random-sampling plan was developed that met these criteria. Counties and job classes were sampled in proportion to their occurrence in the overall population. To ensure reliability, classes with small numbers were oversampled slightly. Within each class, workers were selected randomly, so that each had an equal likelihood of being chosen.

All the data were collected in group sessions preceded by a carefully standardized briefing. Respondents signed their names to questionnaires, but no raw data were ever seen by agency personnel. Questionnaires were obtained from 661 workers, or approximately 16 percent of the total work force. Respondents ranged from human service aides to top-level state and county office personnel. A breakdown of the sample by major job category is presented in Table 2.

Table 2. Breakdown of Sample by Job Type

Job	Number
Program and bureau administrators	11
Department directors (county)	30
Supervisors	70
Caseworker reviewers[a]	131
Eligibility technicians	65
Service workers	229
Aides	55
Total	661

[a] This is a generic department title. It covers a wide range of job activities.

Clearly reflected is the wide range in job levels covered by the data collection. In reviewing other characteristics of the work force (for example, job location, program area, time on the job) reflected by the sample, the researchers increasingly were convinced of its representativeness.

The primary technique used in the analysis of the data was the hierarchical grouping procedure described by Ward (1963) and Ward and Hook (1963), whereby a series of variables (people, items, tests) are grouped together on the basis of profile similarity. At each stage of the grouping, all possible pairs of profiles are considered, and the two most similar are combined. The criterion for combining is the amount of within-group error (or variance). A "jump" in the incremental error from one stage to the next indicates that the profiles combined were dissimilar, and the combinations preceding the jump are selected as the solution. The Ward procedure was used to group the JAS items into clusters to yield practice dimensions and to group workers into job "families."

Findings

The first stage of the analysis concentrated on a reclassification of the JAS to reveal the underlying dimensions of the activities described in it. Accordingly, the seventy-seven items in Part II of that instrument were subjected to the Ward (1963) analysis.* Profiles for each item were constructed across all 661 respondents Each pair of item profiles was compared, and the items were recombined into the fewest possible number of homogeneous clusters. The process roughly is analogous to factor analysis, except that it avoids introducing some of the artifacts associated with that technique.

Each cluster thus consisted of those items that "behaved" the same way (or were highly correlated) across the sample of workers. These were the clusters that captured the similarities and the differences among respondents. We have called them the "di-

* All analyses were carried out at the University of Alabama Computer Center using a UNIVAC-1100 system. I am indebted to Barbara and Harry Barker, of the University of Alabama, for carrying out the analysis through the use of their specialized Program Library.

mensions of practice." The analysis identified twelve such dimensions. They are described in Table 3. The table also shows the following information about each dimension: activities subsumed by it, the number of JAS items contributing to its makeup, and internal consistency reliability. The findings on reliability are encouraging. Eight of the twelve dimensions have reliability coefficients of .80 or above. As can be seen, lower reliabilities seem to be associated with clusters that have few items defining them. Adding JAS items with relevant content should help to increase the stability of those clusters.

Table 3. Major Practice Dimensions
(Based on Cluster Analysis)

1. Linkage—connecting clients with resources, opportunities, and services; evaluating, licensing resources, and trying to improve service to clients. (7 items) $r_{tt} = .78$[a]

2. Instruction—teaching clients skills (money management, personal hygiene, literacy, food preparation) and behaviors (taking job interviews, working in a group). (6 items) $r_{tt} = .88$

3. Counseling, informing—providing information to clients, defining needs, case finding, explaining programs, advising clients, relieving anxiety, choosing courses of action. (8 items) $r_{tt} = .92$

4. Personal care—providing direct, tangible services to clients (assist in dressing, carrying out housekeeping, preparing meals, giving medicines) of a maintenance or custodial nature. (8 items) $r_{tt} = .94$

5. Case management (specific)—preparing records, schedules, files to plan work around specific clients, carrying out intake, determining eligibility for services, public assistance. (7 items) $r_{tt} = .91$

6. External relations—meeting with citizens, client groups, designing and conducting opinion surveys, gathering support for programs, making speeches and presentations. (6 items) $r_{tt} = .80$

7. Compiling information—processing numerical and statistical information, making listings, carrying out studies for costing, reimbursement, planning purposes. (3 items) $r_{tt} = .61$

8. Management of tangibles—taking care of physical components of an operation (inventory control, ordering supplies, transporting property, inspecting facilities, maintaining security). (4 items) $r_{tt} = .81$

Table 3. (continued)

9. Program management—planning details of new programs, designing training, reviewing and preparing budgets, writing policy, conducting meetings, recruiting and screening personnel.
   (8 items) $r_{tt} = .98$
10. Employee supervision—evaluating employee performance, preparing work schedules, teaching workers, giving advice with worker problems, orienting new workers, assigning cases to workers.
    (12 items) $r_{tt} = .98$
11. Case management (general)—reviewing policies and procedures applicable to many clients, planning general work activities, discussing program operations with co-workers.
    (3 items) $r_{tt} = .57$
12. Paper flow—using standard forms to carry out routine procedures (processing vouchers, filling out time sheets, dictating and proofreading correspondence and case records).
    (4 items) $r_{tt} = .57$

ᵃ Kuder-Richardson (KR_{20}) coefficient of internal consistency.

An inspection of the content underlying the dimensions shows that they are diverse. We were interested in learning more about them. It seemed particularly important to find out which dimensions grouped together on the job and which ones did not. This information would add more clarity and detail to any discussion of the generalist/specialist dimension. To accomplish this, a matrix of intercorrelations was generated. Analysis of these intercorrelations suggests a pattern of systematic relationships within the data. There does seem to be a group of interrelated dimensions (clusters) centering on the *direct-service* area (linkage, counseling/informing, teaching, direct care). Another grouping appears in the general area of *management*. Clusters such as program management, supervision, and management of tangibles intercorrelate quite highly. Given the nature of the organization being studied, these preliminary findings were not surprising. These systematic patterns of correlation were taken as an indication that the JAS was reflecting patterns of work activity within the organization and that it should be a useful tool for grouping workers into job "families" based on patterns (profiles) of the twelve practice dimensions.

To group workers into job families, we again used the Ward (1963) technique. This time, profiles were constructed for each of the 661 respondents. Scores for all the items in a given cluster were totaled for each of the 661 workers. The distribution of scores within each cluster was then converted to a distribution of Z-scores; that is, standard scores with a mean of 0.00 and a standard deviation of 1.00. Each respondent's JAS scores thus could be converted to a twelve-point profile expressed in Z-score form. These standardized profiles were the inputs into the hierarchical grouping procedure.

Initially, twenty groups of workers were formed. They ranged in size from eight to sixty-eight respondents. Although each group was distinct (due to the criteria built into the procedure), inspection of the data suggested that many groups seemed to be variations around a more limited set of generic job "families." Five such basic families were identified, and composite "profiles" were constructed for each. The composite profile for the generic job family was constructed by computing a weighted average for each profile point (dimension). The scores averaged were the profile scores for those of the original twenty groups that were assigned to that job family. Weights were based on the number of workers in each of the original groups. The five families were labeled human services workers $(N = 43)$, eligibility workers $(N = 213)$, social service workers $(N = 176)$, supervisors $(N = 89)$, and administrators $(N = 81)$. These families are important because each worker was classified into one job family only; the five families accounted for 91 percent of the work force; and each family constitutes a distinct field of practice, with implications for very different types of skills and knowledges.

The human services workers constitute the paraprofessional cohorts of the department. They are used largely as homemakers and are deployed into clients' homes. Their profile reflects an extremely high loading or involvement in the personal care dimension. Their frequent client contacts enable them to do a good bit of teaching, particularly around specific skills. As expected, the teaching dimension of their jobs is extremely critical. Finally, since they are able to see clients in the home, they also serve as a link between the clients and additional services they need. Hence, the linkage component is quite high. As will be seen, only the paraprofessionals provide to any extent this type of tangible, direct service to the clients. Furthermore, the nature of this service presumes a frequent, prolonged type of contact with clients on a highly interpersonal level.

The second family, eligibility workers (32 percent of the agency's work force), reflects another predictable division of labor in current public welfare practice. These workers provide indirect rather than direct services to people; they are engaged largely in the screening process for determining eligibility for various agency programs, such as public assistance, Medicaid, food assistance, and services. These activities are subsumed under case management, both general and specific, and the management of paper flow.

Social service workers make up the third family. These workers, as expected, have a high loading on the teaching, linkage, and counseling/informing dimensions. They differ from the paraprofessionals in that they provide little or no personal care to clients. Much of their service centers on a more intellectualized process of exchanging information and providing advice and guidance to clients. The interpersonal skill component is extensive. In addition, the profile of this group reflects the heavy investment in case planning and paperwork required by contemporary agency operations. The loadings on case management(s) and paper flow are quite high.

The family characterized as supervisors reflects a concentration on personnel administration activities. This large group consists of individuals whose job functions load heavily in the supervision dimension. The peak in this dimension is distinctive. Also reflected by this group's profile is involvement in program management and in the management of tangibles. In the absence of heavy involvement with the outside public (external relations), this pattern of dimensions depicts management at the program or unit level rather than top management.

The final family, the administrators, carries out the top-level administrative functions of agency practice. The shape of the profile indicates that it is a much broader area of practice than that of supervision. It encompasses supervision, compiling information, program management, and external relations. There also is some involvement in general case management and in the management of tangibles. This is a group responsible for the management of policy, material, and people.

Summary and Implications

As the data have shown, this analysis of the work functions of personnel in a reasonably typical public welfare agency indicates that social work practice is not a simple concept. On the contrary, it is heterogeneous in method, content, and purpose. At a macroscopic level, practice can be divided into three major areas: direct practice, eligibility screening, and management. The first, direct practice, has two components, personal care and the provision of social services. Eligibility determination, the second area, is relatively straightforward. The third area, management, has a personnel administration component (supervision) and a major policy formulation and implementation thrust.

This heterogeneity is not surprising, since most models of practice call for a diverse range of functions. What is important, however, is that these practice streams seem to be relatively discontinuous conceptually, yet they represent the paths along which people normally move as they progress through the organizational job hierarchy. The progression from direct service to management involves a total shift in subject matter and skill focus. To be sure, there seems to be an underpinning of interpersonal skill that is common to the therapeutic, supervisory, and public relations areas. The contexts of these and the problem-solving skills they require, however, seem quite different. Furthermore, the eligibility function is almost totally cognitive, while the personal care activity is concrete, specific, and oriented toward tangibles.

These discontinuities can create problems for the educator and the agency administrator. As currently constituted, organizational advancement generally requires that workers move out of clinical positions into those that are supervisory or administrative. This is true in the agency from which the present data were collected. A person who can master all these functions (or who even wants to) is rather rare. Quite often, as the "cream rises," it begins to go sour, creating problems for the agency administrator who wants to reward good workers with salary and advancement and still retain a cadre of competent service workers. On the educational side, a considerable problem exists for educators who wish to implement curricula representing a continuum of learning that builds on skills imparted at lower levels. If this training is to relate to the true progression of job opportunities, such neat sequences neither will be possible nor particularly desirable.

To deal with these problems, several suggestions can be made: (1) Agencies should take steps to expand career opportunities for people who wish to remain in a clinical track. (2) Entry-level positions in administration that do not require a traditional clinical background as an exclusive credential need to be created. (3) Research should be undertaken to determine what common skills (if any) underlie both the service and the administrative streams. These skills could serve as the building blocks of an educational progression. (4) Job enlargement, to expand the skill base of workers, could be instituted at selected points in a career ladder. This could reduce considerably the likelihood of individuals' being promoted into a job situation for which they are unprepared.

The data generated by the present study have other implications as well. Of the five job families defined in the study, three are highly specialized (the human service workers, eligibility workers, and supervisors). These 345 respondents compose 52 percent of the total sample. The service generalist, as characterized in the SREB material of Teare and McPheeters (1970), is not to be found. A more typical pattern is that of specialization—by program, domain, problem area, or task cluster. At present, however, many undergraduate programs are following the generalist model in developing curricula. Despite the intellectual appeal of the model, there seem to be difficulties in implementing it in agencies. These difficulties need to be studied further. Otherwise, the model may serve as yet another source of discontinuity between agency planners and curriculum designers.

At the graduate level, the data suggest that more emphasis should be placed on the preparation of people for supervisory and management positions. This recommendation evolves from two components of the data. On the one hand, a substantial number of workers do not fit the traditional image of the social worker providing casework services to people. Only 27 percent of the total sample can be characterized as belonging in the social service worker group. On the other hand, a relatively high emphasis can be found in administration and supervision. A substantial portion of the sample, 25 percent, has these two dimensions as primary practice components. As stated earlier, these are the jobs that constitute the advancement opportunities in practice. Since graduate degrees are required for a majority of these jobs, educators would do well to prepare their graduates for these contingencies.

One final point should be made. The data show that a relatively low emphasis is placed on advocacy or any other activities directed toward aggressively changing the nature of the services or service systems. In this agency, workers are not reinforced when they try to bite the hands (or the clients) that feed them. This probably is not unique to this agency. Like the generalist concept, the notion of advocacy has intellectual and emotional appeal to educators. Many programs indoctrinate students to have this thrust as a practice expectation. The gap between expectations and practice realities may be greater than many educators would like to admit. If the tactical skills of being a change agent are taught to students, they should be presented with a full disclosure of the attendant risks. Moreover, the tolerance levels of potential employers should be clearly understood.

In conclusion, it seems clear that the JAS has proved to be a useful preliminary tool for investigating the nature of work in an agency. The practice dimensions and job families thus identified have been most fruitful in sharpening discussions about practice content and its associated skill requirements. As can be seen, there are numerous implications for education, training, job design, and career planning. At present, work is proceeding on a more detailed analysis of the requisite knowledge, attitudes, and skills associated with each task cluster of the JAS. In addition, the tasks are being scaled as to their criticality and relevance. This material is being prepared for future publication in book form, in conjunction with worker bio-data and job-satisfaction information.

II

Designing Human Services Training Based on Worker Task Analysis

Michael J. Austin

The search for accountability in our agencies and on our campuses has led us back to the complex phenomenon of worker competence. Over the past decade, we have stumbled in our search over such terms as *job performance evaluation, competency-based education,* and *task analysis.* This chapter seeks to clarify these terms by describing one approach to defining human services work and preparing a new strategy for curriculum development. The discussion of worker competence, however, must be placed in the context of the human services organizations established to meet the needs of a variety of client problems. This chapter is oriented toward the thousands of persons currently working in public human services agencies under the auspices of state and local governments and toward the thousands of students or future practitioners who will seek employment in the public sector. This orientation is based on an assumption that the vast majority of human services programs are carried out in organizations that Hasenfeld (1974) calls people-processing (in contrast to people-changing) agencies. In essence, very little long-term therapy is conducted or called for in public human services organizations.

The purpose of analyzing issues of competence and task analysis is to identify those attributes of the human services job market useful for educators in the curriculum development process. The data and findings noted in this chapter were derived from a recently completed study (Austin and Skelding, 1975) of one thousand human services workers in the Florida Department of Health and Rehabilitation Services. The study emerged from the realization that educators and administrators did not talk the same language. Educators used terms such as *learning objectives* and *conceptual frameworks for intervention;* the administrators talked in terms of *job performance* and *program accountability.* As a result, considerable effort was devoted to finding a language that would improve communication among educators, administrators, supervisors, workers, and students. The language of Functional Job Analysis, developed by Fine and Wiley (1971), and the descriptive capabilities of the Position Analysis Questionnaire technique of Mc-Cormick, Jeanneret, and Mecham (1969) served as the research and communication tools of this large study. Selected findings will be noted later in the chapter.

Experience indicates that there are important benefits to be derived from improved communication between educators, who are faced with the imperatives of educational programming, and administrators, who must satisfy the demands of agency practice. Admittedly, any research tool carried to its extreme can produce trivia, and any learning objective taken to its extreme can produce irrelevance. The real issue, however, is the ability of educators and administrators to reduce ignorance by finding a common language through which to communicate. Course outlines rarely are shared with program administrators; educators rarely content-analyze the current range of relevant job descriptions or existing documents describing program goals.

The basic issues related to communicating effectively about the nature of human services work include the following: (1) Agency administrators are concerned with service delivery and job performance. (2) Educators are concerned with transforming students into competent practitioners. (3) There is a need for a common perspective on what constitutes competence. (4) The technology of task analysis provides a foundation for improving communication between agencies and universities.

The Language of Agency Administrators and University Educators

The issues of job performance and competence represent the major factors in the communication gap between agency administrators and university educators, since administrators emphasize performance and educators emphasize competence. What, specifically, do they mean by these terms?

Performance on the job can refer to accomplishing something, discharging appointed duties or tasks. It is, in part, a public presentation similar to the performance of actors in a play. From this broad definition, one can delineate more specific boundaries for job performance in the human services: effort, efficiency, and effectiveness. These terms represent the major concerns of human services administrators who seek to make their programs accountable to funding sources and clients. *Effort* in the human services refers primarily to money and time: the cost of delivering services and the time that workers spend delivering services. *Efficiency* means being productive without waste and relates most directly to a minimum number of workers and supervisors delivering services to a maximum number of clients. Human services efficiency also has been assessed in terms of service availability (for example, is the agency open after 5 P.M.?) and service accessibility (for example, can the client easily reach the agency by public transportation and can his or her children be cared for?). *Effectiveness* refers to producing a desired result. In the human services, we tend to make successive approximations of effectiveness; helping a client cope with poverty conditions falls short of helping a client out of poverty and into self-sufficiency. Program evaluators approach such successive approximations in terms of process evaluation and impact evaluation. Determining effectiveness in terms of process evaluation leads to an analysis of the methods used to treat, rehabilitate, or process a client through the human services agency. Impact evaluation addresses effectiveness primarily in terms of outcome regardless of the methods used (for example, is the client self-sufficient, rehabilitated, successfully discharged from the service, and so forth?).

Competence, from the educator's perspective, often refers to the quality of demonstrating the essential abilities necessary for the delivery of human services. While preparation of students for competent practice can be analyzed from various perspectives of expertise—social problem, social science, research, and social policy—the interventive methods used to provide human services to clients provide the context for analyzing competence in this chapter. Irrespective of the type of interventive method (for example, casework, group work, or community organizing), one of the key components of competent practice is the ability to conceptualize the interventive process. While positive impact on a client and/or client situation could be seen as the ultimate test of competence, the focus here is on the ability to tell others, verbally and in writing, exactly what one plans to do and/or has done to help a client cope or rehabilitate himself or herself. From a variety of individual case situations, a practitioner should then be able to conceptualize the job of a human service worker in any agency. In addition to describing the interventive method, the practitioner should be able to place the method in a context of other methods as well as identify the relevant knowledge base (for example, theories of human behavior and social environment, social policy and program imperatives, and related research findings). While educators seek to develop this ability in future practitioners through case analysis, written critiques, oral reports, fieldwork supervisory conferences, term papers, and examinations, it is a skill that is refined and solidified primarily through on-the-job experience.

While administrators focus on effort, efficiency, and effectiveness, educators emphasize the five important audiences with whom the future practitioner interacts: client, supervisor, subordinate, administrator, and general public. Recent efforts in task-oriented casework and behavioral contract setting between the client and the worker represent beginning steps in conceptualizing practice so that a client clearly understands what the worker plans to do *with* and not *for* a client. This process obviously requires a language that can be understood by the client, which means there must be a reduction in or elimination of professional jargon.

The second significant audience for the practitioner is his or her supervisor. In this case, the reporting of the study and the diagnosis, treatment, and evaluating phases of intervention represent the major portion of the agenda of supervisory case conferences. The onus is on the worker to integrate and present the relevant knowledge about clients and show how the interventive techniques relate to a client's situation and stage of development.

Conceptualizing practice for the subordinate, the third audience, is similar to the previous situation with the supervisor. However, the added ingredient here relates to the concept of adult learning. When the practitioner is responsible for supervising workers who have little or no training, the process involves teaching adults, who usually respond well to the experiential aspects of on-the-job, in-service training when new knowledge is related directly to their life or work experiences.

The fourth audience for the future practitioner is the agency administrator. Administrators need hard information, such as the number of intakes completed, the number of discharges, and the number of client goals achieved. They seek these data from workers through reporting forms used in client information systems. Because of this quantitative bias, practitioners assume an additional responsibility to convey to top administration the requirements for effective practice. Significant power and influence can be exerted on administrators through well-reasoned reporting based on a demonstrated ability to conceptualize practice.

Finally, the general public represents a significant audience for the future practitioner. As a beginning, perhaps, the novice social worker might explain to his or her parents what a social worker does. The interrelationship with the public may involve defining a social problem, elaborating on society's response as demonstrated through social policies, describing the range of agencies empowered to implement these policies, and, finally, conceptualizing the role of the line worker who uses different techniques based on a broad body of knowledge to assist a client. The same line of reasoning could be used in speeches to the local Lion's Club, presentation to the county commissioners, or high school social problems classes. Conceptualizing practice for the general public is a critical component of the educator's goal of producing a knowledgeable and competent practitioner who can share his or her expertise in the marketplace of ideas. This is sometimes referred to as preparing for effective citizenship and frequently is a cited educational goal of undergraduate and graduate social work education.

Conceptualizing Human Services Work

To understand the range of procedures and activities central to the delivery of human services, it is necessary to conceptualize a framework for collecting and analyzing data about human services work (M. J. Austin, 1977). Human services work is defined in terms of three basic elements: (1) tasks that are performed by individual service workers, (2) constellations of tasks that make up workers' roles, and (3) the attributes characterizing the total job. These three elements of work constitute the model used in a study of work behavior in Florida's human services organization (Wilson, 1974).

The basic element in this conceptualization of work is the "task." Since a comprehensive system for conceptualizing tasks and their corresponding attributes is included in the Functional Job Analysis (FJA) technology developed by Fine and Wiley (1971), most of the task elements of this technology can be used to analyze human services work. In human services organizations, most of the tasks that workers perform deal primarily with people (interpersonal resources), data (cognitive resources), and, to a limited extent, things (physical resources). The content of a task statement includes the action that the worker performs (for example, asks, listens, writes) and the result or outcome of this action (for example, in order to record identifying information). Using the FJA technology, one can scale a complete task statement according to functional levels that relate to the complexity of the task relative to the three dimensions of data, people, and things.

The second element of human services work, workers' roles,

provides a means of categorizing and describing constellations of tasks. The role model developed by Teare and McPheeters (1970) can be used as a starting point in developing a construct that would conceptualize the elements of human services work. A construct was postulated to include five primary functions of human services work:

1. Linkage—directing, referring, and advocating for clients.
2. Mobilization—developing resources and advocating for change in organizations and social policies.
3. Counseling—instructing, coaching, and supporting clients along with consultation to other care givers.
4. Treatment—maintaining and controlling clients' condition through different therapies and care-giving activities.
5. Administration—collecting and processing client information for service planning and evaluation.

A more complete definition of roles and functions is presented below. The construct assumes that the five functions and related roles represent the total range of work activity performed by service workers in a comprehensive human services organization.*

1. Linkage—helping potential consumers attain appropriate human services. The primary objective of linkage is a confluence between the consumer and an appropriate source of help for the problems indicated. Linkage may take the form of simple communication, via advertising or a formal information and referral source, enabling people to utilize human services resources by helping them negotiate the system; or it may take the form of advocacy— advocating the rights of the potential consumer who is being denied service.

   a. Brokering—facilitating the actual physical connection between the individual or individuals with problems and services that

---

* Task data generated from more than one thousand human services workers in Florida were put into a functional job analysis format, sorted to the eleven roles, and analyzed with respect to existing functional job analysis ordinal scales. As a result, a computerized personnel data system was constructed; the system was based on a task bank of 358 tasks, including multidimensional scaling and related inventory of functional skills.

have the potential for resolving or reducing the problem. The "broker" tries to help the potential consumer of services finesse the service delivery system, which may be relatively unaccommodating at times. Some manipulation may be involved in preparing the potential consumer and/or potential provider for a positive contact. The relationship assumes a standard procedure or a negotiable situation, which may include some discussing or bargaining to reach agreement.

b. Client (consumer) advocating—the successful linking of a rejected consumer with appropriate services. The "client advocate" tries to bring about a change in the stance of the rejecting organization in favor of the person involved. This is a confronting relationship; usually, a formal appeal based on legal or human rights is presented to accountable authorities.

2. Mobilization—working to fill the gaps within the service delivery system by developing or creating resources; that is, programs, services, organizations. The primary objective of mobilization is to modify services to meet current needs. Mobilization includes humanizing services for existing consumers; bringing services to potential consumer groups or classes by changing inequitable or discriminatory practices, regulations, policies, and/or laws; and creating new human service resources or programs.

a. Activating—the development of new human services resources to meet changing social needs. Activating may involve working to define and communicate specific community needs by providing the catalyst for the formation of self-help fellowships. The objectives of the activator include defining problems, organizing interest groups, and seeking public opinion.

b. Systems advocating—changing or adjusting the framework of the service delivery system to accommodate individuals who would otherwise be rejected or denied. Systems advocating may involve making a case for a population of clients by seeking change in practices, rules, regulations, policies, or laws. Preventive and rehabilitative measures are the goals of systems advocating.

3. Counseling—short-term coaching, counseling, teaching, and consulting in a problem-focused framework. The primary ob-

jectives are to convey and impart information or knowledge and develop various kinds of skills in the individual or group. Counseling includes direct-service and consultive activities.

    a. Direct services—teaching, counseling, coaching, or supporting consumers in a short-term, problem-focused situation. The counselor-counselee relationship is usually therapeutic in nature, and improved understanding and skills or increased skill levels are expected. A consensus concerning the problem and desired outcome in these situations usually is agreed on in the initial stages of contact. Contact may be initiated by the counselee or the counselor.

    b. Consulting—a service provided in the colleague or organizational setting. Consulting may involve case conferences to receive or supply relevant information, or consultation may be utilized as an instructive technique to provide specialized knowledge.

4. Treatment—longer-term, disability-focused support, therapy, or control on an ongoing basis. The primary objective is increased status of functioning or humane care. Treatment includes consideration for physically, mentally, or socially handicapped individuals.

    a. Rehabilitating—providing extended disability-focused therapy to dysfunctioning human services consumers. Rehabilitation may involve a variety of therapeutic metholologies. The objective of rehabilitation is increased functional levels, and the goal of treatment is independence and the expectation of continued independence.

    b. Care giving—extending maintenance and/or control to handicapped or maladapted individuals. These physically, mentally, and/or socially deprived persons usually are provided care and treatment oriented toward decreasing their dependency.

5. Administration—the collection of data and the processing of information leading to decision making or monitoring at either the consumer or system level. The primary objective is to generate data as the foundation for reasonable decisions. Adminis-

tration includes information management for monitoring and planning purposes.

a. Client (consumer) programming—planning for client services. Client programming involves data collecting and processing for the purpose of making decisions regarding case disposition. It ranges from simple case data gathering and individual program planning to follow-up.

b. Systems researching—the collection and processing of data relevant to particular areas of programmatic or organizational concern. Systems researching involves research for the purpose of making decisions and taking action. It ranges from gathering information and preparing statistical reports of program activities to program evaluation and sophisticated research.

c. Administering—decision making at all organizational levels and in all organizational contexts. Administering involves decisions concerning program management, personnel supervision, budgeting, fiscal operations, and facilities management. Policy development, program implementation, and organizational decision making also are involved in the administering roles.

One example of the findings from the Florida study can be seen in the role profile of public welfare caseworkers with the same job descriptions: (1) direct services to clients (72.66 percent), including brokering (4.84 percent), treatment (3.33 percent), counseling (8.85 percent), and administrative activities in order to develop service plan (55.64 percent); and (2) indirect services to clients (27.34 percent), including consulting (7.65 percent), administrative data collecting (8.48 percent), and program planning and managing (11.21 percent). From an analysis of the major roles reflected in the work of the caseworkers, one can see a large direct-service component (72.66 percent) featuring the roles of brokering, rehabilitating, counseling, and client programming. The remainder of the caseworker's work involved indirect services (27.34 percent), including the roles of consulting, systems researching, and administering. This profile sheds some different light on the age-old complaint of caseworkers that they do too much paper-work and not enough casework. Half of the caseworker's time appears to be spent in client programming, which involves a range of administrative functions necessary to deliver services to clients. With minimal effort devoted to the counseling and treatment functions, it is apparent from an analysis of one type of worker that the public welfare agency continues to be a people-processing rather than a people-changing organization.

Within each of the roles noted in the profile, there are clusters of tasks that have been given a number of scale values. For example, the scale of worker instruction addresses the prescribed and discretionary components of each task. The more prescriptive (limited authority) the task, the greater is the autonomy of the worker to exercise judgment with minimal supervision. The scale values of 1 (high prescription) to 8 (high discretion) represent another perspective on organizing components of human services work. For example, workers with different levels of training (high school, community college, university, and graduate school) might perform a mix of tasks based on prescription and discretion. At the high school level, one could conceive of a majority of prescribed tasks (80 percent) with a minority of discretionary tasks (20 percent). The reverse might be true for a graduate-level worker. Workers often base their sense of job responsibility on the amount of discretion ascribed to the tasks that make up their jobs. Therefore, a balance often is needed between prescription and discretion to enhance job satisfaction and career development. Tasks that challenge the worker also contribute to an expanding base of competency, which alerts superiors to the potential for career advancement among workers who successfully meet the challenge.

From Job Analysis to Curriculum Development

The task, role, and function of human services work provide an empirical base on which to develop curriculum. However, a careful analysis of "what is" does not take into account "what should be." Job analysis does not account for the fact that workers may be doing the wrong tasks or failing to perform additional roles or that they may represent a mismatch between prior experience and job attributes. For example, very few client advocacy tasks were identified by workers. Moreover, many workers in the human services industry lack either necessary training or career orientation. At the correctional guard and retardation technician level, it was found that guards prefer night duty so that they can work their farms during the day. Similarly, technicians working in retardation facilities often remain on the job only until they can obtain a hotel maid position, which pays better. There are documented cases of baccalaureate-level workers who have had no human services training and are using public welfare casework or juvenile correctional counselor positions as a stepping-stone to a better job or school. While these random observations are not necessarily negative, they do reflect the difficulty of relying solely on persons currently employed in the human services for a definition of the nature of that work.

Despite these limitations, curriculum developers can draw on the current state of empirical knowledge by providing a foundation of practical job-related activities within the traditional theoretical and "practice" wisdom framework of human services education programs. For example, the eleven roles comprising generalist practice were used to develop a practice text useful for entry-level workers, whether they are high school, community college, or college graduates (Austin, Skelding, and Smith, 1977).

For educators who are more interested in developing specific learning objectives for use in course development or individualized units of continuing education, there are important guides from the field of instructional technology that can be employed to build curriculum at the level of individual worker tasks or clusters of tasks. A model for curriculum development utilizing a task or task cluster has been developed and is noted briefly as an example representing one of the most systematic approaches to date (Hyer and others, 1971). Step 1 involves the identification of the level of training to be conducted (that is, starting where the learner is, which is similar to our frequently stated dictum of starting where the client is). Levels can be labeled arbitrarily as entry, middle, and advanced and can signify the range of complexity within one educational program (for example, a bachelor's degree in social work) or reflect a range of educational levels (for example, community college, university, and graduate school). Whatever the delineations, special attention must be given to distinguishing between complex and less complex tasks. Learning objectives can be developed with tasks as the anchor points.

Appropriate training procedures are selected in Step 2. These procedures address the issue of what the learner needs to be able to do or know; that is, (1) identify the agency goals and objectives that relate to a set of tasks, (2) identify any instructions that usually accompany the tasks or the range of prescription and discretion involved, (3) define the role and/or function that includes the tasks, (4) identify the performance criteria utilized to assess successful task completion on the job, and (5) identify for the learner the range of criteria commonly utilized to assess task performance.

Step 3 relates to the selection of a group of tasks from an existing task bank or one developed by the instructor. Task selection can be based on the objectives of a particular course or a continuing education workshop focused on staff training needs.

Learning unit goals are developed in Step 4. The unit could be similar to a particular role, such as brokering or client programming. A unit also could be a group of tasks that cut across a number of roles—for example, interviewing. The key issue is the framing of the goal statements to include the following: Given *what,* the student does *what,* evaluated according to *what* criteria (Mager, 1962a)?

In Step 5 attention is given to formulating specific behavior objectives that relate to the unit goals. These learning objectives can be formed by converting the task statement into an objective by noting the action verb (for example, "teach," "counsel," "advise") and the outcome phase (for example, "in order to accomplish X"). The same principle used to develop goal statements should be used in behavioral objectives: Given *what,* student will do *what,* according to *what* criteria? Additional behavior objectives may be needed to satisfy the skill requirements of a particular task.

In Step 6 the instructor assigns the particular type of training needed to achieve the behavior objectives. Some objectives may be accomplished most successfully through a didactic lecture, in which specific content is presented. Other objectives may be best met by exercises that involve experiential learning (for example, role play, simulation, games, and site visits). Still other objectives may require the application of content or experience acquired in another course or in fieldwork.

In Step 7 subobjectives are written for each behavioral objective, specifying what the learner must know or do before performing or completing the behavioral objective. Since subobjectives based on task descriptions often encompass broad activity, they frequently lend themselves to further classification. The various attributes and scale values assigned to each task also will provide further data for subobjective development.

In Step 8 the instructor determines the learning conditions needed to meet each subobjective formulated in Step 7. Any learning theory or strategy can be useful for determining how the learner can develop the competencies reflected in each subobjective. Therefore, the instructor must have a working knowledge of learning theory, including, for example, Bruner's concept attainment, Taba's inquiry model, Rogers' nondirective model, and Skinner's behavioral conditioning (Joyce and Weit, 1972).

Implications for Research, Teaching, and Practice

The selected findings noted in this chapter represent only a beginning in our efforts to learn more about the nature of human services work. The research to date raises more questions than it answers. If task roles, functions, and job attributes are insufficient descriptors for defining the nature of human services work, we should search for other data in the daily work of practitioners on the firing line. There is an urgent need to legitimate developmental research in which educators and practitioners together select problems, identify sources of information, gather and evaluate new data, produce new understandings about the nature of human services work, and understand the reality of their product with sufficient confidence to communicate it to other practitioners and educators.

The implications for teaching appear to fall within two categories. First, there is an obvious need to ground some aspects of the teaching of interventive methods in empirical evidence. Data from task banks could be systematically used in the human services to better describe and evaluate practice. Second, our teaching in human services education programs ought to benefit, more fully than it does currently, from new developments in the field of instructional technology. The use of videotapes, telecommunications, and other audiovisual techniques represents the tip of the iceberg in instructional technology. Finally, to improve the level of practice found in our agencies, we need to find a common language by which to improve communication between educators and practitioners. The concepts of tasks, roles, and functions reflect a beginning attempt to locate categories of common meaning and areas for collaboration.

12

Case Management and Task-Centered Social Work

B. Jeanne Mueller
Constance H. Shapiro

A Practice Model

Family life is characterized by normal developmental crises (such as the birth of a first child, when spouses must take on new role behaviors as parents) and by situational crises (such as chronic physical illness or economic dependency) that call for help from outside the conjugal unit. In most traditional societies, this help is provided by extended kin. With urbanization and the shift of population into cities, these supportive networks attenuated, although they may continue to exist in modified forms (Litwak, 1965). Conjugal families who move to urban areas usually put together surrogate supportive systems consisting of neighbors, friends, and fellow

Note: The first part of this chapter, "A Practice Model," was written by B. Jeanne Mueller; the second part, "A Performance-Based Assessment of Learning," by Constance H. Shapiro.

workers, who take over some of the functions of less available kin. Even so, sources of stress, both positive and negative, experienced by individuals and families in times of rapid social change may exceed their ability to cope and adapt; consequently, personal and familial breakdown occur.

Chronic mental or physical illness, violence in families, suicide, desertion, and addictions are among the family problems that become recognized as social problems—problems that families no longer are expected to manage on their own. It then becomes a critical function of government to invent new arrangements for social care and rehabilitation. These concerns, and the bureaucratically organized activities that result from them, constitute the institutional domain of social welfare.

Social welfare, in its institutional form, is designed to mitigate the sources of stress in modern and modernizing societies and serves to cultivate, restore, or conserve human resources for use in achieving the priority goals of those societies. Within the welfare sector, the social services are those organized activities that provide linkages among various social programs and help individuals and families deal with or prevent problems that limit their full potential for self-care, a satisfying family life, and successful participation in the mainstream of community life (Mueller and Morgan, 1974). Within the field of social welfare, social work is one profession that has been allocated a major responsibility for delivery of the personal social services (Kahn and Kamerman, 1976).

In the social work profession, the practitioner role is defined variously. The Pincus and Minahan (1973) framework, for example, is a generic approach that emphasizes commonalities across what historically was designated as casework, group work, and community organization. We have found this a very useful perspective in our program at Cornell. For purposes of this discussion, the term *generalist* also implies the notion that social work has the same professional responsibility across settings and fields of practice; namely, a concern for preventing or remediating social disabilities. That is, we are not in the business of treating schizophrenia or diabetes, as such; rather, we deal with the social disability that may be a consequence of chronic mental or physical handicap. Whether we are practitioners in a school, a welfare department, a hospital, or an aftercare clinic, the social work job is the same—to cultivate, restore, and conserve personal resources and mobilize those personal, interpersonal, and community resources to sustain appropriate social behavior. A generalist also may be involved intermittently in community organization activities or neighborhood development work to develop, improve, or expand the supply of human services.

The goals of cultivation, restoration, and conservation are germane to the practice concept of case management (Mueller, 1974). Cultivation comprises all those preventive and developmental activities designed to nourish the personal resources one needs to meet the normal demands of living in a complex society. Developmental day care centers, family life education programs, special education classes, and work-training centers are examples of cultivation. Restoration includes those activities designed to help a person compensate for disability in order to achieve more normal functioning. Mobility training for the adventitiously blind is one example. Conservation concerns activities that help those beyond the restoration of certain functions to conserve their remaining capacities as long as possible. Such activities are designed especially to maximize living for those who are severely handicapped, whether physically, mentally, or emotionally. It is possible to cultivate and conserve appropriate social behavior in seriously retarded, severely physically handicapped, or mentally disturbed children or adults, and the outcomes of service programs can be measured in large part by the extent to which they achieve improvement in social competence and normalize (Wolfensberger, 1972) the lives of the disabled.

In assessing the effects of the use of supportive services to cultivate, restore, or conserve social competence, we must avoid the usual go/no-go judgment. For example, there is no cure for cerebral palsy, but there are ways of diminishing the stress and helping a child cultivate self-help skills and other abilities. We have not discovered a cure for sickle cell anemia, but we can maximize the amount of time that the individual with this disorder spends out of the hospital in family, school, and friendship groups.

As case manager, the generalist (1) provides entry into the service system, (2) makes certain that the client is moved up or down the ladder of sustaining social supports as social competencies wax or wane, and (3) facilitates the client's exit from the services system. The goal is to keep the client at the lowest level of support compatible with his changing needs. We should not expect clients to remain at a given level of dependence/independence, and one case management function is to monitor the client's situation and change it when indicated. For example, a chronic schizophrenic should not be left in an institution if he can function with the help of outpatient aftercare services and a supervised living arrangement. At the same time, he should not be forgotten in a boarding home when some new source of stress has precipitated a crisis that warrants a return to the mental hospital. To the mobilization of resources must be added the provision for continuity in care.

Generalists can be located in a variety of public and private agencies, including neighborhood service centers, where they come to know and be known and trusted by the residents. As generalists learn the folkways of the subculture of their clients' neighborhoods, they can build information bridges between potential clients and the professional world of specialized services. They should have available a cadre of backup human services specialists in community, regional, and state agencies.

The generalist social worker, then, functions as a case manager to provide continuity in care for clients in a service network. Specific activities include (1) providing information and making referrals; (2) following up on referrals; (3) providing a means of access when there are social, psychological, economic, or bureaucratic obstacles to obtaining needed services; (4) serving as an advocate if services to which a client is entitled are withheld or denied; (5) identifying unmet needs for community services and the barriers to delivery of services; and (6) joining with others to develop, improve, or expand the supply of human services.

Information and referral, access, and advocacy services are activities that can be carried out effectively within the context of task-centered, short-term counseling. The Cornell program has field-tested the Reid and Epstein (1972) model. The conceptualization but not the process was modified in some relatively minor ways to make it more compatible for us, assuming that this is the license permitted by the time-honored phrase "the art of social work practice." One such modification relates to the way we conceptualize problem definition. Taking the range of major social roles—but especially family, work, citizen, and friendship roles—we explore during initial interviews for possible sources of stress resulting from interrole or intrarole conflict, role loss, and/or role failure. Role conflict and role failure, of course, are related to norms and values concerning appropriate social behavior. Three major referents validate the appropriateness of the role behavior: oneself—what accords with personal values and personal style; the relevant role-set or reference group for the social role in question; and the American core culture (Loeb, 1961). Intrarole conflict occurs when there are discrepancies between what a person expects of himself as a parent, for example, and how he actually behaves; it also occurs when the person and his spouse have different notions about proper parental behavior. Other examples specific to organizational settings are conflicts between teacher and student, patient and nurse, or client and social worker concerning how one should behave in relation to the other.

Interrole conflict occurs when two roles carried by a person are incompatible and result in interpersonal conflict. An example would be simultaneous but different demands coming from children and spouse, so that one could be a good husband only at the expense of being a less satisfactory father in one's own estimation. Role failure, of course, is the problem of the student who flunks, the spouse who deserts, and the worker who is fired for incompetence. Role loss and role failure cover the situations described as problems in social transition. Listed below are the categories for role analysis used for problem definition, with comparable categories from Reid and Epstein (1972).

Intrarole conflict	Difficulties in role performance
	Problems with formal organizations
Interrole conflict	Interpersonal conflict
Role failure	Dissatisfaction with social relations
	Problems of social transition
Role loss	Problems of social transition

Reactive emotional distress crosses all categories—conflict, failure, and loss—justifying a belief that the purpose of the initial interview should be to locate the sources of stress. Without a sense of distress, a person ordinarily will not be recruited into the client role. This presentation, therefore, will put aside the paradoxical notion of involuntary client. The term *client* as used here is restricted to persons who are willing to enter into a contract for problem solving with a social worker.

The last problem category in the Reid and Epstein model, inadequate resources, is a cause (as reactive emotional distress is a result) of role conflict, role loss, or role failure. Perlman (1962) has identified a series of such causes: deficiency of means—that is, inadequate resources; deficiency of knowledge or preparation; temporary or chronic deficiency of physical, intellectual, or affective capacity; and acute disturbance of capacity and/or motivation due to situational crisis.

The task-centered counseling process can be described briefly as follows: During the initial interview, problems are elicited and clarified. The client then ranks the problems, deciding which to deal with first. The next step is to agree on a contract (Loeb, 1961). Contracts establish a mutual agreement regarding goals and means and clarify purposes and conditions for giving and receiving service. They define tasks, order priorities, set a time duration, and set terms for assessing progress (Perlman, 1962). Contracts can be renegotiated if there is a compelling need to extend the allotted time, and new contracts can be negotiated for a second problem to be worked on.

The task-centered model is based on shared responsibility for problem solving, and clients and social worker have task assignments for the interim between interviews. Major tasks will be divided into subtasks, and immediate goals will be defined as subparts of the larger goals. Reid and Epstein note, and we have verified in practice, that there is a temporal gradient in this process; tasks are revised in the direction of greater and greater specificity.

Termination begins with the initial interview, when time limits are set. These limits have the effect of concentrating efforts on achievable goals and seem to stimulate social worker and client to greater efforts and better planning. In the last interview, achievements are reviewed and future tasks are defined for the client to do independently. A problem-oriented case record (POR), such as that described by Kane (1974), is used to good advantage with this model. The problem-oriented record requires a uniformly gathered, well-defined data base that is collected before problems are defined. The list of problems derived from this information is attached at the front of the record and serves as an index to the subsequent recordings. Each entry in the record must refer to a specific problem, so that one can trace the way it has been dealt with over time. For each listed problem, the closing entry indicates its status, the prognosis, and the recommendation. Kane (1974, p. 418) notes the value of this style of recording for social work education: "By reviewing the records, the instructor would be able to discern the proficiency of the student in gathering and organizing information, the accuracy of assessment, and the appropriateness and resourcefulness of planning. POR gives the instructor the advantage of precisely identifying any weakness . . . and of noting any improvement."

The Cornell undergraduate social work curriculum is built around the generalist definition of the practitioner role and a case management process joined to task-centered counseling. Our thirty cooperating public and private agencies viewed this curriculum as relevant preparation for students coming to them for field placements. It also forms the basis of the curriculum we have developed and are teaching to some 350 caseworkers and supervisors in eleven rural and upstate New York counties. This staff development program is in its fourth year, and undergraduate students now can be placed with agency supervisors who are using this intervention model learned in our agency-based courses.

The Montana Social Work Competence Examination (Arkava and Brennen, 1975; Arkava and others, 1976) has particular relevance for the practice model described above. We are using the examination with our BSW students and plan to use it this coming year in the off-campus course. The eleven categories in the examination are related closely to what is taught in the BSW integrated fieldwork and method course, and they draw extensively on learnings from other courses in the social work curriculum: Community Theory, Organizational Behavior, Small Group Behavior, Social Policy, Program Planning, and Human Behavior. We use the examination in a processual rather than summative manner. That is, students receive the examination at the beginning of the two-semester practice course, and they produce a written assignment for each section, beginning with the Community Context of Practice and the Organizational Context of Practice. These two assignments are completed during the first quarter of the fall semester, and cases are not assigned during the first three weeks in the field, so that students have time to become acquainted with their respective agencies and communities. They attend meetings of school boards, city councils, and county boards; they look at demographic data in census reports; they read current and back issues of local newspapers; and they spend time in various public places, observing the range of political and social attitudes and behaviors characteristic of that community. They also use the Organizational Context of Practice assignment as an excuse to knock on the office doors of various kinds and levels of staff in their placement agencies, make observations of client/staff interaction in the reception rooms, and learn in some detail about the role of the social worker(s) in their particular agency.

Handing in the written units at intervals throughout the year allows time for the students and instructor to identify and remediate weaknesses in perceptual and practice skills or deficiencies in knowledge.

The fieldwork coordinator should make sure that all cooperating agencies will provide students with learning experiences that will enable them to demonstrate the performance competencies. At the end of the year, the students take individual oral examinations. The classroom instructor and the supervising fieldwork faculty participate in these interviews. We expect students to add information to the material submitted earlier in the course. For example, for the section on the Community Context of Practice, we demand more detailed knowledge at the end of the year about the array of human services programs in their communities and possible alternatives when services are not available.

Section 5 of the Competency Examination asks for a demonstration of awareness and utilization of community resources, which, of course, is the information and referral function in case management. Sections 6 through 9 ask for a specific example, a record of service provided by the student social worker to a client system: Problem Identification and Assessment, Development of an Intervention Plan, Implementation of Intervention Plan, and Evaluation and Feedback. These four categories are defined broadly to accommodate a variety of theoretical persuasions, but we ask students to illustrate their comprehension of case management, task-centered counseling, and problem-oriented recording. We caution against interpreting Section 7, "Describe your intervention plan," as meaning that the social worker owns the counseling process. Instead, emphasis is given to the shared responsibility between worker and client(s) for the plan and outcomes. Students may use an individual, a family, or a small group for the client system.

Analogously, as the social worker and client(s) share responsibility for the problem-solving process, so, too, there is shared responsibility between students and instructor for the outcomes of the educational process. The Competency Examination, used with the problem-oriented record (POR), serves to evaluate student proficiencies, but it also is a reflection of strengths and deficiencies in the social work curriculum, and it discloses discrepancies between what the instructor thinks has been taught and what a particular student actually has learned. Thus, it provides us with positive and negative feedback loops to keep our program responsive and responsible.

The personal social services have been institutionalized in modern societies as part of a support system for troubled individuals and families. To some extent, a modified kinship network persists, and surrogate families are created; there is recognition, however, that some family problems also are social problems for which the whole society must assume responsibility. Social work is the profession that has a major responsibility for the delivery of the personal social services. At the point of entry into the service network, a generalist who acts as case manager—giving information, making referrals, providing access, and acting as advocate while helping clients move into various levels of service and out of the system when help is no longer needed—is one appropriate model for social work practice. At times during the case management process, when counseling is advisable, a task-centered, short-term approach, using a problem-oriented style for recording, has demonstrated its worth in the BSW and the Title XX Regional In-Service Training Programs at Cornell.

A Performance-Based Assessment of Learning

As interest in performance-based assessment has grown, social work educators have directed their attention to issues in curriculum development, instructional techniques, and evaluation measures. Amid these efforts at curriculum revision and innovative instruction, however, performance-based evaluation instruments have been slow to emerge. The measures most frequently used to evaluate student learning in social work courses are written measures that assess cognitive mastery of theoretical material. If one purpose of social work education is to improve student competence and ultimately the quality of service delivery to clients, then teaching and evaluation efforts should focus on performance skills in addition to conceptual learning. Moreover, evaluation of in-service training programs for accountability to funding sources, agency administrators, and staff enrolled in the courses readily lends itself to performance-based assessment of learning.

Two issues demand attention: (1) How can one evaluate whether competencies presumably taught in the classroom are being learned by students? (2) What instructional methods enhance competent performance beyond the classroom? Faculty who meticulously examine students on mastery of theoretical material often leave untouched the question of whether students are able to perform more competently in specified social work tasks. One way of learning whether students have acquired the competencies necessary for professional practice is to administer performance-based tests. Such evaluation measures would serve two related functions. In addition to providing specific feedback to students regarding their strengths and weaknesses, performance-based evaluations (as indicated in the preceding section) help educators assess the adequacy of their instructional techniques.

Faculty concerned with student demonstration of competence beyond the classroom can find support in the literature for transfer of learning. Recent reviews (Ellis, 1965; Goldstein, Heller, and Sechrest, 1966; Rose, 1972) emphasize several common conditions that enhance transfer of skills beyond the original learning environment: (1) classroom stimuli that are representative of stimuli outside the classroom; (2) identification of the important features of the desired response (that is, greater effectiveness of transfer will be achieved if strong emphasis is placed in the classroom on eliciting responses considered desirable in other circumstances); (3) provision of a variety of relevant examples of a skill, so that the student is more likely to see the applicability of a concept to a new situation; (4) opportunity for adequate experience with the newly learned skill.

Transfer of learning principles long have influenced the teaching efforts of professional educators. In recent years these principles have been utilized not only to enhance conceptual learning but also to modify behavior—most notably in decreasing fears (Bandura, 1969; Ritter, 1969), increasing appropriate client interview behaviors (Marlatt and others, 1970; Whalen, 1969), increasing empathic behavior (Dalton, Sunblad, and Hylbert, 1973; Goldstein and Sorcher, 1974; Payne, Weiss, and Kapp, 1972; Stone and Vance, 1976), and assertiveness training (McFall and Twentyman, 1973). As in-service training programs attempt to provide knowledge and skills that can be transferred beyond the classroom into real-life situations, we must examine carefully which instructional methods are most successful in teaching for transfer of learning.

Of the instructional techniques available to social work educators, modeling and role playing are particularly well suited to those conditions that have been found to enhance transfer of learning. Modeling occurs when a person (the model) performs the specific skill behaviors we expect the student to learn. As an instructional technique, modeling can provide exposure to new and desirable behaviors that may not exist in the student's repertoire of performance skills. Modeling provides an opportunity to identify the key skills demonstrated by the model and to discuss the circumstances in which it is appropriate to use the skill. The modeling of several different circumstances in which the key skills can be applied helps students generalize the use of newly learned skills to other appropriate situations. Role playing has been defined as a "situation in which an individual is explicitly asked to take a role not normally his own or, if his own, in a setting not normal for the enactment of the role" (Goldstein and Sorcher, 1974). Role playing differs from modeling because it provides a behavioral rehearsal for the learner rather than an *in vivo* display of the desired behavior. With respect to enhancing transfer of learning, role playing provides an opportunity for practice of the newly learned skills and for receiving feedback on one's performance. As with modeling, a variety of situations can be provided as a context for role playing the specified skills.

Although social work educators have utilized modeling and role playing as instructional techniques to help students bridge the gap between theory and practice, the formal evaluation of student learning rarely focuses on the demonstration of practice skills. As we begin to measure the competence of social work students in practice skills, evaluation results, in turn, can enlighten the social work educator regarding the effectiveness of specific instructional techniques.

In an effort to examine the relative efficacy of modeling and role playing on the acquisition of skills by social work students, I studied two groups of twelve caseworkers in county departments of social service; both groups were enrolled in an in-service training course on adult mental health. The course was taught by staff of the Title XX training project referred to in the preceding section and was based on the practice model described. Each group of twelve caseworkers met separately for ten three-hour sessions on alternate weeks. All had been enrolled the previous year in an introductory course that presented the generalist model. Three of the ten sessions were devoted to a review of practice skills derived from Reid and Epstein's (1972) model of task-centered casework: setting time limits, developing tasks, dividing the tasks between worker and client, and summarizing at the conclusion of the interview. This model is particularly well suited to helping professionals who work with multiproblem families and clients in crisis. Its time-limited approach encourages focused intervention on specific problems and seeks to maximize client involvement in the action plan. Skills were taught via lecture/discussion and role playing. In addition, workers in the first group observed a model demonstrating appropriate use of the practice skills being taught. After observing the demonstration, students in the first group were asked to role-play the observed skills. In the second group, an additional twenty minutes of discussion about the role-play exercise were used in place of modeling, so that the time devoted to skill learning was constant in both groups. In each of the three sessions emphasizing practice skills, two separate client-worker situations were presented to student dyads in the class. The use of two role plays per session enabled each student to play the part of the client in one situation and the part of the worker in the other situation. A blackboard was used to specify the skills that students should demonstrate in each role-play exercise. In the group that viewed a model before role playing the specified skills, two models were used in each session, to provide for a variety of examples.

I was concerned with two issues in evaluating learning by students enrolled in the in-service course on adult mental health. One concern was to develop an evaluation procedure that would enable students to demonstrate skills away from the classroom setting. A second concern was to determine whether a difference in the instructional techniques used with the two groups had any impact on student performance. To assess the skill learning of each student, I decided to use audiotaped role-play exercises from sessions preceding and following the course.

Despite the fact that students in the group taught by role playing and discussion had been employed longer and were slightly older than students in the group taught by modeling and role playing, both groups were comparable in educational background and male/female ratio. Since groups had been formed by self-selection one year prior to this study, it was not possible to assign students to groups on a random basis. It is necessary, therefore, to consider that differences in learning among students might be the result of some group differences.

Prior to the course, in order to develop four role plays that approximated as closely as possible realistic client situations encountered by students, I asked each student to submit several brief descriptions of clients with difficult mental health problems. Examples from the students included suicidal clients, clients recently discharged from state hospitals, clients living in family care homes, and clients experiencing problems in mental health. In each role-play situation, students could be expected to demonstrate skills derived from the task-centered casework model. The client role plays were pretested on several welfare caseworkers not enrolled in the course. Based on experience with the pretests, I decided to limit each role play to six minutes, which seemed sufficient time for students to demonstrate specific practice skills.

Undergraduate social work students from Cornell were trained for the client roles. Each client role player was given a printed description of the role, as well as specific instructions regarding responses to anticipated worker interventions. Case records with minimal background information were developed for each client. The client role player was instructed to present the student with the case record before the interview began. Client role players were unaware of the specific objectives of the evaluation and did not know that different instructional techniques had been used with the two groups of students.

Prior to beginning the role-play evaluations, I read aloud several paragraphs of directions while the student read the directions silently. The directions specified the six-minute time limit and instructed the student to interview the client as he or she would in the work situation. Students were given an opportunity to ask questions and familiarize themselves with the cassette tape recorder and the kitchen timer. Tape cassettes used in recording each role play were labeled with the last four numbers of each student's social security number, to ensure confidentiality.

Since students were somewhat apprehensive prior to the pretest experience, the first role play was identified as a warm-up exercise. Although the warm-up role play was not audiotaped, it was monitored by a kitchen timer set to ring after four minutes. The procedure for the taped role plays followed the same format. After the student had participated in the warm-up role play and had asked any questions, the first client role player entered the testing room and handed her case to the students. Although the warm-up role play always was presented first, the order of the three taped client encounters was assigned to each student on a random basis, in an attempt to avoid order effects. The case record contained one page that provided the student with basic background information about the client's age, persons living in the home, and recent client-worker contacts. The student was permitted to take as long as necessary to review the material in the case record. When the student indicated his or her readiness to begin, the client role player turned on the tape recorder and set a kitchen timer for six minutes. The student then interviewed the "client" as if the role play were an actual casework situation. Students could end the interview prior to the allotted six minutes; but when the timer rang, students were instructed to conclude the interview within a few sentences and say goodbye to the client. After one client left the room, another client entered; and this procedure continued until four role-play interviews were completed.

The posttest utilized the same three taped role plays; however, I anticipated that some of the students' changes on the posttest role plays might be attributable to their familiarity with the three role plays from the pretest. In an effort to determine whether students could generalize the newly learned counseling skills to a situation with an unfamiliar client, the warm-up exercise was eliminated and a fourth client role play was introduced to students in each group during the posttest. The order of the four role plays was assigned randomly to each student.

The validity of the role plays was established by postevaluation questionnaires administered to each student. Ninety-six percent ($N = 23$) of the students indicated that the role plays were *typical* of client situations handled by workers in their agency. Sixty-three percent ($N = 15$) said that their responses in the role plays were *very typical* of the responses they would make to actual clients. Of the 37 percent ($N = 9$) who judged their responses to be *somewhat typical,* time limits and awareness of the testing situation were identified as factors influencing their responses. Each role play was scored by me; and a second rater scored one third of the pretests and posttests, selected on a random basis. Interrater agreement of .84 or better was achieved for each skill on which the role plays were scored. Since the tape cassettes of both groups were combined for scoring purposes and identified only with the last four numbers of each student's social security number, both raters ostensibly were blind with regard to which students belonged to which groups. Four counseling skills were measured: setting time limits, developing tasks, dividing work on tasks, and summarizing the content of the interview. Audiotaped interviews were scored for the presence or absence of the specified skills, thereby providing four subtest scores as well as a total score for each role-play interview.

Analysis of the results indicates that the treatment group, taught by modeling and role playing, made greater gains in practice skills than the comparison group, taught by role playing and discussion. The treatment group, which had a lower mean pretest score than the comparison group, actually made sufficient gains in practice skills to surpass the mean score of the comparison group on the posttest measures. When the comprehensive role-play measures were separated into scores for their component skills (setting time limits, developing tasks, dividing work on tasks, and summarizing content), the treatment group achieved higher mean-difference scores than the comparison group from pretest to posttest in all four skills. The unfamiliar client role play presented at the posttest was included, in an effort to determine whether subjects could generalize the newly learned counseling skills to an unfamiliar client situation. In the treatment group, the proportion of students who demonstrated the skills was equal to or greater than the proportion of students in the comparison group in each skill category.

Such findings suggest that instruction by modeling plus role playing results in greater gains in transfer of practice skills beyond the classroom than instruction by role playing and discussion. Due to the limitations of this exploratory study (for example, nonrandom selection of subjects, sample size, and simulated work conditions), analysis of the data is limited to a descriptive statement. The analysis is directed toward revealing those trends and relationships that are most highly suggestive of training effectiveness. Such findings indicate areas that might benefit from more rigorous research and suggest topics for further exploration.

The recent emphasis on competency-based instruction compels educators to consider methods by which competence can be measured. Performance measures, in contrast to the more familiar written measures of cognitive mastery, enable the student to demonstrate skills in a setting that closely approximates the work situation. One can argue that evaluating performance in simulated client interviews is not the same as evaluating actual work performance. However, given most agencies' efforts to protect client confidentiality and student reluctance to having an observer (or even a recording device) present during a client interview, the role-play evaluation measures were considered the most appropriate for the client group studied.

Recent efforts by Rose, Cayner, and Edleson (1977) to utilize a role-play test in evaluating training in interpersonal professional skills indicate that such a test can provide a wide range of highly specific data with which to assess the skills and deficiencies of each of the participants. A general competency score also can be obtained from such performance-based measures. Since evaluation of student learning provides useful feedback to social work educators regarding the effectiveness of curriculum design and instructional methods, it is critical that evaluation procedures keep pace with other efforts in competency-based instruction.

Undergraduate instruction and continuing education are vital components in the social work program at Cornell University. In addition to providing a theoretical framework within which caseworkers can organize their case management and counseling efforts with clients, our undergraduate program is now reaping the rewards from the faculty's continuing education efforts in community agencies. Some caseworkers who have completed in-service training courses are serving as field instructors for social work undergraduates having field placements in nearby departments of social service. The continuity between what students learn in the classroom and what their field instructors emphasize in the agencies helps students appreciate the relationship between theory and practice.

The possibility of utilizing other agency-based experiences to illustrate the value of theory as a guide to practice currently is being contemplated for sophomore social work students enrolled in research methods courses. Faculty who have taught in the continuing education program, now in its fourth year, are eager to conduct follow-up studies to assess the degree to which caseworkers have maintained the skills taught during in-service training. Under-

I3 ❧

Interviewing:
A Scientific, Artistic,
or Mechanistic Process?

Katharine Hooper Briar

The belief that social work interviewing is an art is axiomatic to most social workers. This belief has persisted for several decades and remained unquestioned until recently. Paralleling it has been the assumption that the necessary attributes for effective social work practice—such as empathy, sensitivity, caring, the ability to relate, acceptance, warmth, and support—are innate and unteachable. This chapter will first examine the consequences of these beliefs and then discuss some instructional tools for facilitating acquisition of competence in these interpersonal skills.

While the art-versus-science dichotomy has pervaded the social work literature for decades, close inspection of this distinction suggests that it is superficial, artificial, and misleading. In fact, references to the need for an empirically derived knowledge base to support casework practice can be traced to the Milford Conference of 1929 (American Association of Social Workers, 1929). The conference report suggested that training for social workers should include the adaptation of science and experience from other fields. While this challenge resounds throughout the profession even now, social workers have been reluctant to keep pace with developments in practice that may seem mechanical, systematic, or preoccupied with empirically based findings.

Although there has been a gradual retreat from the preoccupation with casework as an art, the relationship of science to casework still is unclear. Even so, evolving conceptions of casework used terminology more compatible with scientific approaches to social work interventions. By 1942, Garrett's landmark work *Interviewing* defined interviewing as an art but also as a skilled technique. By then, not only casework but the interview itself was being increasingly viewed simultaneously as art, method, process, technique, and skill (Bowers, 1950). Dictionary definitions indicate that a skill may be at the same time an art, a science, or a craft; that terms such as *methods, process,* or *procedure* imply a systematic approach; and that terms such as *technique* suggest artistic, scientific, or mechanical operations. Such definitions illuminate the fact that the static dichotomy of social work as art versus science was in fact spurious. For years, those who insisted on this dichotomy have misrepresented the issue, which would have been better stated as mechanistic versus artistic and scientific endeavors. As the issue is recast in this manner, it seems appropriate to examine how much or how little systematic or scientific knowledge can be brought to bear on the acquisition of interpersonal competence in interviewing. Bowers (1950, p. 125) wrestled with the issue as it applied to the nature and definition of social casework and argued that casework is an art that uses specific techniques not "mechanically as an applied science would but, in the matter of an art, creatively." In other words, systematic, even scientifically derived, knowledge should not be applied mechanically. Few in social work would disagree.

The consequence of equating systematic descriptions and classifications of social worker–client interactions with mechanical, uncaring social work practice can be that the social work profession will not grow because it does not keep pace with relevant new teaching approaches and empirically derived knowledge. Moreover, such views have reinforced the belief that the interpersonal skill component of the interviewing process is the least amenable to scientific study. Consequently, with a few recent exceptions, empirical study of the attributes constituting relationship-building and therapeutic information gathering has not been undertaken in social work. The dearth of systematic studies of interpersonal attributes of social workers has been accompanied by sparse research on instructional methods that promote interpersonal skill acquisition. As a result, there is a paucity of information about the specific behaviors that constitute attributes such as empathy and caring. In addition, there are few, if any, normative standards specifying the levels of competencies social workers should exhibit before working with clients. For example, how much empathy or warmth is necessary before one can become an effective worker?

The question addressed here—"How can students with insufficient interpersonal skills or inappropriate habits acquire more acceptable levels of competence and in what ways can those demonstrating higher levels refine their performance?"—has been a concern of mine for the past two years. In teaching interviewing to undergraduate social work majors, I have tried to help them acquire interpersonal skills. Students also receive initial training and conceptual knowledge in both insight-oriented and behavioral approaches to client problems. Attempts to promote desired levels of competence through the demonstration of skills have been facilitated by the development of competency-based instruction in social work education.

Interpersonal competencies have been viewed traditionally in social work education as symptoms of underlying psychological processes and personality functioning. Students judged to exhibit undesirable interpersonal skills have been encouraged to seek help outside the curriculum through psychotherapy or counseling. The developing literature on procedures for competency-based instruction offers alternatives to those previously utilized methods for promoting interpersonal skill acquisition among social work students.

Competencies are skill patterns that are demonstrable and consistent and adhere to predetermined performance standards linked to the practice context (Ellis and Bryant, 1976). Competency-based instruction necessitates (1) definition of the desired competencies; (2) operationalization of these desired competencies in nonambiguous, specific, observable behavioral terms; (3) development of measures to assess these competencies; and (4) linkages of these measures to some scale of competencies regarding desired levels of performance (Clark, 1976). Clark further suggests that, in addition to developing statements of desired competencies and a system of assessment, a learning environment must be organized explicitly to facilitate acquisition of these competencies.

In recent years, research in psychology and education has made major contributions to the specification of interpersonal competencies and development of instructional methodologies that have utility for social work. Training programs have been developed by Truax and Carkhuff (1967), Carkhuff (1969), Ivey (1971), and Danish and Hauer (1973). A brief review of these major approaches will suggest their implications for interpersonal skill training in social work. Truax and Carkhuff (1967) addressed skill acquisition of accurate empathy, nonpossessive warmth, and genuineness. Their training program relied on skill acquisition by listening to and imitating skilled therapists demonstrating these desired therapeutic attributes on audiotapes. Discussion following brief excerpts from these tapes, along with the actual practicing of responses to client statements, facilitates specific student learning. Students' role playing is taped, and the interaction is critiqued. In the process, according to Truax and Carkhuff, seemingly mechanical techniques ultimately blend into the natural, unique style of the trainee. Truax and Carkhuff's work might be faulted for the lack of specificity regarding the observable processes and behaviors that reflect these desired interpersonal attributes. Even so, the highly developed literature and research utilizing their model suggest that attributes such as empathy, nonpossessive warmth, and genuineness can be taught and subjected to scientific scrutiny. Moreover, their research suggests that systematic analysis of the processes of instruction and skill acquisition does not result in the development of mechanistic counselors.

Later work by Carkhuff (1969), called human relations training, includes training in how to discriminate among a range of client feelings and communicate appropriate responses to these feelings. Lambert and DeJulio (1977) and Gormally and Hill (1974), along with others, have raised some methodological issues regarding research studies utilizing the human relations training approach. Despite these questions, such skill-building programs reinforce the notion that refinement in interpersonal skill development can occur with a variety of training technologies without producing mechanical counselor responses.

Ivey (1971) has developed a training program called "microcounseling," intended to promote acquisition of certain desirable interviewing skills. Microcounseling is an adaptation of microteaching techniques that identify learning tasks in a discrete hierarchy of skill clusters. Each instructional segment relies on the use of direct verbal feedback, modeling, and videotapes to correct responses and suggest more appropriate interviewing behaviors. Programmed material accompanies the videotaped portrayal of desired behavior. Like Truax and Carkhuff (1967), Ivey believes that microcounseling does not promote mechanical interviewing responses but, instead, facilitates spontaneous display of desired attributes that must be acquired. Interviewing behavior, according to Ivey, is extremely complex yet amenable to instruction when broken down into discrete behavioral units. Ivey's microcounseling approach has been utilized with trainees in a variety of settings. Like other models, it has been found to vary in its effectiveness (Authier and Gustafson, 1975).

Toukmanian and Rennie (1975) found that both microcounseling and human relations training were effective in increasing empathy and communication processes but that the microcounseling techniques led to more significant gains in empathy than did human relations training. Such research findings have import for the social work profession, since they call into question the assumption that the more precise and behaviorally specific the identification and measurement of workers' interpersonal skills (as in microcounseling), the greater the chance that the worker will operate on a mechanistic level of functioning.

Technological advances in the use of video equipment for interpersonal skill training also have relevance for social work training. Work by Kagan, entitled Interpersonal Process Recall, offers an instructive guide in the use of videotape playback (Kagan, Krathwohl, and Miller, 1963). According to this process of videotape playback, the client and the worker are able to explore the meaning of verbal and nonverbal behaviors that have transpired during the interview. Feeling states can be discussed openly, because the playback provides cues for recall. Such a procedure is useful for training social workers in interviewing skills, because it helps them to comprehend, without unsubstantiated inferences, the range of feeling states of their clients; it also enables them to test their inferences about clients' feeling states against the empirical reality of client feedback.

More recent work in psychology that builds on the previously cited training models is that of Danish and Hauer (1973). The Danish and Hauer training program specifies the deficits trainers can expect among their students at initial stages of training. For example, the novice trainee may give an overabundance of leading (initiating) responses rather than continuing (mirroring client statements) responses. Such pinpointing of standard deficits displayed by beginning counselors is useful information for social work educators. Not only does some of Danish and Hauer's work suggest how to teach interpersonal skills, but it also specifies the general baseline level of attainment prior to training that educators may encounter.

In addition to the training programs described by Truax, Carkhuff, Ivey, and Danish and Hauer, there are numerous texts that now provide instructional models and skill inventories for courses concerned with the acquisition of interpersonal competencies. Some synthesize the models or inventories developed by authors cited above, while others reflect a specific model or approach to training. Egan (1975) characterizes his work as a "developmental" model for instruction in helping skills; Okun (1976) focuses more on a human relations model; and the Hackney and Nye (1973) programmed text offers a "discriminative" model. Schulman (1978) synthesizes several helping models for explicit skill training on some interpersonal attributes. Brammer (1973) offers guidelines for acquiring interpersonal helping skills along with exercises for experiential learning. All these texts assume that interpersonal skills can be acquired through conceptual and experiential learning. Concerns over students' mechanical display of interpersonal skills are seemingly irrelevant issues for them.

Research regarding the adaptation and testing of some of these instructional models of helping skills inventories in the training of social workers has been reported in the social work and psychology literature. Wells and Miller (1973) utilized adaptations of the Truax and Carkhuff model to train graduate-level social workers. Wells (1975) conducted experimental research on the effectiveness of the Carkhuff human relations training model for training social workers. Mayadas and O'Brien (1976a) utilized Ivey's microtraining model along with Kagan's Interpersonal Process Recall. Experimental research by Schinke and associates (1978) demonstrates that adaptations of Ivey's and Danish and Hauer's models are useful for training graduate social work students. Rosen and Lieberman (1972) examined the performance differences in congruence between workers' and clients' responses along with the content relevance of workers' responses. Rose, Cayner, and Edelson (1977) have developed a step-by-step approach for evaluating interpersonal skills. Other social workers (for instance, Richey, 1976) have developed useful inventories to measure initial interviewing skills of graduate and undergraduate students.

The commitment to competency-based instruction and skill training is not new to the social work profession. In fact, the fieldwork component in social work training reflects a long-standing commitment to the acquisition and demonstration of practice abilities in clinical settings. While competency-based instruction focuses on outcome rather than process, it could run the risk of rendering obsolete some academic learning deemed unnecessary to practice outcomes. For example, knowledge of the Poor Law may not be deemed critical to effective social work practice with low-income clients. Consequently, a narrow definition of desired competency might devalue such content. Despite this potential pitfall, scales developed to measure competence in social work, such as those developed at Montana, encompass a broad spectrum of learning (Arkava and others, 1976).

In my interviewing course, my attempts to help students pinpoint deficits in their display of interpersonal skills were encumbered by several problems. Among these is the fact that these interpersonal attributes may overlap, as may the processes to which they refer. Terms such as *caring* or *acceptance* and their empirical referents do not fit easily into discrete categories. For example, a smile may at the same time be a sign of warmth, support, and empathy. Despite these problems, it still was useful to sketch some examples of what might be meant by these interpersonal attributes. *Empathy* might be reflected in responses such as these: (1) Worker's questions reflect understanding of the events and feelings that accompany the client's problems. (2) Worker suggests to client relevant feelings and events that may accompany problems. An example of *sensitivity* might be reflected in the worker's ability to move the interview from the cognitive to the affective level without creating dysfunctional anxiety for the client. Examples of *caring* might include: (1) Worker states clearly (nonflippantly) a concern for what client is experiencing. (2) Worker asks about any coping problems client has in relation to problematic feelings and events. Ability to give *support,* so important to the social worker's repertoire, might be exemplified as follows: (1) Worker's statements reflect social expectation that client can accomplish agreed-on goal. (2) Worker's supportive comments following client responses are interspersed throughout the interview and frequently are more than monosyllabic. (3) Worker's nonverbal facial expressions mirror the affective component of client's statements (see Hackney and Nye, 1973). *Warmth* may be conveyed when the worker exhibits facial animation, smiles, nods affirmatively, and leans forward to reinforce client statements (D'Augelli, 1974). *Ability to relate* is another attribute presumed essential to the social worker's repertoire and viewed by some as the basis on which client growth and change are facilitated. Examples of ability to relate could include the following: (1) Worker offers spontaneous, anxiety-free responses. (2) The worker rarely interrupts the client when he is talking. Finally, the interpersonal attribute of *acceptance* might be evident when the worker conveys appreciation for the client as a person and separates this from dislike of specific problems that are dysfunctional for the client.

While these attributes do not constitute exhaustive coverage of those interpersonal competencies associated with social work practice, this sample alone suggests the challenge involved in the identification and specification of these and other interpersonal attributes.

Despite assurances to the contrary, students are somewhat reluctant to admit that they lack proficiency in some or all of these attributes in the early phases of the interviewing class. Soon, however, when mutual support among class members has developed, students are able to pinpoint problems candidly. Even though there is consensus among the students as to when interpersonal skill deficiencies are exhibited, the task of helping the student overcome such deficiencies usually falls on the instructor. Curran (1977) cites skill deficits, anxiety, and faulty self-appraisal of performance as the three sources of problems associated with social skills training. Skill deficits among students can be attributed to the fact that they have not learned enough responses or that their responses are inappropriate. Performance anxiety may stem from a panic reaction, which, according to Curran, may be the result of classical conditioning. Faulty self-appraisal of performance may be due to self-deprecation, insufficient self-reinforcement, negative self-evaluation, and unrealistic criteria.

Since skill development in interpersonal competence was only a small component of this interviewing course, students were expected to acquire other kinds of repertoires as well. Thus, while interpersonal skill development was central to the course, the amount of work students invested in overcoming interpersonal performance problems varied according to their deficiencies. Students were encouraged to think of themselves as managers of their own skill building and learning. Due to the variability in students' repertoires, they were encouraged to avoid striving for skill levels too remote from their current level of functioning.

Students experiencing stress or difficulty with interpersonal skill performance were reluctant to identify themselves as "uncaring" or "nonsupportive." Instead, they would cite their "inability to think of what to say next," which could be construed as their "inability to relate." Thus, by focusing on the behavioral referents to these interpersonal skills, students were less likely to see themselves as inept in interpersonal skill performance. To find oneself displaying difficulty with empathic responses might have been personally threatening had there not been specific behaviors targeted for improvement. Terms such as *caring* or *warmth* are so global and ambiguous that students require specific examples of the desired and undesired behaviors constituting these attributes, so that they successively can practice improved responses.

In my course, several instructional tools facilitated acquisition of these interpersonal skills: self-observation via video playback, role playing and behavioral rehearsal, modeling and coaching, cognitive rehearsal, and script writing. The application of these instructional methodologies to the interpersonal skill training of undergraduate students in an interviewing class had evolved over the past two years. These training methods also have been used for the training of clients in social skill acquisition—for instance, in assertiveness or dating skills training. This research, along with the literature covered in psychology and education, provides numerous instructional patterns for interpersonal skill training in the classroom. Since training in assertiveness and dating skills involves interpersonal skill acquisition, technologies useful for training clients in these skills should be useful for student training as well. In fact, some of the literature on assertiveness and dating skills is based on experiments with undergraduate students rather than clients in agencies.

The work of Fiedler (1978), Rose (1975), and Gambrill and Richey (1976) on assertiveness suggests methods for interpersonal skill training of students in the classroom. Rose's work is especially helpful in depicting the utility of modeling, coaching, and role playing. Meichenbaum (1972) discusses cognitive rehearsal. I used script writing, an out-of-class writing assignment, as a way of prompting students to assess effective and ineffective worker interactions in a more reflective and methodical manner than is possible within the classroom.

The following discussion will describe the use of these instructional tools to help students overcome performance problems stemming from skill deficits, performance anxiety, and faulty self-appraisal of performance. The estimations of effectiveness of these instructional tools are tentative; students observations and evaluations along with my own observations form the basis of this analysis.

Self-observation via video playback is critical to the students' awareness of how they present themselves in clinical situations. Comments from students watching playbacks of themselves in the roles of worker and client would include, "I did not realize how cold I looked!" or "What a dead-pan face I have!" This immediate recognition of deficits and areas for improvement by students enables them to monitor their improvement. Students can see their shortcomings, and others are not put in the position of having to persuade them to change. Moreover, they can review at their own pace the frequency of inappropriate responses and the sequencing of them: "Was the probe at the affective or cognitive level appropriate? How did the client respond to it?"

Self-observation via video playback is effective particularly with skill problems due to deficits; students can identify in specific behavioral terms the problem that needs to be corrected and then self-monitor change and improvement. Self-observation also is an effective tool with skill problems derived from anxiety, as the focus on behaviors reduces the sense of enormousness of the performance problem. Furthermore, self-observation is effective with faulty self-appraisal, since it provides a specific baseline of behaviors that need to be improved.

In addition to simulating practice, role playing offers students the opportunity to expand their experiences through vicarious learning. Students whose experiences might have been limited to a few client life-styles, problems, and feelings can assume the role of the client and vicariously try the experiences most remote from their own. Students were provided with several lists of role-playing scenarios. One list contained emotionally intensive role-playing scenarios, such as a battered wife, suicidal or homicidal elderly person, verbally abusive alcoholic parent, or disturbed adolescent. Exercises such as these also encouraged students to identify potential situations where they would be unable to show empathy or warmth due to their anxiety over what to say or do. Some students worked on handling the crying behavior of the client, while others gained confidence in working with the verbally abusive, hostile client. Such role-playing situations enable students to become more skilled in taking both roles simultaneously, which, in a sense, could be viewed as one core ingredient of the empathy attribute. Students struggling with problems over what to say next to the nontalkative client could imagine through dual role taking what was going on with the client and were able to hypothesize possible events and coping problems that might prevail. Anxiety regarding what to say next sometimes will decrease when students consciously can put themselves in the client's place.

Role playing and behavioral rehearsal were effective in helping the student whose problems with interpersonal competencies resulted from skill deficits due to inadequate learning. Through role playing, students were able to rehearse more appropriate ways of interacting and expand their skills rapidly. However, when anxiety was the source of the performance problem, role playing and behavior rehearsal were not effective; students needed to be encouraged step by step to try more complex behaviors. Some needed to be reassured and praised as they attempted a new kind of interaction. This was true particularly when anxiety was due to fear about the impact on the client of certain worker methods. One student had to be reassured that reaching for feelings and permitting ventilation were not mean but acually might reduce the intensity of the client's feelings. Anxiety needed to be dealt with directly. Performance problems stemming from faulty self-appraisal were improved effectively by role playing and behavioral rehearsal. Students could be encouraged to try out different responses and reinforced for each improvement by others, themselves, and the instructor.

Modeling is the demonstration of desirable responses so that they can be imitated by others. Inappropriate modeling can occur in large interviewing classes, since some students may be intrigued by the interactions of other students and imitate them. Controlling what is imitated is a problem in large classes but can be remedied in small groups. Coaching is another technique for teaching alternative ways of responding and behaving. Instead of demonstrating what is being suggested, the coach will merely describe other possible methods. Modeling and coaching are critical to the acquisition of new skills and competencies.

Modeling and coaching are only partially effective when performance problems arise from anxiety. The desired responses must be broken down so that they can be acquired successively, as in the microcounseling approach. Modeling and coaching are futile if the student's deficits are due to faulty self-appraisal. Some students may tell themselves, "I can never do that," "That is too hard," "I'm incompetent," and so forth. Consequently, acquisition of more effective skills may be impeded by this self-deprecation.

The impediment can be reinforced inadvertently by those offering modeling and coaching help if what is conveyed to students is negative evaluation of their behavior. Learning problems stemming from anxiety may require persistent monitoring of students' progress on a step-by-step basis. Coaching may be more effective than modeling when this is the case.

Cognitive rehearsal permits the student to test responses without the risk of being criticized or embarrassed. The imagined response or situation, rehearsed in one's mind, then can be evaluated and compared with the appropriate responses verbalized by someone else. While cognitive rehearsal pervades a practice course in social work, it is only partially effective with performance problems associated with skill deficits, because desired responses are thought through and not behaviorally demonstrated. However, this instructional tool is effective with performance problems due to anxiety, since it permits students to take risks. Similarly, it is successful with problems stemming from faulty self-appraisal, since it permits the student to try new responses without threat of negative feedback from others.

The script-writing assignment required students to write a script for worker and client and then critique the worker's interviewing skills. Students were encouraged to try out worker methods that were not part of their repertoire but might become adopted if effective. Some students referred to this exercise as role playing in slow motion. Script writing was used in conjunction with the video production of a fifteen-minute interview. The videotapes dynamically displayed some of the same worker deficiencies reflected in the scripts. Future use of the script-writing exercise will include review of the student's script and worker critique prior to the production of the fifteen-minute videotapes, since some inappropriate behaviors probably can be pinpointed and eliminated through systematic review prior to video production. As a tool to remediate skill deficits resulting from inadequate learning, script writing was found useful, particularly in encouraging students to try improved or new responses. Some student scripts experimented with task-centered casework, while others used behavioral modification, multimodal therapy, Gestalt, T.A., and so forth. Script writing was helpful to students experiencing performance anxiety because it allowed students time to deliberate on and control each response. Similarly, because risk-taking fears are reduced, script writing was effective when the performance problem was caused by faulty self-appraisal. Students can make mistakes and simultaneously correct them in their critique of the worker's performance.

These instructional tools represent only one attempt to facilitate higher levels of interpersonal competence among social work students in an interviewing class. Programs subscribing to empirical approaches to the development of knowledge for social work facilitate a trial-and-error, step-by-step approach to training social work students to demonstrate competence in interpersonal skills. Research from psychology and education may provide excellent sources of knowledge from which social work adaptations can be derived. But adaptation alone will not reinforce social work's unique contribution to the helping service professions. As long as social workers subscribe to the importance of an array of interpersonal attributes that exceed those addressed by other fields, the social work profession will have to do its own empirical work to ensure that these skills are acquired through effective social work competency-based training programs.

14

Using Videotaped Role Playing to Assess and Develop Competence

Charles Zastrow
Ralph Navarre

A wide variety of approaches for measuring competence in social work are being proposed and utilized. Most approaches attempt to evaluate competence near the end of a student's undergraduate or graduate social work education. Such approaches, for example, measure competence via comprehensive examinations or successful completion of specified tasks in field placement. Some of these approaches are complicated, time-consuming for students and faculty members, and somewhat difficult to administer; moreover, the outcome criteria often are only vaguely specified. In any event, it seems unfortunate and unsatisfactory that a student's competence is not evaluated until he is ready to graduate.

In our undergraduate social work program at the University of Wisconsin-Whitewater, we have been seeking to design a competency approach whereby a student's capacity to perform as a social worker could be assessed in the sophomore year, enabling students who do not meet the competence criteria to transfer to some other major without loss of credits. In addition, we have tried to discover shortcomings that might be eliminated, so that the student could remain in the program; only when it is clear that shortcomings cannot be overcome do we counsel out students. Finally, we have tried to provide competency criteria that are measurable and represent the central core of quality social work practice.

Criteria to Measure Competence

It is our belief that the essential capacity of social workers—whether they be caseworkers, group workers, or community organizers—is the ability to counsel and relate to people. There is considerable support in the literature for this criterion; Wells and Miller (1973, p. 68) state, "There is an almost unanimous emphasis among the helping professions on the central nature of relationship in the helping process." From its inception, social work has viewed the professional relationship between the social worker and the client as the crucial variable in the helping process (Hollis, 1964; Perlman, 1957; Richmond, 1917). Truax and Carkhuff (1967) have demonstrated empirically that it is not the theoretical background of a therapist but rather certain personal attributes (empathy, unconditional positive regard, and genuineness) that make the difference between the capacity to help or harm clients and client groups. Biestek (1957) noted that the casework relationship is "the medium through which the knowledge of human nature of the individual is used" and contended that knowledge without skill in establishing a relationship is inadequate. In a review of the literature on the casework relationship, however, he found no attempt to define operationally the essential skills or components in a relationship. Similarly, Mayadas and O'Brien (1976a, p. 73) concluded recently that the concept of relationship "remains vague and abstract, and interviewing skills are still discussed in highly conceptual and intellectual terms in social work literature."

Our approach uses laboratory training techniques, particularly those involving videotape equipment, as a means of preparing students for contact with clients. Mayadas and O'Brien (1976a, p. 72) observe: "This concept of a laboratory approach is a departure from the traditional social casework presentation of conceptual material followed by or concurrent with the actual practice of casework with live clients in a fieldwork setting. Although efficient as far as it goes, the traditional model neglects the crucial step of teaching the student to operationalize abstract concepts learned in the classroom before sending him into the live practice situation."

There is a growing trend to use laboratory training techniques to facilitate the development of counseling and interpersonal skills. Simulations of counseling situations allow students to try out and develop their skills in a relatively safe and structured situation as well as receive the feedback and guidance of instructors and peers. If videotape is employed, students receive direct feedback from video self-confrontation. The students then are able to assess their strengths and shortcomings and also have the opportunity to conduct additional simulated interview sessions to attempt to improve their performance. In addition, by replaying earlier tapes, a student with potential who had initial difficulties can see his or her growth and development over time. This leads to increased self-confidence for the fieldwork experience to follow.

As a method of helping students develop their counseling and relationship capacities via videotaping, our approach is not unique. As far as we can determine, however (we have located no other studies), videotaping has not been used for simulated counseling situations as an approach to screen out undergraduate students from social work early in their college careers.

Model to Develop Competence

Our program uses a three-step model in developing competence in counseling and relating to people. This three-phase model is similar to the model described by Mayadas and O'Brien (1976a) in teaching counseling skills. The first stage is didactic-conceptual, in which the student acquires a theoretical knowledge of counseling. The second stage is skill learning, in which each student assumes the role of a counselor in contrived counseling situations; in this stage laboratory videotaped equipment is used extensively. The third stage is field placement, in which the student applies social work skills and techniques learned in the first two phases in a closely supervised fieldwork setting. Each of these phases will be elaborated further.

In our program, we seek to assess and develop social work competence (that is, capacity to counsel and relate to people) according to the following format. Prior to taking field placement and generally in the sophomore year, every social work major must enroll in our Methods I (practice) course, which has two objectives. The first is to facilitate the development of a theoretical, conceptual approach to social work practice. The theoretical topics covered are:

* Principles of interviewing
* Confidentiality
* How to motivate discouraged clients (Losoncy, 1977)
* Sigmund Freud—Psychoanalysis
* Carl Rogers—Client-centered therapy
* Eric Berne—Transactional analysis and games people play
* Frederick Perls—Gestalt therapy and encounter groups
* Jay Haley—Double-bind theory
* Albert Ellis—Rational-emotive therapy
* Maxie Maultsby—Rational-behavior therapy
* Thomas Szasz—Mental illness is a myth
* Thomas Scheff—Labeling is the main determinant of functional mental illness
* Thomas Gordon—Effective communication
* Insight versus learning approaches to therapy
* Effectiveness of therapy approaches
* William Glasser—Reality therapy
* Helper therapy principle
* Crisis intervention theory
* Behavior therapy approaches
    Implosive therapy
    Counterconditioning and reciprocal inhibition
    Reinforcement, conditioning, extinction
    Assertiveness training
    Aversive approaches (punishment)

    Issue of self-determination
    Applicability to social work
* Masters and Johnson—Sexual counseling
* Frank Farrelly—Provocative therapy
* Social action

For each therapy approach covered, a summary handout of the theory is provided, and audiovisual tapes are used to demonstrate the theory in a counseling situation. For each theory, we show a film or a videotape of the theoretician counseling a client. Readings further explaining the theory also are assigned.

In this theoretical, conceptual phase, there also are several assignments designed to help students develop their conceptual approach to counseling. For example, the final examination requires each student to present his or her theoretical approach to counseling. The presentation must include answers to the following questions: "How do people develop emotionally? How do emotional problems arise and become perpetuated? What counseling techniques do you believe are most effective, and why? What are the strengths and shortcomings of your counseling approach?" Each student also is asked to write a term paper (or do a class presentation if preferred) on the following subject: "Using theoretical material we have covered in class, describe how you made constructive efforts to modify a personal problem you have or to help someone else modify a personal problem he or she has. Describe the behavior you attempted to modify, describe the theoretical material you used in this effort, and discuss the merits and shortcomings of such a process."

The second objective of our Methods I course is to facilitate the development of students' counseling and relationship skills and capacities. Assignments include role playing (with videotaping) of counseling situations and observation (watching films or videotapes) and discussion of techniques used by recognized authorities in the field of counseling. Emphasis is placed on self-awareness and the professional use of self, interviewing techniques, development of perceptiveness, awareness of values, communication skills, empathy, and professionalism.

Four years ago, after concerted effort, we acquired portable videotape equipment (approximately $4,500 worth) and set up a videotape lab by placing the equipment, along with a desk and chairs, in an office. We are convinced that the lab has immense value, and we use it extensively in our two required methods (practice) courses to assist in assessing and further developing students' counseling and relationship capacities.

In Methods I, students are required to demonstrate their counseling capacities via videotaped role playing. Each student is videotaped in the role of a counselor as he or she attempts to help a counselee (a classmate or a friend) with a contrived problem. This videotape is later reviewed by the student and the instructor. Students are graded on a pass/fail basis for the videotaped role playing. If they fail, they are not allowed to pass the course, even if they receive high grades on tests and other assignments. Students are allowed to videotape a role-play situation as many times as they desire in order to develop their skills to a passing level. If a student feels that the review of the tape by the instructor of the course is not satisfactory, an appeal process is set up, and the tape is reviewed by other social work faculty. (In the three years we have been using this approach, we have not had an appeal.) Students who are not successful in making a passing tape (sometimes after several tries) are encouraged to transfer to another major. (Frankly, they have little choice, since they must pass Methods I to enroll in future required courses.)

During the videotaped role playing, students are required to demonstrate skill in establishing a working relationship, exploring problems in depth with the counselee, and exploring alternative solutions to the problem with the counselee. When the videotape is reviewed by the student and instructor, the instructor fills out a rating sheet, which is used as an aid to judge the student's performance on certain specific components of the counseling process. Students receive one of three ratings (Focus Attention on This, Doing OK on This, Right On!) for each of the following skill areas:

- Opening remarks
- Explanation of counselor role
- Voice quality and volume
- Body posture
- Eye contact

- Behavioral congruence with facial expression (therapist's words match his/her outward appearance)
- Frequency of open-ended questions (not yes-no or multiple-choice questions)
- Amount of therapist's verbal activity
- Verbal following behavior (sequencing questions with clients' answers, preparing client for shift in subject matter)
- Clarity of questions
- Ability to confront client with inconsistencies
- Use of humor
- Warmth; ability to put client at ease
- Use of silence
- Ability to help client define problems
- Ability to have client specify goals
- Paraphrasing
- Reflection of client's feelings
- Summarization of client information
- Ability to answer client questions—provide useful information
- Extent to which interviewer presented him/herself as a professional
- Extent to which necessary data about the problem were obtained
- Ending the interview; length of interview
- Completeness of interview
- Extent to which a helpful relationship was developed
- Extent to which alternative solutions to the problem were explored

This information is shared and discussed with the student, enabling him or her to obtain further feedback on counseling strengths that were demonstrated and identify specific areas needing attention in the future.

In spite of our efforts to spell out the criteria used to assess counseling competence, the final decision regarding whether a student receives a pass or fail for the simulated counseling is a subjective judgment. Initial efforts to objectify the specific components have been made by Truax and Carkhuff (1967), Ivey (1971), and Kagan and others (1969). Our specification of the variables of quality counseling also can be viewed as an effort to add objectivity to deciding whether a student displays an "acceptable" level of counseling skills. As yet, however, no approach that is fully objective has been developed for measuring the quality of counseling skills.

This subjective judgment has several implications: (1) Instructors using a videotape approach similar to the above must be skilled clinicians (with extensive training and experience) in order to have the background for assessing what is an acceptable level of counseling competence. (2) An appeal procedure must be established wherein other clinicians can review a tape of a student who feels that his or her tape was rated too unfavorably. (3) If a large number of students receive passes on their videotapes and later experience considerable difficulty in counseling situations at their field placement, the instructor's subjective judgments of who should pass are called into question.

(Our attempts to provide the theoretical knowledge and skill practice in one course proved overambitious. Students had to absorb vast amounts of material, and instructors had to spend considerable time videotaping sessions individually for each student outside of regular classroom hours. Consequently, we are planning to replace the Methods I course with two courses, one focused on the theoretical component and the second focused on the skill-learning segment.)

In fieldwork the student applies the theoretical concepts and skills learned in the first two phases. Since our fieldwork program is similar to most other undergraduate programs, our description will be brief. We offer three types of field placement for interns: a two-semester placement, two days a week for thirty-two weeks; a block field placement, four days a week for sixteen weeks; a block field placement during the summer, five full days a week for twelve weeks. Interns are required to enroll concurrently in a second methods (practice) course while in field placement. Additional videotaping of simulated counseling and interpersonal situations frequently is used in this second methods course.

Reactions of Students to Videotaped Role Playing

Last semester in our Methods I class, we used a questionnaire that was given to the students twice, once at the beginning of the course and again at the end. There were thirty-three students in the class. One of the questions asked was:

At this time, how ready (prepared) do you feel you are to counsel clients?

1	2	3	4	5
Not ready				Ready

At the beginning of the course, the mean score was 2.32; at the end it had increased to 4.16 (significant using a Wilcoxon test).

The second question asked was:

Do you feel at the present time that you have the necessary counseling skills to be able to successfully counsel people today about their emotional/personal problems?

1	2	3	4	5
Do not have				Have
necessary				necessary
skills				skills

The mean score increased from 1.94 at the beginning of the course to 3.96 at the end (significant with a Wilcoxon test). Both responses indicate that students' confidence in their counseling capacities had increased substantially.

A question that was asked only at the end of the semester was "How, *specifically*, did the videotaped role playing help you to develop your counseling capacities?" Responses included:

It helped make me comfortable in a counseling situation. I was able to test out different ways of helping a client and when reviewing the tape I saw what things I did well, what I did badly, and what I needed to change to become a better counselor.

I became aware of my own voice, posture, and gestures and the importance they play in counseling.

I was able to see an actual picture of myself, not what I thought I looked like, and was able to see where I made my mistakes and could have done something different.

It was helpful to be put in situations or forced to counsel, which I think helped us to rapidly develop counseling skills. I feel that the best way to learn something is to actually do it instead of just talking about it. I also thought it was useful to watch the tape and look for my mistakes. This is the best way to correct them.

I became aware of exactly how I came across to the client, and I noticed that I was suggesting things to him— which I didn't even realize before reviewing the tape.

Made me more aware of my self-presence (mannerisms).

Gave me the opportunity early in my academic career to have a slight taste of what counseling is about and what I might be in store for!

I was not confident in my counseling skills at first. But after seeing the videotape, I saw that I could do it. Videotaping is a good confidence builder.

All thirty-three students thought that the videotaped role playing was a valuable learning experience.

Responses to other questionnaire items revealed that at the beginning of the course students were apprehensive (some students were extremely apprehensive) about participating in the videotaped role playing. This apprehension was reduced partially by didactic material and discussions in class on "how to counsel" and by role playing counseling situations in class (generally two students counseling two other students who had a contrived problem). Following the videotaped role playing, students expressed increased confidence in their capacities to counsel and a substantial reduction in apprehension about being videotaped in the future.

Interestingly, those playing the role of the "counselee" frequently presented real situations they currently were facing or had encountered in the past. ("Counselees" informed their "counselor" of this after the role playing, and the "counselor" mentioned this to the instructor when the tape was being reviewed.)

Of the thirty-three students in class, thirty-two received a pass on their videotaping. Two were referred for counseling for personal problems they had expressed during the review of the tape (videotaping sets up a structure whereby the instructor gets to know each student). Twelve of the students made more than one tape to further develop their counseling capacities. At the end of the course, a few students were considered to have marginal counseling skills, but they are expected to make further improvement in the second methods (practice) course, which also uses videotaped playing. If improvements do not occur following continued intensive efforts to develop their counseling capacities, the students will be counseled out of social work.

Outcome

Assessing precisely the effectiveness of videotaped role playing in developing counseling capacities is difficult, because many other factors influence the development of these capacities: observing other therapists, learning didactic material on interviewing skills and therapy approaches, counseling "real" clients in field placement, and receiving feedback from supervisors. Yet, as indicated above, students believe that videotaped role playing is a valuable learning technique. Furthermore, social service agencies in our area actively seek our students for field placements; they believe that our students are well prepared and view them as an asset.

In using "capacity to counsel and to relate to people" as our selecting-out criterion, we have found it necessary to counsel very few students out of social work. In the past three years, we have had an average of two hundred student majors and over that period have counseled out twelve students. An additional small number of majors, once they understood the nature of social work and the required counseling skills, have self-selected themselves out of the program. The use of videotaped role playing to assess and develop social work competence appears to have the following advantages:

- Students report that it is a valuable tool in learning how to counsel, since it provides considerable feedback on themselves and their manner of relating to others, builds their confidence for counseling "real" clients, and gives them an opportunity to test their skills and interpersonal behaviors in a relatively safe setting.

- Problems that students have in counseling and relating to people can be identified and shown to the student; efforts toward improvement can then begin.
- Students whose capacities lie elsewhere can be identified early in their college careers and counseled into some other major.
- The instructor becomes personally acquainted with each student and thereby receives feedback about the course and becomes aware of individual needs of each student.
- Videotaping links theory with practice and thereby makes the course more meaningful and relevant.
- The approach provides assurance to field placement agencies that student interns will have an acceptable level of counseling capacities.

Conclusion

In our undergraduate program, we are using "capacity to counsel and relate to people" as our criterion for competence in social work. This capacity is assessed via videotaped role playing of a contrived counseling situation. All students are required in the first practice course (generally in the sophomore year) to make a tape that demonstrates their counseling capacities. They are permitted to continue making tapes until a "passable" one is made. The thrust, however, is on developing their counseling capacities rather than on a grade. Those students who are unable to develop the necessary competence capacities are selected out of the program. We have found this approach to be highly effective in assessing and developing students' counseling capacities.

15

Laboratory Training to Enhance Interviewing Skills

David Katz

A crucial element in the practice of clinical social work is competence in the helping interview. In addition to natural talent and motivation, competence as an interviewer requires lengthy training, experience, and supervision. Formal training in interviewing is a relatively recent development in professional social work education. More traditionally, beginning students armed primarily with conceptual knowledge have been placed in practica where they have had to learn interviewing by trial-and-error interactions with clients and after-the-fact supervision. In recent years, there has been a move toward the use of school-based laboratory training for teaching basic interviewing skills to beginning students (Burian, 1976).

The growth of laboratory courses is based on an assumption that beginning students can be taught helping skills by demonstration, practice, and feedback under optimized learning conditions. Since teaching takes place in a school laboratory, the sequence of instruction can be controlled, performance standards can be identified clearly, and learning problems can be addressed without placing a real client at risk. The rationale for laboratory training for beginning social work students is that it provides them with a basic repertoire of helping skills that will ease their transition into the practicum and serves as the foundation for practice. This chapter is based on a study of three cohorts of beginning students who completed a laboratory course in interviewing skills as part of their graduate-degree program (MSW) in social work.

The laboratory is particularly suited to the training of beginning interviewers, because their actual performance as interviewers serves as data for peer and instructor feedback and self-critique about personal style, sensitivity to others, and use of skills. This is possible for several reasons. First of all, unlike practice in agencies, the learner's behavior in the laboratory is public and open to observation by instructor and peers rather than private and unobserved except by the client and occasionally by a supervisor. Also, since the interview situation in most laboratory training groups involves the use of other learners as clients, learners receive feedback from peers about the effects of their helping behavior on a client and have the opportunity to observe the effects of various other helper styles on themselves while in the client role. Furthermore, because it is a training setting with many learners, the laboratory can make efficient use of modern audiovisual technology. Videotape replay of interviewing sessions has some very distinct advantages for beginning interviewers. The videotape replay alters the perspective of a participant in an interaction from that of actor to that of observer. The interviewer who has some knowledge of what she or he was thinking, feeling, or saying while in a session has no direct knowledge of how his or her behavior appeared to an observer. Since the tape can be stopped during a videotape replay, the learner has the opportunity to think about and discuss the relationship between what he or she (as well as the peer-client) perceived, thought, and felt during the interview and the observable interviewing behavior. With skillful instructor and peer feedback related to the videotape replay, the learner has an unparalleled opportunity to integrate internal cues with observable behavior and gain additional mastery of and control over interviewing style. Videotapes of interviews also provide instructors with a means of evaluating student competency from actual interviewing performances and researchers with a source of data about variables related to student performance.

Even though laboratory training has many advantages over didactic methods, there are numerous questions confronting the instructor who wishes to utilize this approach.

1. What skills shall be included in a training program?
2. In what order shall they be presented?
3. What training techniques are best for promoting acquisition of skills and awareness of personal style?
4. What shall novice interviewers be expected to learn as a result of training?
5. What interviewer behaviors shall be measured and how?
6. How shall the overall competence of the learner be evaluated following training?
7. Does the final learner performance at the end of laboratory training predict future performance in the practicum?

Several of these issues will be discussed in the light of observations and research findings from the training laboratory, and similar methods for extending the findings to field settings will be suggested.

Interviewer Training Programs

Finding a prepackaged interviewing skills training program presents far less difficulty than choosing from the number of models available. Several programmatic training models that emphasize humanistic and behavioristic approaches to the helping relationship (Carkhuff, 1972; Danish and Hauer, 1973; Egan, 1975; Ivey, 1971; Kagan, 1972a; Okun, 1976; Schulman, 1978) are available to the social work instructor. These training models tend to be developmental, stressing to a greater or lesser degree the sequential acquisition of facilitative helper characteristics and skills (for example, self-awareness, sensitivity to others, communication skills, specific techniques) and a conceptual framework for applying these skills appropriately at different stages in the helping process. They tend to stress experiential learning, using demonstration, practice, and feedback, with more or less behaviorally specific criteria for measuring learner performance. There is some evidence that brief training programs do lead to improved learner performance in the measures specified in the trainer's objectives, at least in the laboratory (Clubock, 1978; Danish, D'Augelli, and Brock, 1976); but their generalization to practice settings is questionable (Spooner and Stone, 1977) and related to the specific skill measured.

Although these training models have much in common, each tends to stress a different aspect of the helping process. Some (Carkhuff, 1972; Kagan, 1972b) stress sensitivity to client affect, while others (Egan, 1975; Ivey, 1971) stress particular behaviors said to facilitate client communication and movement.

The number of different models for training students in interviewing skills places the instructor in a dilemma. The instructor wishes to provide students with those skills that will provide the best basis for competent practice, but there is little concrete evidence to guide the choice of particular skills over others as most relevant to beginning social work interviewers. Some skills may be essential to good practice; some may be inconsequential or subsumed under other skills. Thus, instructors often are left to their experience or intuition in selecting appropriate skills for the training laboratory.

Although laboratory training models emphasize the acquisition of specific skills, which makes the evaluation of the parts of student performance more reliable, instructors also are called on to make overall evaluations of student performance. Little is known about how social work instructors weight various skills to judge overall performance. Some skills may have more importance than others for particular judges; some may be universally crucial to the overall evaluation because they precede, and are the basis of, a number of higher skills. This issue scarcely has been addressed in social work education even though students traditionally have been subjected to such evaluations. It probably is a safe assumption that overall evaluations of students' ability as interviewers are based in part on some idiosyncratic instructor bias and in part on some shared but not well-explicated norms of the profession, drawn from observed differences in behavior between novices and experienced interviewers (Kadushin, 1972, p. 17). The way in which effective use of particular skills is related to the overall evaluation of students as good interviewers emerged as a major research issue for our studies of interviewer training, and our research findings will focus on this problem.

The Training Laboratory

The development of a training laboratory in a professional school of social work depends on the presence of at least two major elements. The first of these is faculty resources. Laboratory training is a labor-intensive instructional activity. It requires a small student-to-instructor ratio and additional hours of instructor contact outside the classroom in the form of conferences and feedback sessions. The second element is a physical facility. Optimum laboratory training requires a nonstandard classroom setting with a relatively open arrangement for group exercises, interviewing areas where smaller groups may practice as participants or observers in simulated interview sessions, and recording and playback facilities for feedback sessions. While audiotape may suffice as the minimal technological component, videotape is preferable and necessary to capture nonverbal behavior. The site of our training laboratory, the George Warren Brown School of Social Work at Washington University, was fortunate to have excellent physical facilities and the resources to provide instructors for the small laboratory training sections. While most of the instructors taught on a part-time basis, each had an excellent grasp of interviewing technique and relevant literature.

The laboratory is a one-semester course for entering MSW students who have had no formal interviewer training. The course was structured, particularly at its inception, to utilize elements from a variety of interviewer training models. It is taught in small sections (fifteen or fewer students) and has three major components. The first component is taught in workshop format, stressing structured exercises, peer feedback, and group processing of experiences. Its purpose is to increase students' awareness of their styles in social interactions (for example, in making contact with others, in exploring thoughts and feelings, and in self-expression) and to serve as a foundation for later training in professional role behavior. This initial component also facilitated the development of group trust, which is helpful to students who must risk self-exposure (as interviewers and clients) in later training activities. The second component adopts a microcounseling (Ivey, 1971) approach to teaching basic interviewing skills. Modeling, practice, and peer and instructor feedback are used as vehicles for teaching skills of verbal and nonverbal attending behavior, reflecting behavior, and summarizing behavior. This component was meant to be an introduction to the basic repertoire of the interviewer. These skills usually are not practiced in the context of an ongoing interview but rather as an interviewer response to discrete communication by a client. The third component stresses a developmental approach to phases in treatment (Egan, 1975). Students are taught techniques for facilitating client self-exploration, for use in early treatment stages; client self-understanding in middle treatment stages; and goal setting, contracting, and implementing action plans in later treatment stages. This component extensively utilizes simulated interviewing to help students conceptualize and practice skills such as primary and advanced accurate empathy, confrontation, and concreteness. The third component takes up two thirds of the training time. In addition to identifying helpful interviewer skills and personal characteristics, it provides a framework for their purposeful application. For example, "primary-level accurate empathy," or accurate perception and reflection of the overt content and feeling in a client's communication, is identified as a skill that facilitates client self-exploration in the early phases of treatment. Confrontation, or reflecting inconsistencies or distortions in client communication, is identified as a skill that facilitates client self-understanding in the middle stages of the treatment, after a trusting treatment relationship has been established.

Instructors experimented with a number of methods for interviewing practice. Early in the history of the laboratory, pairs of students would videotape an interview in one room for the first hour, while the rest of the class would practice exercises in another room. During the second hour, the tapes were criticized by the instructor and the entire class. This practice had several undesirable features. Students often were defensive and found it difficult to discriminate their behavior or recall their thoughts or feelings before so large an audience. It also was difficult to schedule many replay sessions during the semester, since class time was limited. By far the most serious drawback of this method, however, was the tendency of students to practice only the initial interview. This was understandable, since students had the opportunity to interview and receive videotape feedback in class two or three times a semester and did not know their partners well enough to advance beyond the first interview in practice, although they could do so conceptually.

To remedy some of these drawbacks, a few instructors began to schedule interviewing sessions outside of class time, with tapes reviewed in class or in tutorial sessions. This had the effect of increasing practice time, but students still lacked continuity in their helping relationships and tended to stay in the initial interview throughout the semester. With later cohorts of students, the instructors evolved a more satisfactory method of interviewing practice. The class was divided into small training groups of three to five students for the third component. These groups met separately and were able to tape and critique two interviews for each class session. Because the small groups became acquainted with each member's personal issues more intimately in worker and client roles, more continuity was provided in the interviewing process. This, in turn, enabled a greater number of students to begin working with skills appropriate to later treatment stages. Since instructors could not participate in all the simultaneous feedback sessions, students frequently were responsible for running their feedback. Teaching students how to give feedback, then, became an increasingly important aspect of the course. Utilizing Kagan's (1972a) Interpersonal Process Recall, we asked the students to stop the videotape at crucial points, and encouraged the interviewer and the client to recall what they were thinking and feeling at that point in relation to their behavior. Group process helped an atmosphere of trust, so that students generally felt free to reveal themselves and also became accurate observers of one another.

One drawback of the structured small-group experience is the occasional student who becomes more self-revealing than she or he had intended. While this often is a valuable learning experience for the student interviewer, more time than the ten to fifteen minutes allotted for each interview is needed. On occasion, the instructor must be available to provide some closure for the issue and perhaps see the student alone after class.

Development of the Research Instrument

The research instrument grew out of an attempt by the training laboratory instructors to develop a means of scoring student performance on a final videotaped interview, which accounted for 50 percent of the course grade. Reliance on a final performance test was based on the school's philosophy of trying to grade, wherever possible, on the basis of identifiable student competencies. Two issues emerged in attempting to evaluate the skillfulness of students: what to measure and how to measure it. Since we did not know with any degree of certainty which of the skills the students were learning, we decided to include in our evaluation instrument all the identifiable skills that had been covered in the course. From the literature, and from observation of the students, we also were aware that personal characteristics (genuineness and warmth) and states (anxiety) seemed to affect the quality of performance; therefore, we included these as items in the instrument. Finally, almost as an afterthought, we included a single item called Overall Effectiveness, based on how skillful an interviewer was judged by an instructor after viewing that student's performance.

The instructors primarily were interested in an instrument that would enable them to obtain a profile of learner strengths and weakness from judgments of a final videotaped performance and have information on which to base (and defend) their grading of students. Therefore, we designed an instrument that attempted (1) to tap the raters' anchored judgments about the presence or absence of particular skills or characteristics in the interview, together with some admittedly subjective estimates of the effectiveness with which each skill is used, and (2) to evaluate the overall quality of the learner's total performance.

The evaluation and research instrument we developed initially consisted of a series of scales for rating twenty-three variables. The first eleven items refer to variables that are associated with interviewer characteristics or states present or absent but that usually are not employed selectively to some specific purpose by an interviewer:

1. Attentive to Client: Physically paying attention
2. Eye Contact: Looks at client's facial expression
3. Relaxed: Posture and manner looks comfortable
4. Self-Conscious: Seems ill at ease in role
5. Fidgety: Nervous mannerisms
6. Distracted: Seems inattentive, self-absorbed
7. Genuine: Open and spontaneous, no mask of impersonality
8. Respect for Client: Projects respect for client
9. Sensitivity to Client's Feelings: Seems to really know what client is expressing
10. Mutuality: Easy give and take in interviews
11. Warmth

These items are judged for their presence in the session on a four-point scale: 0 = almost never present, 1 = present less than half the time, 2 = present more than half the time, 3 = almost always present.

The second set of items refers to variables associated with discretionary skills:

12. Verbal Following: Responds to client communication rather than asking questions or directing discussion
13. Exploratory Responses: Minimal prompts that elicit further elaboration from the client
14. Understanding Responses: Paraphrases and reflections that elicit clarification
15. Primary-Level Accurate Empathy: Accurately perceives and communicates overt feeling and content of client's communication
16. Summarizing Responses: Reflects major themes in client communication
17. Self-Disclosure: Models self-disclosure; connects own experiences with those of client
18. Advice: Suggests options for client behavior
19. Confrontation: Points out distortions or inconsistencies in client's communication

20. Advanced Accurate Empathy: Accurately expresses the implicit meanings of client communications and the implications of the client's behavior; moves the client beyond self-exploration to self-understanding

21. Immediacy: Direct, mutual talk of what is happening here and now in the helping relationship

22. Concreteness: Relates client verbalizations to real situations rather than to generalities

These items first are rated for appropriateness of use. Overuse or underuse is rated 1, while appropriate use is rated 2. Where a skill is not appropriate to a situation and is *not* used, it is rated 0, and the item is not counted in the analysis. Where the skill is appropriate and is not used, it is rated 1 (underuse). Each appropriateness score then is multiplied by a four-point effectiveness score. High effectiveness (4) is defined as use of a skill that facilitates client movement toward self-exploration or insight. Low effectiveness (1) is defined as use of a skill that misses the mark, is inaccurate, sidetracks, or otherwise hinders client movement. Where a skill should have been used but was not, an automatic low effectiveness score (1) is assigned. Thus, scores for discretionary skills range from 8 (appropriate use × high effectiveness) to 1 (inappropriate use × low effectiveness). The twenty-third item on the instrument asks for an overall judgment about the student's competence as an interviewer compared with other students. Ratings are made on a seven-point scale ranging from excellent (7) to poor (1).

The instrument was intended for use with the student's final videotaped performance. Judges can take notes or stop a videotape at any point prior to filling out the instrument, but where more than one views a tape, judges are enjoined from collaborating. Ratings are made from recall after each interview is completed.

Preliminary Studies

The research aspect of the training course focused on the way in which instructors and other judges weighted various skills and characteristics in evaluating student competence. Preliminary studies of posttraining ratings were conducted for the first two student cohorts completing the training laboratory course. We hoped to use the findings to revise the training sequence by increasing our emphasis on those skills most related to overall judgments of interviewer effectiveness.

The posttraining videotapes were made in the following manner. Taping was done outside of class hours in a small video studio. Pairs of students (client-worker) interacted in privacy and were videotaped by an unmanned camera having a wide-angle lens. The recorders were in an adjacent room. Interviews lasted ten minutes. "Clients" were fellow students in the course who explored their life issues rather than role playing other people. Since the performance test served as a final examination that accounted for 50 percent of the course grade, a high degree of motivation was assured (and probably heightened anxiety as well). The format was that of an initial interview. Interviewers were instructed to help the client explore life issues, utilizing as many of the skills they had learned as were appropriate to the situation. Students had received copies of the evaluation instrument several weeks earlier and had spent two class sessions using the instrument to rate each other's previous videotapes. Rating of the first cohort was done by five instructors and a teaching assistant working in pairs. To eliminate rater bias, each pair of judges rated twenty students from another section. Since the judges were fully familiar with course content, only brief training sessions were held prior to rating to improve reliability.

A second rating of three videotaped interviews (similar to those previously described) randomly selected from the following semester's cohort of students was undertaken several months later. Since the researchers felt that course instructors were a homogeneous group, another set of judges with greater practice experience was used. Judges for this rating were sixteen practicum instructors associated with the School of Social Work. They underwent a three-hour training session, following which each instructor rated each of the three videotapes, which were shown to them in a group. Practicum instructors also were encouraged to take notes while watching; they could ask for the tape to be stopped at any point but could not discuss the interview prior to completing the instrument.

Results. The primary interest of this research was to determine which combination of performance skills or characteristics was associated with being judged a good beginning interviewer. The data from the twenty-three-variable instrument were analyzed by means of a step-wise multiple-regression technique, with variable 23 (Overall Judgment) as the dependent variable. Step-wise multiple regression first searches for the variable contributing the most variance to the regression equation. In subsequent steps, it searches for the variable contributing the next highest amount of variance, controlling for variables already in the equation, until additional variables no longer account for significant amounts of variance. Analysis of results for variables contributing at least 1 percent of additional variance to the regression equation, based on the mean item scores of six judges rating sixty students (Cohort I), showed that Verbal Following alone accounted for 65 percent of the variance in predicting the Overall rating. It was followed by Primary-Level Accurate Empathy (7 percent), Confrontation (4 percent), Relaxed (2 percent), Concreteness (2 percent), and Summarizing Responses (2 percent).

For Cohort II, item scores of the sixteen practicum instructors were regressed against their Overall ratings. Results for variables contributing at least 1 percent of additional variance to the regression equation showed that Verbal Following accounted for 81 percent of the variance in predicting the Overall rating. It was followed by Summarizing Responses (6 percent), Genuine (3 percent), and Concreteness (1 percent).

Discussion. At first glance, the finding that a single variable, Verbal Following, accounted for a very high proportion of the variance in predicting Overall judgment of student ability may seem at odds with the current concept of a good interviewer as a person who has mastered a repertoire of skills. If we consider, however, that we are looking at good *novice* interviewers, the finding is consonant with literature describing the transition from novice to experienced interviewer. "Experienced interviewers are apt to manifest less control, be less active, and less inclined to offer advice than are inexperienced interviewers. Inexperienced interviewers are apt to talk more, and to take more responsibility for the interview" (Kadushin, 1972, p. 71). Inexperienced interviewers tend to be more patently manipulative and try to get clients moving in a particular direction, while experienced interviewers tend to respond more communicatively to client thoughts and feelings. Inexperienced interviewers may ask questions, while experienced interviewers are likely to make statements about their perception of client communication (Ornston, Cicchetti, and Towbin, 1970). Experienced interviewers allow clients more opportunity to initiate interaction and are less likely to assert themselves by interrupting (Mattarazzo and others, 1968). Novice interviewers rely primarily on "prompts," or closed-ended questions, and respond to client communication in an interrogatory manner. They use directive and leading responses and show little concern for feelings (D'Augelli, Danish, and Brock, 1976). With training, novice interviewers reflect more, give less directive responses, and focus more on client affective state (Danish, D'Augelli, and Brock, 1976). In summary, there seems to be consensus in the literature that training and experience lead to less directiveness, fewer closed-ended questions, less manipulativeness, and more attentiveness to client communication.

These conclusions are very similar to instructors' observations of the behavior of novice interviewers in the laboratory course. Novices have difficulty listening consistently to clients' thoughts, feelings, and experiences. They tend to rely on questions to size up the problem. The questions often are leading, since the novice seems interested in verifying his or her hunches rather than clarifying client communications. Preoccupation with asking the "right" question often leads a novice to withdraw inwardly to think of a subsequent question before a client has responded to the current one. This behavior may communicate lack of concern or understanding to the client, although often it is related to the novice's fear of not knowing what to say next and appearing incompetent.

The Verbal Following variable, which is defined simply as "responds to client communication rather than asking questions or directing discussion," may have such a high degree of predictive power because it corresponds to the raters' internal model of an experienced interviewer who listens and follows client communication and does not engage in the typical novice behaviors of questioning, leading, and overlooking important aspects of client communication. It is safe to assume that students who look like more experienced interviewers look like better interviewers to judges.

While the results of these first two ratings seem quite impressive, some statistical questions arise, since many of the skills in these studies were highly intercorrelated. Because of the high intercorrelations, the true predictive effects of each of the successive variables in the regression equation are diminished. It probably is true that some of the other variables could predict overall evaluations almost as well as Verbal Following. However, the precedence of that single variable makes sense not only statistically, because it is the best predictor, but also instructionally, since it would appear to be a necessary but not sufficient condition for higher skills. For example, interviewers cannot be empathic if they do not follow clients' communications, but they can follow clients without being empathic. Thus, the study strongly suggests that for our students the ability to listen, follow client communication, and not engage in novice behaviors were the crucial variables in determining overall ability.

Notwithstanding the statistical caveat, the findings led the instructors to undertake revision of the emphasis of the training laboratory and gave impetus to the development of a more rigorous research design to try to clarify the sequences of skill learning leading to a student's being judged a good interviewer.

Training and Research with the Third Cohort

Beginning with the third cohort, students were given a pretest the second week of classes, following the same format as the posttests of previous cohorts. While this pretest also was intended for research purposes, it was used extensively in feedback sessions in which students were sensitized to their novice behavior. They proved for the most part to be acutely sensitive to the discomfort they felt as interviewers and clients when the interviewer style was marked by leading, reliance on prompts for information gathering, problem solving, and directiveness. The early and continuous emphasis of instructors reinforced accurate listening and understanding of the client experience and affect; interrogating prompts and premature problem-solving activities were discouraged.

To increase the students' sensitivity to client communication, greater amounts of time early on were devoted to videotaping interviews and feedback. To avoid the problem of repeatedly engaging in initial interviews, students were encouraged to work with steady partners; several instructors instituted the practice of utilizing smaller training groups that interviewed and gave feedback to their members. As a result of these changes, a larger number of students were enabled to practice advanced skills and develop more confidence in their ability to relate to each other in a therapeutic manner.

Several changes in research design were undertaken to study the third cohort of students. Pretraining and posttraining videotaped interviews for the twenty-six students in this cohort were duplicated in random order on video cassettes. These duplicated tapes were rated by judges who were unaware of the temporal sequence of the original taping and the previous findings. Two raters (doctoral students in social work and clinical psychology) were given six hours of training in identifying interviewer skills and characteristics and understanding each other's rating criteria. Each judge rated each interview segment separately.

Since both pretraining and posttraining interview performances were available for each student, the data were analyzed for two types of change: level of performance and pattern of variables predictive of the Overall rating. We hypothesized that individual variable scores, particularly for those skills emphasized in training, would reflect improved performance, as would the Overall score. We also hypothesized that the pattern of independent variables predictive of the Overall score would change as a result of training. This hypothesis was based on the assumption that training would substantially reduce the level of novice behaviors that load so heavily on the Verbal Following variable. If we were successful in training students to follow rather than lead in their interview style, this variable would lose much of its predictive power; other variables based on higher skills would emerge to account for a greater amount of variance in the regression equation.

Results. Pearson product-moment reliability coefficients for interrater reliability ranged from moderate to good (.48–.82), with a mean reliability of .74. Scores were averaged between raters for the following analyses.

Changes in scores between pretraining and posttraining conditions were analyzed for each variable, using t tests for correlated means. The results are presented in Table 1. Six of the ten variables relating to interviewer characteristics showed significant change. Several anxiety-related variables (Self-Conscious, Fidgety, and Distracted) decreased significantly, while several variables related to therapeutic conditions (Genuine, Sensitivity, and Respect) increased significantly. Of the variables relating to more elementary interviewer skills (Verbal Following, Exploratory Responses, Understanding Responses, Primary-Level Accurate Empathy, Concreteness, and Summarizing Responses), only Concreteness failed to show a significant positive change. The Overall variable showed a highly significant increase.

For the purpose of reducing the number of variables by eliminating the least important ones, a step-wise multiple regression was undertaken with combined conditions. As a result of this analysis, the following variables were eliminated from further regression analysis: Self-Disclosure, Advice, Attentive, Eye Contact, Relaxed, Self-Conscious, Respect, and Sensitivity. All subsequent regression analyses were performed on the remaining fifteen variables.

Step-wise multiple-regression analyses then were performed separately for the pretraining and posttraining conditions. The purpose of these analyses was to define a linear combination of the minimum number of variables accounting for a maximum amount of variance in predicting the Overall rating. Results of this analysis are presented in Table 2.

In the pretraining condition, Verbal Following alone accounted for almost 60 percent of the variance; together with five other variables, it accounted for 82 percent. The remaining variables accounted for 2 percent additional variance. Deleting Verbal Following from the equation resulted in a substantial reduction in the amount of variance explained.

In the posttraining condition, Primary-Level Accurate Empathy accounted for almost 50 percent of the variance; together

Table 1. Means, Standard Deviations, and t Scores for Pretraining and Posttraining Ratings (Cohort III)

Variable	M, Pretest	SD, Pretest	M, Posttest	SD, Posttest	t	P (2-tail)
1. Attentive	2.79	.35	2.81	.24	.27	N.S.
2. Eye Contact	2.87	.30	2.98	.10	2.00	N.S.
3. Relaxed	2.12	.45	2.13	.41	.17	N.S.
4. Self-Conscious	1.39	.49	1.02	.38	-3.72	<.002
5. Fidgety	1.23	.52	.90	.57	-2.36	<.05
6. Distracted	.67	.50	.46	.39	-2.17	<.05
7. Genuine	1.52	.64	1.83	.67	3.19	<.01
8. Respect	1.60	.48	1.90	.48	3.07	<.01
9. Sensitivity	1.23	.40	1.87	.43	7.40	<.001
10. Mutuality	1.62	.45	1.78	.40	1.81	N.S.
11. Warmth	1.62	.40	1.78	.50	1.98	N.S.
12. Verbal following	3.52	1.50	4.81	1.41	3.80	<.001
13. Exploratory responses	3.62	.93	4.52	1.48	2.44	<.05
14. Understanding responses	3.44	1.75	5.44	1.16	4.70	<.001
15. Primary Empathy	2.33	1.36	4.31	1.53	6.51	<.001
16. Summarizing responses	1.96	1.01	3.08	1.49	3.42	<.01
17. Self-Disclosure	1.33	1.57	1.13	1.53	-.44	N.S.
18. Advice	1.70	1.71	2.92	2.37	2.34	<.05
19. Confrontation	1.56	.58	2.13	1.42	1.89	N.S.
20. Advanced Empathy	1.27	.59	1.73	.75	2.99	<.01
21. Immediacy	1.62	.80	1.94	1.22	1.37	N.S.
22. Concreteness	3.94	1.30	4.25	1.62	.71	N.S.
23. Overall	3.73	.79	4.83	.66	7.60	<.001

Table 2. Step-Wise Multiple-Regression Summary for
Pretraining and Posttraining Conditions

Variable	Multiple R	R Square	R Square Change	Simple R	B
		Pretraining			
Verbal following	.76	.58	.58	.76	.37
Genuine	.84	.70	.12	.22	.24
Summarizing responses	.87	.76	.06	.56	.17
Concrete	.89	.79	.03	.44	.12
Distracted	.90	.80	.02	−.52	−.44
Understanding responses	.91	.82	.01	.52	−.10
Constant (overall)					1.49
		Posttraining			
Primary empathy	.70	.49	.49	.70	.10
Understanding responses	.79	.63	.14	.63	.08
Summarizing responses	.85	.72	.10	.49	.20
Confrontation	.88	.78	.06	.61	.03
Genuine	.90	.81	.03	.57	.23
Distracted	.91	.83	.02	−.28	−.44
Advanced empathy	.92	.84	.01	.44	.09
Constant (overall)					2.00

Note: Variables listed contribute at least 1 percent additional variance to the regression equation, with overall rating as the dependent variable (Cohort III).

with six other variables, it accounted for 84 percent. Remaining variables accounted for 2 percent additional variance. However, there was no substantial drop in variance explained until Primary-Level Accurate Empathy, Understanding Responses, and Summarizing Responses had been deleted from the equation, indicating that no single variable by itself seemed crucial in the posttraining regression equation.

In addition to trying to account for the maximum amount of variance with the minimum of variables in each training condition, we also were interested in investigating the relative contributions of each of the major skill variables to the prediction of the Overall rating in relation to a conceptual model of interview training. This model assumes a sequence of learning from the lowest- to the highest-level skills in the following order, based on the sequence of instruction: Verbal Following, Exploratory Responses, Concreteness, Understanding Responses, Primary-Level Accurate Empathy, Summarizing Responses, Confrontation, Advanced Accurate Empathy, Immediacy. To identify pattern changes between the trained and untrained conditions, each of these variables was entered *in sequence* in a hierarchical multiple-regression design. This procedure yields the additional variance added to a regression equation by each successively higher skill when the lower ones already are in the equation. The results of the analysis for both conditions are presented in Table 3.

In the pretraining condition, Verbal Following accounts for the bulk of variance explained, with succeeding higher-level variables adding relatively small increments of variance. In the posttraining condition, the pattern appears changed. The lowest-level skill accounts for only 25 percent of the variance, and, with the exception of Concreteness, the entry of almost each successive higher-level skill adds substantially to the variance explained by the equation. On the level of single variables, Understanding Responses adds a great deal more variance in the posttraining, while Concreteness does so in the pretraining condition. In the trained condition, the most advanced skills account for only small amounts of additional variance.

Discussion. Significant changes in skill level between pretraining and posttraining occur primarily in the elementary skills and overall rating. There also is significant improvement in several therapeutic conditions and significant reduction in several anxiety-related behaviors. While these changes are consonant with training objectives, in the absence of a control group they cannot be attributed specifically to training.

Physical attending and advanced skill variables did not seem to increase much following training. It seems likely that the former did not increase because they were already at a high level, while the latter simply showed no improvement. The mean posttraining levels of the elementary skills (scale mean = 4.5) indicate at least a medium degree of competence as well as significant change after training.

The major finding from the step-wise multiple-regression

Table 3. Hierarchical Multiple-Regression Summary

Variable	Multiple R	R Square	R Square Change	Simple R	B
Pretraining					
Verbal following	.76	.58	.58	.76	.33
Exploratory responses	.77	.60	.02	.49	− .22
Understanding responses	.78	.60	.01	.52	− .62
Concreteness	.81	.66	.06	.44	.16
Primary empathy	.85	.73	.07	.67	.11
Summarizing responses	.87	.75	.03	.56	.13
Confrontation	.87	.76	.01	.31	.19
Advanced Empathy	.88	.77	.01	.28	− .79
Immediacy	.89	.79	.02	.17	.22
Constant (overall)					1.19
Posttraining					
Verbal following	.50	.25	.25	.50	− .87
Exploratory responses	.55	.30	.05	.46	.16
Understanding responses	.72	.51	.21	.63	.15
Concreteness	.72	.51	.00	.34	− .37
Primary empathy	.80	.65	.14	.70	.89
Summarizing responses	.88	.77	.12	.49	.20
Confrontation	.90	.80	.03	.61	.12
Advanced empathy	.91	.83	.03	.45	.22
Immediacy	.91	.83	.00	.34	− .44
Constant (overall)					2.26

Note: Variables are sequentially entered into the regression equation, beginning with the lowest skill (Cohort III).

analysis is the emergence of Primary-Level Accurate Empathy as the leading predictor of outcome in the posttraining condition, even though it cannot be considered a crucial variable as could Verbal Following in the pretraining condition. It also was determined that a relatively small number of learner characteristics and skills were almost as effective in predicting outcome as the larger set.

Changes in the pattern of variance explained by independent variables in the hierarchical regression analyses support the hypothesis that training increases the power of higher-level skills to predict Overall Effectiveness. Verbal Following accounts for less than half of the variance posttraining that it did pretraining, while Understanding Responses, Summarizing Responses, and Primary-Level Accurate Empathy account for substantially more than they did in the pretraining condition.

These findings can be conceptualized in the following way. Before training, interviewers' scores are significantly lower on a number of variables and on Overall Effectiveness than they are after training. However, within that lower range, novices scoring high on Overall Effectiveness tend also to score high on Verbal Following. The absence of typical novice behaviors makes them look more effective than other novices who manifest these behaviors, even in the absence of specific skills. After training, interviewers score higher on skills and Overall Effectiveness. The findings suggest that better Overall Effectiveness after training is accounted for by the addition of the previously mentioned elementary skills to the student's repertoire. Whether this pattern change is due to training cannot be determined adequately on the basis of this uncontrolled design without replication. However, the finding that pattern change moved in the predicted direction is a hopeful sign and worthy of future research. The finding that advanced skills (Confrontation, Advanced Accurate Empathy, and Immediacy) did not seem to gain significantly in posttraining ratings or account for much additional variance in the regression equations suggests that we had not trained our learners adequately in these skills or that they cannot be performed adequately in our simulated interview format.

Implications for Training

With the data at hand, we may at least begin to speculate about answers to some of the issues previously raised as those confronting the social work educator who uses a laboratory training method for teaching interviewing skills.

Based on observation of learners and the empirical evidence gathered in this research program, it is clear to us that Verbal Following, or the ability to communicate responsively with a client without interrogating or leading, is the lowest level of beginner skill that predicts how well a novice will be judged as an interviewer. Once this lowest-level skill is achieved, mastery of the skills of reflection of content and feeling (Understanding Responses, Summarizing Responses, and Primary-Level Accurate Empathy) predict favorable judgment about a student interviewer's competence. These skills, together with the ability to concentrate on the client's communication (low Distracted) and the ability to be open and spontaneous (Genuine), seem to form the core of what makes a beginning interviewer's performance look good. It would appear reasonable to expect students to show mastery of these skills after a one-semester course and for instructors to concentrate on them, perhaps to the exclusion of more peripheral skills. For example, there does not seem to be much profit in spending time on physical attending behavior, which seems well established in most students.

The research we have reported here is just a beginning. The program is continuing, and with each cohort of students we hope to refine the methodology and further validate our findings. The next steps also include leaving the laboratory and going into the field. We want to train practicum instructors to rate student skills by observation, and we want to examine the relationship between field and laboratory ratings. If it can be determined that laboratory performance predicts field performance, we will have some basis for beginning to ask the most crucial question we face as educators: "What student skills make a difference to client outcome?"

16

Developing Administrative Competence

Jean M. Kruzich

Since the early 1960s, the growth of cash and in-kind programs has resulted in an expansion of the number and complexity of human services organizations. These changes have placed new demands on the administrator's ability to guide an agency through political and legislative complexities. Agency staff and educators are faced with the issue of determining the kinds of skills administrators need to successfully move the organizations toward their goals.

A review of the literature suggests that different sets of skills are necessary for human services administrators. Austin and Lauderdale (1976, pp. 14–15) suggest that administrators must possess skills in the areas of management and accountability, policy development and coordination, and public relations. Shapiro (1971, p. 66) emphasizes an educational program that focuses on the acquisition of scientific orientation, integration of analytical concepts and technologies from management sciences with knowledge of welfare organizations, and development of intellectual skills and habits to manage complex systems. In general, however, the literature in this area has not provided empirical data to help educators make informed curriculum decisions.

The purpose of the study reported in this chapter was to provide a data base for decision making on content and sequencing of administrative curricula in the School of Social Work and the School of Social Development at the University of Minnesota. The study's objectives were to determine what administrators (that is, all individuals having job classifications above and including first-line supervisors in social services, income maintenance, and support payments in state and county welfare agencies in Minnesota) do; what training they need to do their jobs better; and how size of agency, educational level, area of agency involvement, and years of employment affect their need for training.

Our first step was to develop a questionnaire to send to welfare administrators. We did so by reviewing all administrative job classification specifications, listing all the task descriptions from the job classifications, and adding subsequent modifications to incorporate a more behaviorally explicit statement of responsibilities. In addition, a few items that reflect the administrator as a change agent but that were not included in job descriptions were added. For example: "Act as advocate for client needs when in conflict with agency policy." An attempt was made to group activities into categories aimed at specific functions with a minimum of overlap with other functions. In consultation with administrative staff in public welfare, we developed nine categories or functions: staff supervision, community and agency coordination, fiscal management, internal operations, program development and planning, staff training, evaluation and research, staff management, and intergovernmental activities. Each of these administrative categories included four to eight task items. These items, in effect, represented an operational definition of the categories.* Welfare Administrators were asked to rate each task in terms of two factors: the importance of the activity in their work and the importance of the

* A more detailed description of administrative functions and tasks used in this study is available from the author.

activity in terms of the need for additional training. In the last section of the questionnaire, administrators also rated the nine broad administrative functions on these two factors.

The questionnaire was sent to the total population of 560 administrators. Of that population, 323 (58 percent) responded in a form that was usable. A review of the number of respondents by job classification indicated a sufficiently similar percentage to the overall response rates to provide a sample representative of the larger population.

Most of the administrators in our study (67 percent) have completed four years of college, and an additional 32 percent hold an advanced degree. As a category or group, the Department of Public Welfare (DPW) has the most highly educated staff, with 60 percent of its administrators holding a graduate degree. In contrast, the vast majority of administrators in the eighty-four rural counties have only a bachelor's degree. Of those with a graduate degree, more than one third from graduate programs other than social work came from schools of public affairs or public administration. Outside of the metropolitan area, however, the MSW is virtually the only graduate degree held by administrators. This information can be interpreted as an effort by large welfare agencies to hire individuals from areas that offer more training in managerial or administrative activities than has been offered traditionally in schools of social work.

Importance of Administrative Functions in Work

Analysis of the data included a breakdown of administrators' responses by agency into the nine administrative categories used in the questionnaire. A review of the rankings indicates that in the two large metropolitan counties staff supervision was considered the most important area of administrative function. For DPW staff, a higher priority was given to areas of program planning and intergovernmental activities than to staff supervision. The difference in priorities between the counties and DPW reflects their differing roles in the delivery of social services. The majority of county welfare administrators are involved in supervision of the delivery of cash or in-kind services. In contrast, DPW administrators are involved in assistance to counties in the development and planning of federal and state program activities.

A review of the specific tasks included under the broad administrative functions reveals the most important tasks in these areas. The task "maintaining an organizational climate conducive to effective job performance" was thought to be a very important skill; more than half of the respondents in both the county and the DPW felt that this activity was important in their work. It also is interesting to note that eleven administrators independently included (in a fill-in item marked "other") "methods of effectively handling disciplinary problems with subordinates" as an important role in staff supervision. Under program development and planning, development of long-range goals and program objectives was seen as the most important activity.

A review of the rankings when stratified by educational level indicates that staff supervision remains the most important (that is, it receives a ranking of 1) for individuals with four years of college or less. Yet, for administrators holding advanced degrees, staff supervision is not even rated as one of the most important areas in their work. All educational levels, except those with fewer than four years of college, believe that program development and planning is an important function in their work. While the number of individuals with fewer than four years of higher education is only eighteen, an earlier working paper (Kruzich, 1975) revealed that this group is made up of income maintenance supervisors. Clearly, their work revolves around the training, management, and supervision of staff as opposed to more technically specific functions.

Importance of Administrative Functions
for Additional Training

Analysis of the data provides a breakdown of administrators' responses to the nine administrative functions and their importance in training. Staff supervision is the most important area for skill development for administration in the two largest metropolitan counties. For DPW staff, a higher priority was given to areas of research, program planning, and fiscal management than to staff supervision. While fiscal management was not viewed as one of the more important functions in their jobs, it was seen as a top priority for training at DPW.

Although staff supervision is seen as the most important function for individuals with four years of experience or less, it is not viewed as an important area for administrators with advanced degrees. The same is true in the area of training.

One possible interpretation of the relatively low ranking of staff supervision for administrators with MSW degrees relates to their training. Since few schools of social work have offered academic training in administration until recently, administrators with MSWs probably have been trained for direct-service work. Thus, their clinical background may have prepared them for the tasks involved in staff supervision as administrators but not with skills needed in the more technical areas of planning and fiscal management.

The importance of program development and planning as an administrative function already has been noted. With the exception of those with fewer than four years of college, it is considered by all educational levels to be of major importance for additional training. The fact that intergroup comparisons reveal little variation concerning this area may suggest that advanced-degree programs, both MSW and other graduate degrees, have not adequately addressed these areas. Another possible interpretation is that program development and planning is an ongoing and demanding function requiring constant retraining as an administrator moves to new levels of management. It also is revealing that individuals with MSWs express different needs for additional training than do individuals with other graduate degrees.

A comparison of responses by area suggests that, while program development and planning is not the most important current function for those now in administration, support services, or staff development, they do consider it the most important training need.

Regardless of the number of years of employment, staff supervision remains a vital area for training. Program planning and development continues to be an important area regardless of years of experience in public welfare. Fiscal management and program development and planning take on greater importance as needs for additional training for those employed more than ten years. For those individuals with twenty or more years of experience, research and evaluation also are considered priorities. The emphasis on these areas may be less amenable to on-the-job learning than staff supervision. However, internal operations loses its importance with an increase in years of employment. This could imply that a familiarity with an organization aids in studying and initiating changes in an agency but does not help in mastering technical skills such as fiscal management and program planning.

Implications for Curriculum Development

A basic assumption made in performing such a survey is that individuals' reports of their needs are accurate and provide data that are important for decision making. But practice needs may change rather quickly; respondents at the time of measurement may have been influenced by a special set of situational factors. One also needs to decide to what extent the results of this study can be generalized to welfare agencies in other states. Caveats aside, however, this kind of approach does raise a number of points germane to developmental issues in an educational program or service agency. Such information encourages a school or agency to be more responsive to the needs of students and social welfare personnel and provides an impetus and rationale for seeking out new resources to meet these identified needs.

One local outcome of this needs-assessment study was the recognition that the School of Social Work in Minneapolis was not in an immediate position to adequately meet the contemporary needs of public welfare staff in Minnesota. Subsequent discussions between faculty from the Minneapolis school and the School of Social Development in Duluth resulted in a collaborative grant proposal to support the development of administration curricula through Title XX training monies.

Another consequence was to increase curricular emphasis on administrative tasks identified in the study. For example, by actually requiring students to develop needs assessments, program objectives, and agency budgets in the classroom, and by designing field-learning contracts that include administrative tasks for student learning and practice, the curriculum moved closer to a competency-based focus building on traditional knowledge through active development of relevant practice skills. The lack of faculty resources in certain areas necessitated the hiring of community practitioners to develop and teach courses in areas like financial analysis, forecasting, and assessment of agency needs. The needs-assessment study minimized the ad hoc use of community faculty by providing an empirical base for the deliberate integration of existing course work with new offerings, providing students with an optimal mix of administrative theory and skill building. Similar use of the study has been made by staff development personnel in public welfare to plan relevant seminars, workshops, and institutes for employees.

17

Assessing Management Competence

Robert W. McClelland
Carol D. Austin

A number of procedures have been employed for the identification and selection of managers. The use of an assessment center to rate performance and identify potential candidates for positions of administrative responsibility is one approach that has grown in popularity. The literature reports extensively on the use of assessment centers in a variety of settings (Bray, Campbell, and Grant, 1974; Bray and Grant, 1966; Byham, 1970; Howard, 1974; Huck, 1973; Meyer, 1974; Michigan Bell Telephone, 1962; Office of Strategic Services, 1948). To more systematically select administrators for positions throughout state government, the state of Wisconsin approved the establishment of an executive assessment center designed to assess general management skills. A description of the process employed at the center, the results of the project, and a critique of its operations follow. A brief history of the development of assessment centers provides a useful backdrop for the Wisconsin experience. The empirical work in this area was developed primarily in business and industrial settings.

The idea of systematically assessing attributes associated with management competence was addressed first in the 1940s. During World War II, the Germans, British, and Americans attempted to select candidates for special assignments by utilizing an assessment center process, which was refined by industrial psychologists in the early 1950s. In 1956 Bray established the first assessment center in American industry. A major research contribution was made by this center; its staff developed and implemented a longitudinal study of the careers of managers who had been assessed at the center. The Management Progress Study (Bray and Grant, 1966) is of particular interest because it was conceived and implemented purely as a research project. In contrast, results of many subsequent studies are biased, since they also were used to select and promote managers. Bray's work remains a major contribution to the field of management assessment. Many of the tests, exercises, and performance dimensions he utilized have been incorporated into recent assessment center efforts.

The Management Progress Study assessed 422 men employed by six Bell System telephone companies. The subjects spent three and a half days at the center, during which time a series of tests, structured exercises, and simulations was administered to the group. Individuals were assessed on twenty-five performance dimensions believed to be associated with management competence. Compelling evidence is provided by the accuracy of the original predictions after eight years. Of the fifty-five men who had achieved middle-management positions, forty-three (78 percent) had been predicted correctly by the assessors. Eight years later, seventy-three of the original group had not advanced beyond the first level of management. The assessment staff had predicted correctly that sixty-nine (95 percent) would not be promoted to middle-management positions. (Follow-up data on this sample are available only for those men who remained employed by the Bell System eight years later.)

The assessment center established by the State of Wisconsin has incorporated many of the features of Bray's center. It was established in an attempt to improve the screening of applicants for top-management positions in state government. Prior to the development of the assessment center, candidates for career executive-level positions were evaluated by a panel comprised of three persons selected for their familiarity with the requirements of the job. Three candidates were identified and certified as eligible for the vacant position; generally, the opening was filled from this group. The process was seen as undesirable for several reasons. It was time consuming, often requiring several months from job announcement to job placement. The process required reapplication and screening of candidates for each new vacancy, a lengthy and duplicative procedure for the applicant. The panel and/or personal interview approach could assess only a limited number of characteristics believed necessary for the job and frequently was limited to personal statements of competence by the applicant and intuitive judgment by interviewers. The assessment center, in contrast, provided a method by which key performance dimensions could be more objectively identified and rated. Furthermore, the assessment center approach was not dependent on the existence of a vacant position and could provide a pool of prescreened candidates for career executive jobs.

The career executive pool was composed of incumbents (196) and candidates (239). Incumbents were in executive-level positions, usually at the bureau director level. Candidates aspired to executive-level positions and held section chief or senior analyst jobs. Incumbents were slightly older (48.1 years) than candidates (44.8 years). Both groups had attained similar levels of education (16.5 and 16.7 years, respectively) but differed significantly in their length of service to the state of Wisconsin, with incumbents having served 21.9 years and candidates having served 13.6 years.

Neither group included many minority group members or women. There were only four women in the incumbent group and twelve in the candidate category; for minorities, the numbers were six in the incumbent group and five in the candidate group. These data reflect clearly the disproportionate number of white males in high-level administrative positions, which is typical of most organizations today.

Participants were drawn from all departments of Wisconsin state government, including diverse organizations such as the Departments of Health and Social Services (Aging, Family Services, Mental Hygiene, Vocational Rehabilitation, Health, and Corrections), Public Instruction, Revenue, and Agriculture.

There were three major components in the Wisconsin assessment program: identification of performance dimensions from a job analysis process, selection and implementation of an assessment method, and integration of the career executive candidate pool and specific executive vacancies. Each of these will be discussed in turn.

Prior to the implementation of the assessment program, a comprehensive analysis of top-echelon management positions was conducted through interviews, workshops, and an extensive questionnaire. This effort was designed to identify performance dimensions common to all high-level management positions. Sixteen dimensions identified as most significant fell into four categories: management skills, communication skills, orientation skills, and interpersonal skills. A definition of each follows:

Management Skills:

1. Planning and organization—effectiveness in approaching, arranging, and relating work in a systematic and situationally appropriate manner
2. Management control—appreciation of the need for controls and maintenance of control over processes, including use of tools such as records, forms, and instructional manuals
3. Use of delegation—effective assignment of decision-making authority and accountability
4. Problem analysis—effectiveness in identifying, seeking out, and relating data pertinent to the solution of a problem
5. Decisiveness—readiness to make decisions and render judgment when necessary
6. Decision making—extent to which conclusions reached reflect communication of the evidence at hand, the alternatives available, and the potential ramifications

Communication Skills:

7. Oral communication—effectiveness of expression in individual and group situations

8. Oral presentation—effectiveness of expression of ideas or facts, planned or unplanned, in a speaker-to-audience setting
9. Written communication—effectiveness of expression in writing; correctness of grammar, syntax, and other basic English skills

Orientation Skills:

10. Responsiveness—appreciation of and positive response to the needs and concerns of various publics served

Interpersonal Skills:

11. Stress tolerance—stability of performance under pressure and opposition
12. Leadership—effectiveness in guiding groups or individuals to accomplish goals cooperatively and have ideas accepted; manifestation of consistent behavior and style that inspire long-term respect and willing cooperation
13. Sensitivity—awareness and consideration of the needs and feelings of others
14. Risk taking—the extent to which calculated and logically defensible risks are taken
15. Tenacity—the tendency to stay with a position or line of thought until the desired objective is achieved or no longer reasonably attainable
16. Initiative—active efforts to influence events rather than passive acceptance; self-confidence to operate with independence within broad policies or instructions

The methods chosen for use by the assessment center included simulations, exercises, and written analyses designed to evaluate cognitive and behavioral as well as written and oral communication skills. Specifically, the Wisconsin program utilized the In-Basket Exercise, Assigned Role Group Discussion, Non-Assigned Role Group Discussion, Problem Analysis, and Speech and Writing Exercise. These exercises were chosen because they provided data on several performance dimensions.

The In-Basket Exercise is a simulation that has been used consistently in assessment centers. It is designed to include tasks typically encountered on a new job that require interaction with superiors, subordinates, peers, and representatives of external organizations. It is a time-limited, high-stress exercise. After the In-Basket Exercise is completed, the subject is interviewed by the assessor concerning actions taken and reasons for various decisions made during the simulation. The Assigned Role Group Discussion is a simulated situation in which participants are assigned a point of view to sell to other team members. The setting is a city council meeting where a million-dollar federal grant must be allocated. Various proposals are considered, and there is opportunity to bargain and trade off projects for support. The Non-Assigned Role Group Discussion Exercise is designed to assess candidates' skill in eliciting cooperative problem-solving behaviors. The group must resolve problems described in four case studies presenting management issues frequently encountered in public human services agencies.

Candidates' analytical skills are evaluated through their performance on a specific exercise in problem analysis. Data on the field operations of a state agency are provided for examination. The subject is asked to scrutinize the relevant information and make appropriate recommendations. The Speech and Writing Exercise requires subjects to prepare a written response and formal oral presentation. Detailed background information concerning three problematic situations is the content for the written and oral products. The oral presentation takes the form of a press conference.

Statistical relationships among performance dimensions, assessment exercises, and final scores for the pool of candidates indicate that, although assessors drew on all relevant exercises for data on specific performance dimensions, they relied more heavily on the In-Basket Exercise and the Problem Analysis (Huett, 1975). An unanticipated finding emerged from an examination of the composite overall ratings of the sample. The candidates' ($N = 311$) performance in the management skills category fell below their performance in the communication skills area (management skills scores ranged from 2.39 to 2.87; communication skills scores ranged from 2.71 to 3.05 on a five-point scale. Of all performance dimensions, candidates were rated highest in oral communication (3.05 on a five-point scale) and lowest on risk taking (2.25 on a five-point scale).

Composite scores for the sample on all sixteen performance dimensions were as follows (on a five-point scale):

Management Skills:
Planning and organization	2.54
Management control	2.39
Use of delegation	2.58
Problem analysis	2.45
Decisiveness	2.87
Decision making	2.39

Communication Skills:
Oral communication	3.05
Oral presentation	3.00
Written communication	2.71

Interpersonal Skills:
Stress tolerance	2.95
Leadership	2.45
Sensitivity	2.60
Risk taking	2.25
Tenacity	2.84
Initiative	2.70
Responsiveness	2.73

At present, there are no data on the predictive ability of the dimensions included in the Wisconsin program. A study by Wollowick and McNamara (1969), however, used similar variables and found predictive strength among many of the dimensions. Correlations between overall performance rating and change in position level were significant for the Leaderless Group, the In-Basket, Written Communication, Decision Making, Resistance to Stress (all found significant at the .01 level), Planning and Organization, and Oral Communication (both significant at .05) Exercises.

Reliability among assessors is essential to the success of a center. Wisconsin's assessment center trained high-level management staff to serve as assessors through a three-day intensive training program. Assessors who had not gone through the assessment center were given five days of training. This approach raised concerns about the advisability of utilizing managers rather than professional assessors in the process. Huck (1973, p. 206) has addressed this issue and concluded: "A few studies have been reported in the literature dealing with the background of managers serving on the assessment staffs. These studies have been aimed at the question of whether or not professional psychologists provide a higher degree of interrater reliability than the trained line managers serving as assessors. The available evidence suggests that they do not." Despite these assertions found in the literature, concerns remained regarding interrater reliability of participating management assessors in the Wisconsin program. A report on the program's reliability and validity stated, "While reliability estimates were not generally available, . . . such estimates proved disappointing where they were: the possibility exists that a participant's exercise scores may be as much a function of who does the scoring on the exercise as of the characteristics of the participant" (Wisconsin State Bureau of Personnel, 1975). If this in fact is a systematic pattern in scoring, it may call into question the validity of the assessment process in Wisconsin.

On completion of the assessment, the participants returned to their jobs, and assessors remained to discuss their observations of candidates' performances. Each assessor contributed observations, and the assessors as a group identified the subjects' strengths and weaknesses. A numerical score (on a scale of 1 to 5) was assigned to each performance dimension, and an overall average was computed. Persons whose composite score was 2 or above were included in the career executive pool and became eligible for consideration when career executive vacancies needed to be filled. Persons with an overall score of less than 2 were not included in the pool. Candidates who were deficient in particular performance dimensions were helped to develop a plan for strengthening skills in the specified areas through university extension courses. Reassessment after one year is possible if an approved employee development plan was established and the candidate has demonstrated progress toward meeting the plan's goals. If no formal employee development plan was pursued, a candidate must wait three years for reassessment.

The selection of an applicant to a high-level management position involves the integration of two streams of activity: the results of applicants' assessments and a job analysis of the vacant position. This is a crucial step in the process because it matches the specific requirement of the vacancy with particular skills of candidates in the career executive pool. Performance dimensions believed to be particularly important were given extra weight on the analysis of the vacant position. Candidates rated highly on the specified dimensions were selected for consideration.

The process involved several tasks. First, an analysis of the vacant position was conducted, including the identification of knowledge, skills, and abilities needed, a determination of training and experience required, ranking of relevant performance dimensions, and a weighting of those performance dimensions. The top one hundred candidates from the career executive pool were identified according to their assessed skills. Candidates' performances were weighted by multiplying their scores on selected dimensions by the weight given to each dimension for the vacant position. Ten candidates scoring highest on the weighted performance dimensions were identified through this procedure. They then were interviewed, and additional data were collected by the appointing authority, leading to selection and appointment.

The literature (Bray, Campbell, and Grant, 1974; Huck, 1973; Wollowick and McNamara, 1969) confirms the notion that a variety of nontechnical and interchangeable management skills can be isolated and assessed. The Wisconsin assessment center was founded on this concept. Wisconsin's Administrative Code (1971, Section Pers. 30.01) states three generic goals for the career executive program: "(1) To provide state departments with a pool of highly qualified executive candidates for appointment on a competitive basis to executive-level positions. (2) To provide employees a broad opportunity for advancement as well as flexibility and mobility within and between state agencies and units of state government. (3) To make use of employees' managerial and administrative skills." Has the program been successful in accomplishing its mission?

In terms of the first goal, it appears that, rather than providing employee flexibility through interagency exchange, the program primarily has benefited agency management in reorganization efforts. A pool of candidates was created. It consisted of 164 executive incumbents, 419 candidates, 21 unclassified state employees, and 91 nonstate employees, totaling 695 (Hanson and others, 1976). The size of the pool will increase as more people are assessed. Since participants rated below 2 (on a scale of 1 to 5) in overall scores were dropped from the pool, the review process has eliminated the weakest candidates. Evidence regarding the quality of the candidates who remain in the pool has yet to be established. Concerns over interrater reliability continue to pose questions about scoring consistency. Taken together, these issues leave an observer somewhat skeptical about the program's claims.

The second goal addresses as desired outcomes advancement opportunity, flexibility, and mobility within and between state agencies. Since the program has not been in operation long, the results are inconclusive. Available data indicate that advancement from the candidate pool to career executive positions has been minimal. Out of forty-eight career executive appointments since the inception of the program, only twelve were filled by new candidates. Most were filled from the ranks of career executive incumbents. Consequently, only about 3 percent of the assessed pool has been promoted to career executive positions (Hanson and others, 1976, p. 5).

Finally, the assessment center approach sought to make effective use of employees' managerial and administrative skills. The desirability of movement among executive positions in different state agencies is controversial. If the assessments developed at the center are to be utilized as originally conceived, belief is required in the generic nature of management at top administrative levels. Moreover, appointment decisions must be based primarily on managerial and administrative skills. Commitment to this philosophy has met with operational resistance. A sample of twenty career executive vacancy announcements issued between April 1974 and

January 1976 revealed that eleven positions required restrictive training and experience (Hanson and others, 1976, p. 6). Inclusion of specific technical skills and narrowly defined training or experience in position descriptions for vacancies dramatically limits access to vacant positions for candidates in the assessed pool. Operationally, the generic management skills assessed by the center have not been congruent with the conception of skills required for vacancies.

Despite general agreement that assessment center operations are exceptionally well managed, there has been mixed reaction to using the center as the sole process for certifying candidates for career executive positions. Comparing assessment center procedures with testing and selection methods used previously indicates that the center provides more data on applicants and allows for more systematic comparison of candidates on important performance dimensions. Performance evaluation under simulated conditions appears preferable to the short panel interview used previously, but it also has an artificial quality. A concentrated period of role playing may distort the "reality" that is being simulated and may not accurately reflect job performance. For example, supervision requires assessment of staff strengths and weaknesses over an extended period; role plays do not reveal this. Further, people vary in their role-playing skills. Social workers may be familiar with the technique, while candidates with other backgrounds may find it foreign. One must question whether the center's simulation exercises assess administrative skills or role-playing proficiency.

Candidates who performed less well in the assessment center complained of being "branded." The previous system allowed a candidate to apply for each new vacancy without being labeled by a numerical competency score. Remedial training efforts prescribed for candidates with low assessment scores have been criticized as superficial, and on-the-job training opportunities have not developed.

Promoted as a cost-effective recruitment and selection system, the assessment center has consumed more state funds than had been anticipated. The average cost per assessee was $686. This figure is 29 percent more than the $533 average cost reported by centers in the private sector. Cost per appointment varies from

$11,644 to $20,642, depending on whether appointment of career executive incumbents is included (Hanson and others, 1976, p. 6). Either figure demonstrates the high cost of the program. As more appointments are made, these costs will drop. Whether the high cost is justified by significantly improved selection of candidates is debatable and can be judged only by the long-term performance of appointees. Clear evidence of the superiority of the assessment system will be necessary if the program is to justify its continued existence.

The creation of a pool of readily available candidates had some unforeseen negative consequences for affirmative action. After two years of assessments, it became clear that there were few women or minorities in the pool; their rank in the system was not high enough to make them eligible to compete for career executive positions. A second problem involved providing access to the assessment center and personnel system for persons outside state government. Potential candidates from other states and from nongovernmental agencies were unlikely to initiate the assessment process because they could only hope to be considered for a career executive position at some later time. Yet the short span between announcement of a vacancy and appointment made it difficult for people outside the system to be included. The ability to draw highly qualified candidates into the state governmental system appeared to have been reduced by the assessment center, thus limiting the state's ability to attract new blood.

Research Implications

A number of research implications emerge from an examination of the executive assessment program. There is a need for more longitudinal studies to track what happens to participants over time. The true test of the value of this executive selection system lies in the job performance of the people selected. Considering the cost of the program, it will be essential to document the long-range benefits. Bray's pioneering efforts in this area merit replication. Another area for examination involves the match between the candidates' assessed skills and the performance dimensions identified as central in specific job vacancies. This is a key step in the selection process. An analysis of the congruence of this match would assist in determining the degree to which the isolated performance dimensions reflect actual work requirements of the position.

A fruitful yet neglected area for research that is not addressed in the formal assessment center approach is a candidate's competence in what Pawlak (1976) has called "organizational tinkering." Competence and effectiveness in administrative roles may have as much bearing on a person's ability to "work the system" as skills that can be evaluated more directly. Developing techniques for the assessment of competence in these informal, subtle, and tremendously important skills would be a useful contribution.

Implications for Social Work Education

The experience of the Wisconsin assessment center provides case material for a much broader discussion than should be undertaken here regarding the training of social workers for management positions in large public bureaucracies as well as smaller organizational settings. For a profession such as social work—which is torn between simultaneous trends in education, one generic and the other specialist—the Wisconsin experience highlights a historical professional paradox.

The traditional route to administrative positions within social welfare agencies has been promotion up the professional career ladder. Rising in the ranks and eventually moving into management roles, often without the requisite training, has been a frequent experience among social work executives. The idea of training for entry-level management positions (for example, budget analyst, planner, policy analyst, program analyst) is a more recent development spurred by the growing demand of large public social welfare bureaucracies for competent middle-level administrative personnel. Administrators' career development experiences often are mediated by the kinds of agencies in which they work.

Patti (1977) provides a differentiated analysis of how management-level personnel allocate their time in a range of agency settings. As one might expect, his data indicate substantial differences in the ways managers in public, private, and voluntary social welfare agencies spend their time. One major explanatory variable, agency size, accounts for much of the variation. The depth of the administrative hierarchy, directly related to agency size, can alter significantly the kinds and range of tasks a manager performs. Flatter organizations require generalist-oriented administrators, while agencies whose hierarchies are steep can accommodate greater specialization. The Wisconsin experience may be generalizable to other large public bureaucratic settings but less applicable to small private and voluntary agencies. This may present a dilemma for social work educators who train students for administrative positions in the range of social welfare agencies.

Two major sets of issues surface from this review of the executive assessment process in Wisconsin. First, how generic are management skills? Should social workers trained as managers be able to demonstrate a specialized expertise? Do all kinds of public programs require the same sets of skills of their administrators? The assumption that management skills are generic and can be assessed without regard to the specific program area in which an administrator works is basic to the career assessment approach. The sixteen performance dimensions identified and used by the Wisconsin assessment center were seen as applicable to any management position. It is here that administration as the operational arm or policy is overlooked. Administration can be a highly discretionary activity through which even the most benign policy can become punitive and possibly destructive. Witness the broad range of variation along which programs such as Food Stamps, AFDC, and General Relief are administered. Can we entrust such sensitive programs to administrators who possess only generic management skills without a social work perspective? Perhaps it is this specialized sensitivity to the humane translation of policy into practice via enlightened administration that provides the foundation for a management specialization for social work. In this way, we will be able to differentiate the social worker with administrative training from the student prepared in business administration, public administration, or planning.

The emphasis on generic management skills also raises some issues for the development of social work education designed to prepare students for careers in management and administration. Comparison of the performance dimensions used in the Wisconsin center with generic social work models such as that of Pincus and Minahan (1973) shows many similarities (data collection, problem assessment, exercising influence, forming and maintaining action systems). Generically oriented social work schools that wish to initiate management concentrations should find present many of the necessary curriculum resources. A focus on interpersonal skills, which is basic to all social work education programs, also is a major component of the generic management skills identified by the Wisconsin assessment center.

The assessment center approach supports a systematic process whereby social work education can test and evaluate skill acquisition. The performance dimensions could be used in the development of a pretest-posttest design for assessing students' progress. Many of the exercises are valuable teaching tools. Simulation exercises allow students to practice necessary skills in a sheltered setting before attempting them in an agency. On a broader scale, the social work profession is struggling to design a method of assessing professional competence. The assessment center approach suggests a valuable addition to the paper-and-pencil tests currently utilized in social work certification and licensure.

The second set of issues concerns the functions that assessment centers fulfill for large public bureaucracies and whether they should provide guidance for the development of management and administration curricula in schools of social work. One must question the function performed by management assessment centers for the large organizations in which they operate. They do serve the overt function of assessment for promotion; however, the relationship between promotion and competence is not necessarily direct. Peter and Hull (1969) have addressed this point at length. Within the context of a civil service personnel system, a more objective assessment of candidates' credentials, skills, and experience is consistent with merit-based promotion. Even here, the data indicate that promotions based on assessment of generic management skills have been fewer than anticipated (twenty career executive vacancy announcements revealed eleven with very restrictive training and experience requirements). The assessment center provides a certified pool of applicants from which candidates for high-level administrative positions can be drawn. In the absence of longitudinal data, it is impossible to determine the extent to which appointees perform competently in their new positions. At the appointment stage, the pool is standardized by the assessment center process rather than by a shared level of competence.

While generic performance criteria provide significant dimensions on which management curricula can be based, they should be incorporated in a critical fashion. Although public bureaucracies indeed may be the largest employers of administratively trained social workers, we must be aware of the danger of allowing the market to influence too directly our curriculum-building efforts. Generic skills may provide a baseline for managers from several backgrounds. Social workers trained as managers should be equipped with more highly developed skills and sensitivities based on their social work orientation. Significantly, there is only one assessment center performance dimension concerned with orientation (responsiveness). Yet, if a manager is to be identified as a social worker, important values (for example, ensuring that people have access to the resources, services, and opportunities they need to meet various life tasks and that these resources are provided in ways that respect clients' dignity and individuality) must be stressed. Too much emphasis on generic aspects of management skills may obscure the importance of the congruence and fit between managers' professional affiliations and the programs they administer.

18

Training Financial Counseling Specialists

Joan M. Jones
Susan C. Richards

When Scott Fitzgerald made his well-known statement, "The very rich are different from you and me," he capsulized a still pervasive myth that a positive correlation exists between the size of individuals' incomes and their financial and emotional security, their freedom of choice, and their physical comfort. The realities of life in the 1970s challenge this assumption daily. Money, if not the root of all evil, poses sufficient problems that researchers and marriage counselors report economic stress as the primary cause of conflict in American families (Saxon, 1972, p. 299). For families earning below a minimum subsistence income, the etiology of financial stress is a deficit of funds to provide even their most basic needs. For families ranked in middle- and upper-income brackets, the explicit causes of financial problems generally can be related to deficiencies in knowledge and skills of money management or to impulsive or compulsive spending behaviors that are dysfunctional expressions of emotions.

250

The statistics of bankruptcy courts substantiate that in 1975 more than 250,000 individuals bought, borrowed, and charged themselves into financial ruin (U.S. Department of Commerce, 1976, p. 526). Some families earning comfortable incomes find themselves in the oppressive state that Hill (1970) labeled "secondary poverty." For these families, "financial stress is due to imprudent management of resources rather than to inadequate income" (Hill, 1970, p. 222). Individuals in this category have spent themselves into a state of debt, in which their monthly payments for past expenditures require so great a percentage of their paychecks that the income remaining is insufficient to finance daily life essentials. Clients surveyed by the Consumer Credit Counseling Service of Greater New York had an average cash-and-credit purchase expenditure level that exceeded their monthly income by $397 (*Wall Street Journal*, August 1, 1977). Laughlin and Bressler (1971, p. 617) reported that "the number of families afflicted by severe money problems is reaching epidemic proportions. If the estimate is correct that for every bankrupt family twenty more are on the brink of bankruptcy, then nearly three and one-half million people are facing financial crises."

We live in a money world—a credit society, a token economy—in which circular pieces of metal and rectangular pieces of green paper are the medium of exchange. The temptation to live beyond one's means is fostered by advertising agencies and facilitated by credit card companies that hold fast to the motto "In Debt We Trust—Buy Now, Pay Later" ("Merchants of Debt," 1977, p. 36). Psychologically sophisticated advertising campaigns capitalize on basic human desires for wealth, power, and status. They assure consumers that wealth is commensurate with money spent, that success is inextricably interwoven with luxury sedans and Caribbean vacations, and that taste and status are evidenced by designer clothes and vintage wines. Reliance on the purchasing power of plastic cards is evidenced by a 600 percent increase in the ratio of consumer installment debt to personal income between the years 1946 and 1975 (U.S. Department of Commerce, 1977, p. 103).

Overspending to purchase identity, status, and even dreams is only one form of money mismanagement. Within families, financial stress also may occur when money serves as an outlet or a substitute for expression of feelings. During the past decade, there has been an increased interest in exploring the dynamics of money and its use in the manipulation of intrafamilial relationships (Goldberg and Lewis, 1978; Ward, Wackman, and Wartella, 1977; Weinstein, 1976). Parents whose life demands or pressures estrange them from their children may offer large allowances or material possessions as substitutes for, or expressions of, affection. Weinstein (1976, pp. 37–38) notes: "Because money is linked with personal standing, with self-worth, it has to be important—much more important than its function as an economic tool, as a medium of exchange. . . . It has become entangled with early sensations of love and affection, with positive and not-so-positive family relationships. The result: for our children, as well as for ourselves, money becomes a synonym for security and, sometimes, a symbol of love."

Marital conflicts also may be rooted in conflicts over control of the purse strings. Marriage traditionally has placed women in the position of financial vulnerability because "without a doubt, the term of the unwritten marriage contract which cripples the largest number of women is the absolute economic power most husbands have over their wives" (Fleming and Washburne, 1977, p. 125). Indeed, husbands have lorded their earning capacities over nonworking wives, sometimes justifying their purchase of expensive "man toys" as reasonable rewards for their labors. In retaliation, these same women may spend excessively or seek employment to prove their own worth and to avoid "the economic dependency . . . which can breed resentment and mistrust" (Fleming and Washburne, 1977, p. 126).

Finally, economic-based stress may be precipitated by differences in individuals' financial orientations. The extremes of this condition occur when a conspicuous consumer marries a stringent saver. In a comparative study of "Areas of Marital Conflict in Successfully and Unsuccessfully Functioning Families," disputes over finances were the primary source of disagreement for both groups (Mitchell, Bullard, and Mudd, 1962, p. 90). According to *The General Mills American Family Report for 1974–1975* (General Mills, 1975, p. 43), 54 percent of randomly sampled families stated that they argued about money.

Despite thorough documentation by researchers from various disciplines of the need for comprehensive financial counseling programs, at present there is a dearth of professionally trained people in this field (Hall, 1968, p. 6). Individuals experiencing financial distress find themselves consulting a wide range of professionals—bankers, investment consultants, home economists, ministers, social workers, psychologists, and credit counselors—whose financial counseling services reflect their individual conceptions of the function of money and are consistent with their professional training. As might be supposed, the services offered by individuals with such varied expertise are fragmented; in general, they offer only one of three services: education, therapeutic intervention, or credit counseling (Richards, 1975, pp. 2–5).

Home economists, investment counselors, and bankers most often view financial management skills as learned behaviors. Believing that with sound economic knowledge individuals will be able to make wise financial decisions, they employ various educational techniques to expand consumers' decision-making capacities and money management practices. Psychologists, social workers, and clergymen tend to emphasize the psychological components of dysfunctional spending behaviors. They conceptualize overspending and faulty money management as symptomatic of anxiety or emotional distress. "The goals of treatment within this context are to help clients consider reflectively the cathartic effects of compulsive or impulsive spending and gain awareness of the underlying causes of their maladaptive use of money. They rarely attempt an analysis of budgetary practices, for identifying deficits in money management is seen as a useful adjunct to the relief of immediate pressure but not to the resolution of the problem" (Richards and Tomdro, 1975, p. 4).

Because available financial counseling services are limited in number and focus on isolated aspects of financial distress, numerous families in states of debt, exacerbated by repeated financial misjudgments, seek assistance from one of 210 credit counseling agencies associated with the National Foundation for Consumer Credit. The primary goal of these programs, subsidized by fees and monies from creditors, is the resolution of problems between the client and his creditors. Typically, clients may be placed on pro-rated financial plans, relinquishing to the budget counseling agency large percentages of their incomes for dispersal to creditors. Studies of these programs indicate that such an approach to financial distress meets only the immediate crisis and fails to equip clients to avoid future financial problems (Krueger, 1970; Olson, 1968). Ideally, it has been suggested, "credit counseling programs should provide leadership to develop strong educational programs for groups which will enable many families to avoid serious credit difficulties, as well as initiate more effective individual services" (Hall, 1968, p. 22).

Recognizing the deficits in existing counseling programs and responding to the training requests of several human service agen-cies, the University of Wisconsin-Milwaukee School of Social Wel-fare developed an interdisciplinary option to train bachelor's-level social workers in the specialized skills of family financial counseling. This option reflects the educational rationale articulated by Specht (1977, p. 1): "Following achievement of competence at [the generalist] level, professional development should focus upon *spe-cialized* elements in practice which consist of in-depth knowledge and skill." It essentially is a problem and population-group ap-proach (Specht, 1977, p. 23), calling for specialization along the lines of improving financial functioning of individuals, families, groups, and communities.

By combining the knowledge and practice base of social work with the expertise of specialized areas of home economics, the option helps students develop competencies that may be subsumed under two broad categories: (1) acquisition of knowledge basic to sound financial practices and (2) adaptation of skills of assessment, intervention, and evaluation to assist clients experiencing financially based stress. Identification of the competencies was accomplished by a committee comprising faculty members from home economics, social work, and undergraduate field programs. The process that was followed may be useful to various university task forces charged with the responsibility for developing specialized skill packages.

Initially, committee members sought to identify the optimal financial counseling services requested by public and private agencies and specify the specialized skills essential to the delivery of these services. Three potential sources of this information were identified, and interviews were arranged with individuals who described what they believed would be useful content and experiential material for the proposed financial counseling specialty. The first group of interviewees comprised social workers, credit union employees, and home economists who were providing financial counseling services or financial management education. Committee members specified that students would need to be empathic listeners, skilled in developing individualized financial plans, knowledgeable about legal solutions to overindebtedness, and cognizant of community resources. They suggested that students be assigned to field settings in which they would be able to practice newly acquired financial counseling skills. Next, potential employers of students who would receive financial counseling training were surveyed. They described various money management services—such as budgeting, prorating, and educational seminars—that would be useful to their customers, and they suggested that students master the content relevant to such services.

Finally, members of the Advisory Committee of the Consumer Budget Counseling Service (composed of representatives from the legal profession, labor unions, the University of Wisconsin Extension System, and banks) were questioned. These individuals had been instrumental in developing and launching the Consumer Budget Counseling section of the Milwaukee Family Service Agency. In this capacity, they were aware of the financial counseling requirements of a broad spectrum of clients, including low-income minority groups, middle-income union workers, and affluent executives. They recommended that the Financial Counseling Option focus on the needs of families, because a survey undertaken by the Consumer Budget Counseling Service had indicated that the majority of individuals seeking financial counseling are married.

The survey of existing financial counseling services and potential agencies under whose auspices more expanded services might be offered clarified considerably the concrete tasks that financial counselors should be equipped to accomplish. It was at this point that the Financial Counseling Option's eleven competencies were defined, and the context within which they were to be acquired were specified.

Through special content courses, students are expected to:

1. Demonstrate comprehension of the relationship between personal resources (such as earning potential, fringe benefits, skills, education, health, available time, and value priorities) and the level of living an individual or family unit can achieve
2. Demonstrate knowledge of specific expenditure areas (food, housing, clothing, transportation, insurance, credit, and so forth) that increase rational consumer decision making
3. Explicate marketing techniques, the psychology of selling, and procedures utilized by advertisers to create wants
4. Differentiate problems that are common to many consumers (including limited mobility, discrimination, lack of assertiveness in the marketplace, and lack of consumer sagacity) from problems that are unique to the low-income and/or minority consumer
5. Exhibit knowledge of the legal remedies for overindebtedness—bankruptcy, Chapter XIII of the Bankruptcy Act, and prorating

Within structured field settings, students must:

6. Identify the components a family deems essential to daily living and develop skills related to assisting families in the evolution of workable financial plans
7. Acquire assessment skills specifically relevant to:
   a. Evaluation of a family's individual financial desires, needs, goals, values, and priorities.
   b. Specification of the relationship of these priorities to maladaptive patterns of money management.
   c. Determination of the focus of intervention geared to altering existing dysfunctional budgetary practices and establishing more functional spending patterns.
8. Practice specifying treatment objectives and developing contracts with clients that identify the change goals

9. Articulate the ramifications of poor money management and demonstrate techniques for the reeducation of families with dysfunctional spending behaviors
10. Enumerate diverse types of community resources available to financially distressed families and practice advocacy techniques essential to assisting them
11. Practice explicating the process of credit granting and collection and the legal implications of clients' becoming enmeshed in the credit system

After formulation of the competencies that should be developed by students electing the option, members of the Interdisciplinary Course Development Committee explored which existing courses might be utilized or adapted to provide the specialized content. They evaluated ways in which field settings might be structured to enable students to apply new knowledge to practice situations. Finally, with faculty members from economics, sociology, and business administration, they identified courses in those departments that might be pertinent to the option's knowledge requirements.

As ultimately designed, the Family Financial Counseling Option requires that, in addition to BSW courses, students complete six credit hours in economics; six credit hours in home economics, including nutrition and one elective; and the three newly developed special content courses: Management in Family Living, Family Financial Management, and Methods of Family Financial Counseling.

The introductory course, Management in Family Living, enables students to study management concepts and their applicability to family functioning. From this knowledge base, students explore various means of assisting individuals and families with managerial responsibilities to optimally utilize all their resources for the realization of their specific life goals.

Family Financial Management surveys the concepts and principles relevant to maximizing the use of one's resources, both human and material, in the attainment of financial goals. At the end of the course, students should be able to (1) understand their personal goals, values, standards, and resultant money management behaviors; (2) demonstrate knowledge of specific content areas (for example, insurance) increasing rationality in the consumer decision-making process; (3) develop family budgets and explain components composing "typical" spending patterns; (4) comprehend the relationship between the use of resources and the level of living an individual or family is able to achieve. Students analyze their financial management behaviors by following a process similar to the one they will employ with clients. They are required to maintain a monthly log of all expenditures and use this information as a basis for developing individualized financial plans.

In the final course, Methods of Family Financial Counseling, students expand treatment skills (communication, assessment, goal specification, contracting, and evaluation) developed in their first field experiences to include those essential to financial counselors. They study the causes of a range of financial problems, alternatives for resolving overindebtedness, and methods for training clients in sound money management practices. Since the attainment of the option's competencies requires the mastery and integration of complex personal economics material and practice skills, a variety of training materials were developed in conjunction with innovative teaching methods to facilitate students' accomplishment of the instructional objectives (Mager, 1962a).

The training process involves extensive utilization of case materials collected in various field agencies. These records expose students to individuals and families with an assortment of financial problems: welfare mothers endeavoring to eke out an existence from an insufficient AFDC check, unmarried college students with temporary poverty-level incomes, professional families whose dual incomes have prompted them to spend beyond their combined salaries, and blue-collar workers with erratic employment and wage patterns. Experience with such a range of problems demonstrates to students that financially based stress is not unique to any client group but is generalized across class and economic lines.

After analyzing case records in class, advanced students are required to assist an individual or family requesting financial counseling. The client generally is seen during the course of a semester, thus allowing sufficient time not only for goal specification and intervention but also for evaluation of the treatment outcome. Presentation of their cases in class creates for students a forum for sharing experiences while expanding their awareness of impediments to service delivery and highlighting particularly successful interventive strategies. Role-playing exercises are designed to give students the opportunity to be on both sides of the counseling relationship, thereby sensitizing them to the anxiety experienced by clients with severe financial problems.

An additional instructional technique is the use of videotapes developed by faculty members instructing in the option. One video presentation, a cartoon series, delineates the competencies essential for financial counselors. Other videotapes of counseling sessions are employed to further develop students' understanding of the steps of the process of successful intervention with clients experiencing financial problems.

Concurrent with enrollment in the specific content courses, students are assigned to field settings in which they apply their expertise in a variety of treatment situations with different client groups. Students in placement at the Department of Public Welfare offer budget and credit counseling and teach simplified systems for resource management to recipients of financial aid. For many of this clientele, poverty is a chronic state, and predictably they are pessimistic about the possibilities of improving their deprived lifestyles. In contrast, clients, primarily students, at the University Financial Counseling center are considerably more optimistic. Because their monetary difficulties are temporary, they are more confident about their resolution. The field students in this setting provide information relevant to meeting immediate shortages of funds, payments of tuition, and daily living expenses.

A third group of field students, assigned to the Consumer Budget Counseling Program of the Family Service Agency, offer crisis counseling to young middle-income families whose financial distress stems from their having fallen victim to the credit society. These individuals, living in the aforementioned state of "secondary poverty," have amassed debts that consume 50 to 100 percent of their incomes. Counseling is directed to the exploration of means of resolving the immediate financial crises and to the acquisition of more adequate money management skills.

At the beginning of each semester, field students, in conjunction with a faculty field supervisor with family economics expertise, develop written contracts. These contracts identify the learning objectives of experience in a particular agency and specify the tasks related to their attainment. The practical tasks assigned to field students may include production of printed materials for clients, maintenance of a daily log or diary of field experiences utilizing newly developed skills, and tape recording of individual counseling sessions for later critique or self-evaluation.

Because direct observation of students' conducting counseling sessions is disruptive, students meet regularly with their faculty supervisors to review current cases, discuss problems of new clients, and determine if services are consistent with agency policies. In addition to conferences with faculty supervisors, students prepare written case records describing the financial problems identified by clients, their conceptualizations of the sources of stress, possible solutions to the crises, analyses of the counseling sessions, and final evaluations of the success of the treatment process.

Since the inception of the Family Financial Counseling Option in the spring of 1976, student enrollment has increased steadily. Although it is too soon to substantiate all the employment and professional advantages its graduates may gain, students' responses to the special content courses have reinforced their validity and function in a social work curriculum. Statements in postcourse evaluations emphasize the value of acquiring money management skills in the reorganization of students' lives as well as in the lives of their clients. Several students have suggested that the Management of Family Resources course should be required for *all* graduate and undergraduate social work students; one student urged that it be made a prerequisite for marriage.

The employment opportunities for graduates of this specialization are increasing as the community becomes aware of their special training. Examples of new employment opportunities are financial counseling positions at the Hemophiliac Society, where a new graduate provides full-time financial counseling to parents overwhelmed by the chronic and exorbitant medical expenses of their hemophiliac children, and at an alcoholic rehabilitation center. These unique employment opportunities, only two of many, strongly suggest that in our money world, where the poor stay poor and the rich receive credit, financial counselors shall not want for clients.

19

Preparing Social Workers
for Effective Practice
in Integrated
Human Services Agencies

Peter Hookey

In the context of this chapter, a generalist is a practitioner who functions competently in integrated-services agencies—agencies that provide a wide range of services that under other organizational arrangements would be provided by several categorical service agencies.

Several authors have bestowed the status of the label "movement" on the recent multiplicity of efforts to integrate human services at the local community level (see, for example, Gage, 1976). Services integration certainly has become a professional goal for a broad band of idealists—and for a few pragmatists. *Integration* is a generic term covering a variety of more specific concepts. For present purposes, just three such concepts are important.

Coordination is defined as the integration of services via one or more of the following: meetings of multiagency boards; centralized case files or data banks; shared reception and/or telecommunications facilities; joint agency publicity; shared staff responsible for interagency liaison and/or centralized public relations and/or client intake and/or client follow-up functions. *Colocation* is defined as the physical siting of the offices of several agencies' service providers in one building or in closely adjacent facilities. *Fusion* is defined as the integration of the work of two or more different types of human service agencies such that the resulting multidisciplinary work group(s) give(s) group members their primary functional identity.

In some instances, there may be *lateral-plus-vertical fusion;* that is, lateral work fusion at the primary-service-provider level and also some degree of vertical fusion involving multifunctional supervisory hierarchies and/or legal mandates and/or funding mechanisms. In other instances, there may be *solely lateral fusion.* In this case, each type of professional in the primary-level work group is separately supervised, funded, and legally mandated through different agency structures. Solely lateral fusion may be a result of two types of arrangements. One alternative is *hosting fusion.* In this case, a host agency fuses into its service-provider work force a clear minority of additional workers of other professions who are outposted from one or more other types of agencies. A second alternative is *no-host fusion.* In this case, the fused multidisciplinary work group has no clear domination (by virtue of host, numerical, or prestige status) by one professional group.

Developments in Four Countries

England. The "Seebohm reorganization" in England is known throughout the Western world as the largest-scale and perhaps most dramatic example of social services integration.* The reorganization legislation flowed from the report of a central government committee chaired by Frederick Seebohm (Committee on Local Authority, 1969). The original decision to convene the

---

* For briefer discussions of some comparable developments in a wider range of countries, see Hookey, 1977a.

Seebohm Committee stemmed from the central government's "concern to devise a family-oriented service to deal with the problems of juvenile delinquency" (Barr, 1977, p. 1).

Prior to 1970, each city and county local government unit (known as a local authority) deployed its social workers in separate children's, general welfare, and mental welfare departments. (Income maintenance services were, and still are, administered separately through central government social security offices.)

The Local Authorities Social Services Act of 1970 mandated that these several local government departments be amalgamated in one fell swoop into integrated-services departments. The former specialist job designations were changed to the generalist term *social worker*. Literally overnight, "child care workers" and "mental welfare officers" became "social workers." They were called on to perform many additional functions for which they had at best very brief in-service training. They were required to relate internally to many new, unfamiliar, and untrusted supervisors and externally to a bewildered public, confused clients, and frustrated and often belligerent professionals in other types of agencies.

In my assessment, the reorganization was justified and, on overall balance, has led to better services to clients. If it were to be done at all, it had to be done all at once. An incremental approach probably would have been halted or at least unduly delayed by political challenges stemming from the inevitable transitional inconveniences. As it was, the logistics of the amalgamation itself were planned with military precision, and generally there were few client casualties. There probably could have been better advance publicity, but in such situations there always are many who await the impact of such changes before confronting how to deal with them.

The Seebohm reorganization led to lateral-plus-vertical fusion of services. Many direct service workers and many of their supervisors went into a state of disorientation that appropriately might be labeled "fusion shock." While a few are still in a state of chronic "fusion shock," the vast majority have emerged from it; many now prefer their broader responsibilities and the markedly enhanced status of their department in the local government agencies' pecking order. "In the senior ranks of local government, directors of social services are full chief officers involved in corporate management decisions that impinge on the life of the whole community" (Barr, 1977, p. 3).

The Seebohm Committee hoped that social services reorganization would be accompanied by changes in the National Health Service that would make its local units structurally compatible with those of the new social services department. The National Health Service was reorganized at a later date, in April 1974, but there still are major incompatibilities between the two structures. Each area health authority must appoint a specialist in community medicine whose duties must include liaison with local social services departments. The latter are encouraged to appoint a senior officer with responsibility for liaison with the National Health Service (Brown, 1976). Thus, there is considerable official incentive for the coordination of health and social services at supervisory levels.

For many years, there has been experimentation with voluntary, small-scale fusion of health and social services at the primary care level. In many instances one or more general practitioners have acted as host(s) to a social worker outposted (or, in British terminology, "seconded") on full salary from his or her social service agency. These programs have both predated and postdated the Seebohm reorganization. Originally, social workers tended to be the initiators who convinced a few more or less skeptical general practitioners to try such arrangements. More recently, many general practitioners have become attracted to such schemes, which cost them virtually nothing financially but may considerably ease their work load. This trend, coupled with recent budget cutbacks and hiring freezes in many social services departments, has meant that several departments now maintain waiting lists of general practitioners requesting social worker secondments. Cooper and others (1975) have reported on a controlled-intervention outcome study of a social worker secondment program in a general practitioner group practice in a London suburb. The results were supportive of this type of secondment program.

There have been some recent efforts to improve coordination between local authorities' housing and social services departments. About half of the housing stock in England is publicly owned, mostly by local authorities, and demand for it far exceeds the supply. Social workers traditionally have spent a good deal of time entreating skeptical housing officers to look favorably on their clients' housing applications. These representations typically are drawn out and mutually frustrating. Interagency tension at the service-provider level often has been manifested in acrimonious exchanges between social services and housing department directors at local authority council meetings. Many battle-weary local authority chief executives have been watching with interest the performance of the controversial "supremos" who have been appointed recently by two London-area local authorities. In each case, the supremo, or super-director, is responsible for coordinating the activities of the social services department and the housing department and acting as a buffer between the department heads and the chief executive. Currently, the debate on the merits and demerits of this high-level coordination innovation is in full swing; it is too early to say whether such appointments will become commonplace.

Shortly after the Seebohm reorganization, a visiting United States delegation "reported favorably on the form reorganization was taking, but a case could be made for a more thorough appraisal now that the new social services departments have had time to settle down" (Barr, 1977, p. 1; for the delegation's report, see Morris, 1974). Such research currently is in progress at the National Institute for Social Work in London and at the Universities of Keele and Aberdeen (Barr, 1977, p. 2). Barr (1977) has provided a critical review of the Seebohm reorganization and subsequent practice and policy developments. His paper was prepared partly as a response to an earlier draft of this chapter, and as such it is a valuable complementary document.

The Netherlands. For many years, the Dutch have been experimenting with a wide range of approaches to the integration of primary human services. The language barrier has thwarted international recognition of many of their achievements, especially outside of Europe.

Holistically oriented general practitioners consistently have been well represented among the more conspicuous innovators. Nearly two decades ago, Huygen (1962) published a short but highly influential article on the "home-team" model. He docu-

mented and espoused a services-integration model that was suited
particularly to rural areas. His model capitalized on the fact that
rural parish boundaries often delineated the service areas of four
key types of primary human services workers—priests, general practitioners, social workers, and district nurses. These professionals
typically used their homes as their main office. Huygen proposed
that these workers in each rural parish should constitute themselves
into a "home team" and develop a schedule of weekly case conferences to be held at the home of one or other of the team members and supplemented whenever necessary by more frequent bilat-
eral face-to-face or telephone contacts.

    In such home teams, a great deal of constructive service
coordination has occurred. While such arrangements do not involve
any agency integration in a formal organizational sense, many such
teams legitimately may be described as examples of informal fusion
by virtue of the degree of the team members' commitment to and
identification with the home-team practice concept.

    In more recent years, integration efforts typically have
involved larger groups of primary human service professionals.
Primary-level services integration in the Netherlands is very much a
grass-roots sociopolitical movement with its own catch phrase, "de
eerste lijn." Literally, this means first or front line (care), but a
more liberal translation also might include the concepts of "avant
garde" and "cutting edge." The movement has spawned periodic
national conferences, and its own bimonthly subscription journal,
De Eerste Lijn, which provides its clientele with an engaging mix of
erudition and cutting satire. Gijsman (1976) has provided an over-
view of 257 "eerste lijn" project reports that were published during
1971–1975 in a wide variety of social work, social science, and
medical journals.

    Social workers and general practitioners are key service pro-
viders in most "eerste lijn" service centers. Descriptions of developments at Gezondheidscentrum Hoensbroek (Hoensbroek Health
Center), which opened in 1970, provide rich illustrative material
(deGroot and Maertens, 1975; Dubois, 1971, 1976). The purpose-
built center is designed to accommodate all the medical and social
service personnel serving the approximately ten thousand residents
of North Hoensbroek, a coal-mining center in the southern tip of

the Netherlands. Currently, five general practitioners, two social workers, five district nurses, and one midwife work at the center.

The staff members at the Hoensbroek Center (and staff at several similar centers) are a fused team. They have a strong commitment to each other, in both a professional and a personal sense. The seriousness of their commitment is reflected in weekly team meetings, lengthy daily discussions over coffee, the hiring of outside group-dynamics consultants to advise them on intrateam role and personality clashes, and the involvement of team members' spouses in team planning conferences at a similar center in Venlo.

The Hoensbroek Center's director has drawn attention to the role of the team as an advocate for social change (Dubois, quoted in deGroot and Maertens, 1975). The complex medico-psycho-social problems of many of the team's clients were considered to be partially the result of cruel and exploitive practices in the local coal mines. The team's advocacy against these practices was seen by mine managers as potentially damaging to their interests, and pressure was put on team members to stifle their criticisms. Prior to the formation of the center, the general practitioners recognized this social problem but perhaps thought it was social workers' business to become involved. However, the social workers may have lacked the power base from which to challenge the mine managers. The initiation of the center created a situation of "strength in unity," in which the team was capable of more than the sum of the prior capabilities of its members.

Sweden. In Sweden the services-integration theme is manifested particularly in the "oppen vård" ("open care") movement. The movement originated in the central government's desire to reorient the health care system away from costly and dysfunctional institutional care toward greater emphasis on "open" (community) care (National Board of Health and Welfare, 1970). Purpose-built primary care centers are being erected in many areas of the country.

The emphasis on construction of new facilities has provided the opportunity for colocation of primary health and social services. Furthermore, there have been serious efforts to achieve not only colocation but also fusion of services. Describing the plans for a primary care center in Luleå, Inghe and Rolander (1974) have emphasized the importance of good functional cooperation in patient care—something, they point out, that is not necessarily achieved just by colocating the offices of various primary-level service providers.

Perhaps the best-known examples of integrated primary care facilities are the Tierp and Skara centers, which are located in rural areas in central Sweden. In both cases, care is delivered by fused no-host groups of approximately equal numbers of social workers, general practitioners, and district nurses. At Tierp, the staff is divided into area teams comprising one each of each type of professional (Berfenstam and Smedby, 1976; Lindblom, 1974). The teams hold weekly case conferences chaired by social workers. At Skara, there also are frequent team conferences, and staff members have found it necessary to keep in check a tendency to focus too much on their life-style problems rather than those of their patients (Westrin, 1973). They have evolved a guideline of a maximum of two to three hours per week spent in all types of team conferences (clinical, policy-oriented, and educational).

The Swedes also are experimenting with the hosting approach to fusion of services. In Tynnered, a Gothenberg suburb, a social worker employed by the local public social services department has been outposted into a medical group composed of three general practitioners, whose office is located in a high-rise apartment building (Falklind and others, 1974). This program is of particular interest in that the outposting has been accompanied by devolution of statutory powers and responsibilities. The social worker is empowered to exercise directly her employing agency's responsibilities under Sweden's child abuse and alcoholism laws. This obviates costly and duplicative referrals of clients to the main social service agency in such circumstances. Under the child abuse law, for instance, the social worker has powers to place a child in emergency protective custody. When the social worker and a general practitioner colleague are aware of a case of child abuse, both are obligated to report the case to the appropriate legal authorities. If there is a dispute over whether certain behaviors constitute abuse, neither can veto the other's right to make a report.

United States. Several years ago in the United States, the federally mandated separation of financial and nonfinancial public welfare services stimulated many states to reassess the organizational structure of their services. In New Jersey, for instance, separation of services led to the establishment in 1971 of county social services departments. Shortly thereafter, the Atlantic County department outposted several of its service workers into other local public and private agencies—to a migrant farm program office, a hospital, high schools, the county jail, a Catholic ghetto agency, and an ethnic social center. Hoshino and Weber (1973) have described this program in detail. It constitutes a multifaceted version of the hosting fusion approach to services integration.

Other services integration projects have involved a linkage-agent approach, in which specially hired linkage agents have been charged with coordinating the activities of existing agency professionals. One of the most comprehensive of these projects has served the six-county Devils Lake area of northeast North Dakota (Jensen and others, 1973). During 1971–1974 a three-year federal demonstration grant led to the construction of the Devils Lake Human Services Center. Under the impetus of the project, the offices of ten preexisting area agencies, most of them public, were colocated in or very near the new purpose-built Human Services Center. A group of service counselors were hired with grant funds, deployed throughout the six-county area (some in satellite offices), and supervised by senior project staff in Devils Lake. The service counselors' function was to facilitate clients' use of the area's preexisting human services. They provided intake, information, referral, followup, and evaluation services. They also acted as catalysts for cooperative activities among area human services staff.

The network of service counselors was disbanded after the cessation of the federal grant. The center itself remains, with its group of colocated agencies and an administrator. In 1973 the North Dakota legislature passed a bill (House Bill 1031) encouraging the joint exercise of governmental powers through the establishment of a network of human services centers throughout the state.

Some services-integration projects have evolved largely through the dedicated efforts of voluntary organizations committed to enhancing community cohesion. The Countryside Council in southwest Minnesota is illustrative of this kind of organization. The council is a voluntary "67-member organization of concerned individuals . . . engaged in a rural community development process to learn the ways of achieving agreed-upon objectives in resolving problems affecting their 19-county community" (Countryside Council, 1975, p. 28).

In 1973 the Minnesota legislature passed the Human Services Act, encouraging the establishment of Human Services Boards throughout the state. In a joint memo circulated in September 1973, the state's health, public welfare, and corrections commissioners encouraged county commissioners to consider setting up Human Services Boards. Since 1973 the Countryside Council has been spearheading the development of these boards. Typically, a board's members are lay individuals who employ a professional administrator to coordinate the services of several agencies within a one- to three-county area. Under the act, a Human Services Board has the power to assess the unique needs of its service area and then, where necessary, to reorganize the service zoning arrangements of its constituent agencies and reapportion according to local priorities the available categorical public funds.

Service coordination and some degree of colocation have been part of the objectives of the projects in North Dakota and Minnesota outlined above. Each of them has been involved primarily with public-sector services. A services-integration approach of a markedly different character is demonstrated by the holistic health centers in Hinsdale and Woodridge, Illinois (both Chicago suburbs). The centers are situated in church buildings and are predicated on the symbiotic nature of medical, sociopsychological, and spiritual problems (Cunningham, 1977; Tubesing, 1977; Westberg, 1970). They offer a fused-team approach to care, featuring therapy planning conferences involving the client/patient and each center's family physician, nurse, and pastoral counselor.

The centers were launched with private foundation funds but are intended to be self-supporting on a fee-for-service basis. The centers' staff members are in nationwide demand as consultants to community groups interested in starting similar centers.

The holistic health center model is illustrative of the additive approach that characterizes most services-integration developments in the private sector in the United States. In the above case, perceptive professionals saw a need for a new form of services integration and established a new agency to provide it. Another version of the additive approach occurs when a private service agency decides to provide more holistic services and hires additional staff (rather than seeking out an outposting arrangement involving existing staff of another local agency). The tendency of many group medical practices to hire their own social workers is an example of this latter type of additive approach to services integration (Hookey, 1977a, 1977b, 1978).

The additive approach to services integration raises some interesting policy and value questions. Few would quarrel with the merit of most additive services-integration projects in and of themselves. But from a broader perspective, it is questionable whether the ideal of services integration is furthered by additive private sector projects that effectively add to the complexity of choosing among available human services in a given area. Furthermore, such projects may result—via a personnel siphoning-off process—in the dilution of the quality of the services of traditional public agencies. This latter point is particularly important in view of the fact that the price factor may preclude poorer consumers from availing themselves of the services of the more expensive private sector services-integration projects.

The debate over value issues notwithstanding, in the short term there undoubtedly will be further experimentation in the field of additive services integration. At the same time, there will be increased efforts to promote coordination, colocation, and linkage at various levels of human services hierarchies. These approaches to services integration have been endorsed by the National Council on Social Welfare's Task Force on the Future for Social Services in the United States (National Council on Social Welfare, 1977). The task force's scenario of networks of coordinated but autonomous agencies plus centralized case management is reminiscent of the Devils Lake arrangements described above (Jensen and others, 1973).

In the years ahead, it is likely that there also will be further experimentation with the hosting fusion approach—for instance, along the lines of the Atlantic County model (Hoshino and Weber, 1973). In the longer term, such developments may pave the way for fusions involving mergers of two or more primary human services agencies. The first wave of such mergers probably will involve public and voluntary agencies, leading to the creation of departments of social services in the English sense (of a more comprehensive scope than those currently so designated in some states). Such a department might be formed by vertical and lateral fusion of county public welfare, mental health, public health, and senior citizens' agencies. Subsequently, there may be further fusions involving social services departments and private-sector agencies, including primary health care agencies. Such fusions would be consistent with the developments in the Netherlands and Sweden described above.

Implications for Education

Certain curriculum areas will need to be given particular emphasis as educators train or retrain social workers for competent generalist practice in integrated primary human services agencies. (Hereafter, such practitioners will be referred to as integrated services generalists—IS generalists for short.) In the following discussion of curriculum issues, the frame of reference will be the "Montana List of Social Work Practice Skills" (Cummins, 1976). While the Montana List was developed in the context of competency-based baccalaureate education, it also has considerable utility in the graduate education context. The following discussion should be interpreted as applying to baccalaureate and graduate education. The discussion is organized so as to relate, in turn, to the first, second, and seventh of the seven skills categories covered by the Montana List—namely, the organizational, community, and professional contexts of practice.

IS generalists need to be prepared to function as creative conceptualizers and planners of various forms of integrated service networks. They need to recognize the potentially stultifying nature of the "practitioner-in-agency" mind-set—the tendency for experience in a particular kind of agency structure to stifle receptivity to alternative structures. In more general terms, what is needed is an emphasis on lateral possibility thinking, or what de Bono (1972) calls "PO" thinking.

IS generalists also need an in-depth understanding of the goal of holistic care and of the rationales, advantages, and disadvantages of the various organizational maneuvers—coordination, colocation, and fusion—that may facilitate progress toward this goal.

Certain groups of services lend themselves more to a particular kind of services integration than others. However, it is necessary to differentiate between what is more readily achievable and what is more worthwhile. An integration of two or more services that is achieved easily may be beneficial rarely, and vice versa. In between the extremes, fusion of two particular services may be desirable in view of the professionals' frequently felt needs for face-to-face planning of services to shared clients. However, sometimes the value of that time-consuming face-to-face planning is less than the value of the extra services that could be provided during the time saved by operating within a nonfused structure. (The above argument is predicated on the assumption that fused relationships are more time consuming than other less intimate relationships, an assumption that is likely to be true in most but not all types of settings.)

Gage (1976, p. 30) has provided a thorough discussion of the concept of "service clusters"—for instance, "hard" services as distinguished from "soft" services and "core" services as distinguished from "supportive" services. Services in each such category may be "compatible for potential integration" (Gage, 1976, p. 32). Services that have substantive interdependencies also are sensible targets for integration initiatives. For instance, medical, sociopsychological, and spiritual care services form a meaningful cluster of fused services, in view of the symbiosis of the soma, the psyche, and the soul (Huygen, 1962; Westberg, 1970). It must be recognized, however, that what makes sense on substantive grounds often is difficult to achieve because of services incompatibilities in relation to economic, political, or administrative considerations (Gage, 1976, p. 32).

IS generalists also need to be well exposed to quantitative issues: intrateam and team-clientele staffing ratios, preferable service population sizes for areas served by various types of services-integration projects, and so forth. Much of the existing literature on such projects does address these quantitative issues. However, there is a need for much more original research in this area and for the systematic aggregation of the experiences reported in existing publications.

Educators of IS generalists need to place special emphasis on the issue of "awareness of the unique social characteristics of the community and the region" (Cummins, 1976, p. 66). Rural and ghetto communities often provide the potential for services-integrated opportunities, yet many prospective IS generalists lack experiential knowledge of such communities. To a limited but significant extent, this knowledge gap can be narrowed by exposure to rural- and ghetto-oriented fiction, films, and professional literature.

IS generalists need to be aware of the activism and advocacy potentialities of their practice settings. They often will have opportunities to identify and speak out about "the relationship between private troubles and broader community issues" (Cummins, 1976, p. 66). This kind of opportunity was seized in the Netherlands by the Hoensbroek Center team in its confrontation with local coal mine managers (deGroot and Maertens, 1975). The team's efforts are illustrative of the politically involved, establishment-challenging tenor of the Dutch "eerste lijn" movement—a nationwide movement that warrants the attention of social work educators in other countries (Hookey, 1977c).

IS generalists have the responsibility to identify oppressive corporate practices in their service area, awaken (if necessary) the dormant social consciences of their colleagues in other professions, and mobilize the considerable advocacy potential inherent within multiprofessional interest groups (whether fused, colocated, or coordinated). Especially in very rural areas, the staff members of an integrated-services center may be the only human service professionals serving a wide geographical area. As such, they have a collective responsibility to fight social repression and work to improve the quality of community life.

In many integrated-services projects, the professional context of practice is that the social worker is in a professional minority of one, has no on-site professional supervision (in the intradisciplinary sense), often is identified by a designation other than social worker, and belongs to a team that allocates tasks more on the basis of role/personality fit than on disciplinary preparation. Education for such milieus indeed is a challenge. Curricula must maximize disciplinary security and autonomy while minimizing disciplinary self-consciousness, rigidity, and narrowmindedness. Therefore, more interdisciplinary courses and practica (Bassoff, 1976; Hookey, 1976) are needed. Through these experiences, students learn to interact assertively and constructively with members of the other professions that share in integrated-services projects. In such settings, agency standards and guidelines often are much less formal than in many traditional social work agencies. IS generalists need to develop the maturity and self-awareness that will enable them to set self-expectations and self-limits that are professionally responsible yet humanly realistic.

Many IS generalists will be employed under outposting arrangements (Hoshino and Weber, 1973). They need to be encouraged to negotiate for themselves the maximum feasible devolution of their sending agency's statutory powers—in the style of the Tynnered project in Sweden (Falklind and others, 1974). If outposted social workers suffer statutory disenfranchisement, their clients are inconvenienced, and it is more difficult for the social workers to develop.

In the years ahead, integrated-services settings are likely to account for an increasing proportion of the social worker work force. In the United States, most social work education programs no longer place major emphasis on the production of designated specialists (medical social workers, psychiatric social workers, and so forth). It is unlikely that expansion of the services-integration approach will produce as glaring and pervasive needs for generalist retraining as those brought about by the Seebohm reorganization in England. Nevertheless, there is likely to be a significant demand for basic professional training programs to be supplemented by continuing education programs designed to provide in-service retooling for generalist practice in integrated-services agencies. The curriculum content issues discussed above are those essentially of degree of emphasis rather than novel issues as such. Nevertheless, they could form the nucleus for the development of worthwhile and enjoyable continuing education courses and seminars.

Extensive research is needed to complement curriculum development efforts. At present, the services-integration field is replete with evaluations of individual projects. Aiken and others (1975) and Gilbert and Specht (1977a) have begun the task of aggregating the experiences acquired during these projects. Much more aggregative research needs to be done. The "case survey" approach is well suited to the aggregation of the experiences reported in single-project evaluations, both published and unpublished (Lucas, 1974; Yin and Heald, 1975). In addition to this aggregative research, there is a need for closely monitored social experiments involving the integration of primary human services in a wide geographical area—as has occurred, for instance, in the Tierp area of Sweden (Berfenstam and Smedby, 1976).

Services integration and holistic care are popular topics for professional debate, particularly among those of us who choose to season our pragmatism with the spice of idealism. However, we need to remind ourselves frequently that, in allegorical terms, we are talking about different ways to cut a pie whose size clearly is finite and may even shrink in the years ahead. Zald (1977, pp. 121–122) recently predicted that "labor-intensive social welfare services will find it increasingly difficult to be funded. . . . In the overall priority of things, the welfare state in Western industrialized countries will be in low gear." Even if Zald's analysis is accepted, there still is every reason to promote and staff truly functional positions for generalist social workers within integrated primary human services agencies. This policy will facilitate the responsible use of scarce professional resources.

References

ABELS, P. *The New Practice of Supervision and Staff Development.* New York: Association Press, 1977.

ABELS, S. "Utilization of Grounded Theory as a Methodological and a Substantive Approach to Social Work Education." Paper presented at the annual program meeting of the Council on Social Work Education, Phoenix, Ariz., Feb. 1977.

AD HOC COMMITTEE ON ADVOCACY. "The Social Worker as Advocate: Champion of Social Victims." *Social Work,* 1969, *14,* 16–22.

AHRONS, C. R. "Interpersonal Skill Development: Establishing the Skill Base." Paper presented at the annual program meeting of the Council on Social Work Education, Phoenix, Ariz., Feb. 1977.

AIKEN, M., and others. *Coordinating Human Services: New Strategies for Building Service Delivery Systems.* San Francisco: Jossey-Bass, 1975.

ALAMSHAH, W. H. "The Conditions for Creativity." *Journal of Creative Behavior,* 1967, *1,* 305–313.

277

ALINSKY, S. *Reveille for Radicals.* Chicago: University of Chicago Press, 1946. (Reprinted by Vintage Books, 1969.)

AMERICAN ASSOCIATION OF SOCIAL WORKERS. *Social Casework— Generic and Specific: An Outline. A Report of the Milford Conference.* Studies in the Practice of Social Work, No. 2. Washington, D.C.: American Association of Social Workers, 1929.

ANDREWS, T. E. "What We Know and What We Don't Know." In W. R. Houston (Ed.), *Exploring Competency Based Education.* Berkeley, Calif.: McCutchan, 1974.

ARGYRIS, C., and SCHÖN, D. A. *Theory in Practice: Increasing Professional Effectiveness.* San Francisco: Jossey-Bass, 1974.

ARKAVA, M. L., and BRENNEN, E. C. "Toward a Competency Examination for the Baccalaureate Social Worker." *Journal of Education for Social Work,* 1975, *11,* 22–29.

ARKAVA, M. L., and BRENNEN, E. C. (Eds.). *Competency-Based Education for Social Work: Evaluation and Curriculum Issues.* New York: Council on Social Work Education, 1976.

ARKAVA, M. L., and others. *Montana Social Work Competence Scales: A Summative Examination for Baccalaureate Social Workers.* Missoula: Department of Social Work, University of Montana, 1976.

ARMITAGE, A., and CLARK, F. W. "Design Issues in the Performance-Based Curriculum." *Journal of Education for Social Work,* 1975, *11,* 22–29.

AUSTIN, D. M. "Identifying Research Priorities in Social Work Education." Paper presented at the Conference on Research Utilization in Social Work Education, Council on Social Work Education, New Orleans, Aug. 1977.

AUSTIN, D. M., and LAUDERDALE, M. L. "Preparing Public Welfare Administrators." *Public Welfare,* 1976, *34,* 14–18.

AUSTIN, M. J. "Defining the Nature of Human Service Work for Personnel Systems Management." *Administration in Social Work,* 1977, *1,* 31–41.

AUSTIN, M. J., and SKELDING, A. H. *Personnel and Staff Development Planning for the Human Services.* Tallahassee: State University System of Florida, 1975.

AUSTIN, M. J., SKELDING, A. H., and SMITH, P. L. *Delivering Human Services: An Introductory Programmed Text.* New York: Harper & Row, 1977.

AUSTIN, M. J., and SMITH, P. L. *The Florida Human Service Task Bank*. Vol. 2. Final Report of the Florida Board of Regents, Office of Career Planning and Curriculum Development for the Human Services. Tallahassee: State University System of Florida, 1975.

AUSUBEL, D. P. "Some Psychological Aspects of Curriculum Theory." *Samplings* (entire issue). Albuquerque, N.M.: Future Schools Study Project, Albuquerque Public Schools, 1968.

AUTHIER, J., and GUSTAFSON, K. "Application of Supervised and Nonsupervised Microcounseling Paradigms in the Training of Paraprofessionals." *Journal of Counseling Psychology*, 1975, *22*, 74–78.

AYLLON, T., and AZRIN, N. H. *The Token Economy*. New York: Appleton-Century-Crofts, 1968.

BAER, B., and FEDERICO, R. C. *Educating the Baccalaureate Social Worker: Report of the Undergraduate Social Work Curriculum Development Project*. Cambridge, Mass.: Ballinger, 1978.

BANDURA, A. *Principles of Behavior Modification*. New York: Holt, Rinehart and Winston, 1969.

BARKER, R., and BRIGGS, T. (Eds.). *Manpower Research on the Utilization of Baccalaureate Social Workers: Implications for Education*. Washington, D.C.: U.S. Government Printing Office, 1972.

BARR, H. "The Reorganization of the Social Services in England and Wales: In Search of the Lessons for Other Countries." Paper presented at the Big Sky Summer Symposium, Big Sky, Mont., Aug. 1977. (Available from the author at the Central Council for Education and Training in Social Work, Derbyshire House, St. Chad's Street, London WC1H 8AD, England.)

BARLETT, H. M. *The Common Base of Social Work Practice*. Washington, D.C.: National Association of Social Workers, 1970.

BASSOFF, B. Z. "Interdisciplinary Education for Health Professionals: Issues and Directions." *Social Work in Health Care*, 1976, *2*, 219–228.

BENSCHOTTER, R., and others. "The Use of Closed Circuit TV and Videotape in the Training of Social Group Workers." *Social Work Education Reporter*, 1967, *15*, 26–29.

BERDYAEV, N. *The Meaning of the Creative Act*. (D. A. Lowrie, Trans.) London: Gollancz, 1955.

BERFENSTAM, R., and SMEDBY, B. "Collaboration Between Medical and Social Care." *Socialmedicinsk Tidskrift,* 1976, *53,* 365–372.

BERGIN, A. E. "The Evaluation of Therapeutic Outcomes." In A. E. Bergin and S. L. Garfield (Eds.), *Handbook of Psychotherapy and Behavior Change.* New York: Wiley, 1971.

BIESTEK, F. P. *The Casework Relationship.* Chicago: Loyola University Press, 1957.

BISNO, H. *The Place of the Undergraduate Curriculum in Social Work Education.* New York: Council on Social Work Education, 1959.

BISNO, H. "A Theoretical Framework for Teaching Social Work Methods and Skills, with Particular Reference to Undergraduate Social Welfare Education." *Education for Social Work,* 1969, *5,* 5–17.

BLOOM, B. S., and others (Eds.). *Taxonomy of Educational Objectives.* Handbook I: *Cognitive Domain;* Handbook II: *Affective Domain.* New York: McKay, 1956, 1964.

BLOOM, M. *Paradox of Helping: Introduction to the Philosophy of Scientific Practice.* New York: Wiley, 1975.

BLOOM, M. "Analysis of the Research on Educating Social Work Students." *Journal of Education for Social Work,* 1976a, *12,* 3–10.

BLOOM, M. "Practice Through Measurement." In B. Ross and S. K. Khinduka (Eds.), *Social Work in Practice.* Washington, D.C.: National Association of Social Workers, 1976b.

BLOOM, M. "Choices in the Evaluation of Clinical Practice." Paper presented at the annual program meeting of the Council on Social Work Education, New Orleans, Feb. 1978.

BLOOM, M., and BLOCK, S. "Evaluating One's Own Effectiveness and Efficiency." *Social Work,* 1977, *22,* 130–136.

BLOOM, M., BUTCH, P., and WALKER, D. "Single-System Designs for One-Time Contacts: N = 1, T = 1." Unpublished manuscript, 1978.

BLOOM, M., and GORDON, W. E. "Measurement Through Practice." Paper presented at the annual program meeting of the Council on Social Work Education, Philadelphia, Feb. 1976.

BOEHM, W. *Objectives of the Social Work Curriculum of the Future.* New York: Council on Social Work Education, 1959.

BOULDING, K. E. "Toward a General Theory of Growth." *Canadian Journal of Economics and Political Science,* 1953, *19,* 326–340.

BOWERS, S. "The Nature and Definition of Social Casework." In C. Kasius (Ed.), *Principles and Techniques in Social Casework.* New York: Family Service Association of America, 1950.

BRAGER, G. "The Indigenous Worker: A New Approach to the Social Work Technician." *Social Work,* 1965, *10,* 33–40.

BRAMMER, L. M. *The Helping Relationship.* Englewood Cliffs, N.J.: Prentice-Hall, 1973.

BRAY, D. W., CAMPBELL, R. J., and GRANT, D. L. *Formative Years in Business: A Long-Term AT&T Study of Managerial Lives.* New York: Wiley-Interscience, 1974.

BRAY, D. W., and GRANT, D. L. "The Assessment Center in the Measurement of Potential for Business Management." *Psychological Monographs,* 1966, *80* (Whole No. 625).

BRENNEN, E. C. "Is the Work Sample Approach Feasible?" In M. L. Arkava and E. C. Brennen (Eds.), *Competency-Based Education for Social Work: Evaluation and Curriculum Issues.* New York: Council on Social Work Education, 1976.

BRIAR, S. "The Current Crisis in Social Casework." In S. Briar (Ed.), *Social Work Practice.* New York: Columbia University Press, 1967.

BRIAR, S. "Social Casework," *Social Work,* 1973a, *18,* 4.

BRIAR, S. "Effective Social Work Intervention in Direct Practice: Implications for Education." In *Facing the Challenge.* Plenary session papers from the 19th Annual Program Meeting of the Council on Social Work Education, New York, Council on Social Work Education, 1973b.

BRIAR, S. "Generalists, Specialists, and Territory." *Social Work,* 1976, *21,* 262, 341.

BRIAR, S. "Social Work Practice: Contemporary Issues." In J. B. Turner (Ed.), *Encyclopedia of Social Work.* Vol. 2. Washington, D.C.: National Association of Social Workers, 1977.

BROWN, R. G. S. "Collaboration Between the National Health Service and Local Government." *Local Government Studies,* 1976, *6,* 15–25.

BURIAN, W. A. "The Laboratory as an Element in Social Work

Curriculum Design." *Journal of Education for Social Work*, 1976, *12*, 36–43.

BURKE, J. B. "Curriculum Design." In R. Housman (Ed.), *Competency Based Teacher Education*. Chicago: Science Association, 1972.

BURNS, E. "Social Welfare Is Our Commitment." In *The Social Welfare Forum*, 1958. New York: Columbia University Press, 1958.

BURRILL, G. C. "Competency-Based Curriculum Development: An Experimental Model for Social Service Workers." *Alternative Higher Education*, 1977, *1*, 17–26.

BUTLER, H., and BILORUSKY, J. "Experimenting Community: A New Curriculum for Human Service Professionals." *Education and Urban Society*, 1975, *7*, 117–139.

BUTLER, H., and RICHMOND, S. "Concrete Comparison, Generalization, and Validation in Social Research and Practice." *Philosophy in Context*, 1977, *6*, 82–105.

BYHAM, W. C. "Assessment Centers for Spotting Future Managers." *Harvard Business Review*, 1970, *48*, 150–160, plus Appendix.

CALLAHAN, R. E. *Education and the Cult of Efficiency*. Chicago: University of Chicago Press, 1962.

CAMPBELL, D. T., and STANLEY, J. C. *Experimental and Quasi-Experimental Design for Research*. Chicago: Rand McNally, 1963.

CANADIAN ASSOCIATION OF SOCIAL WORKERS. *Competence in Social Work Practices: Report on a Study of Competence*. Ottawa, Ont.: Canadian Association of Social Workers, 1969.

CANNON, I. M. *Social Work in Hospitals*. New York: Russell Sage Foundation, 1923.

CANNON, I. C. "Medicine as a Social Instrument: Medical Social Service." *New England Journal of Medicine*, 1951, *244*, 715–725.

CARKHUFF, R. R. *Helping and Human Relations*. (2 vols.) New York: Holt, Rinehart and Winston, 1969.

CARKHUFF, R. R. *The Development of Human Resources*. New York: Holt, Rinehart and Winston, 1972.

CARR, L. W. "The Montana Experience: A Critical Analysis." In M. L. Arkava and E. C. Brennen (Eds.), *Competency-Based*

Education for Social Work: Evaluation and Curriculum Issues.
New York: Council on Social Work Education, 1976.

CATTELL, R. *Manual for Forms A and B, Sixteen Personality Factors Questionnaire.* Champaign, Ill.: Institute for Personality and Ability Testing, 1962.

CHASE, A. *The Legacy of Malthus.* New York: Knopf, 1977.

CHICKERING, A. W. "Developmental Change as a Major Outcome." In M. T. Keeton and associates, *Experiential Learning: Rationale, Characteristics, and Assessment.* San Francisco: Jossey-Bass, 1976.

CHOMMIE, P. W., and HUDSON, J. "Evaluation of Outcome and Process." *Social Work,* 1974, *19,* 682–687.

CHURCHMAN, C. W. *The Systems Approach.* New York: Dell, 1968.

CLARK, F. W. "Characteristics of Competency-Based Curriculum." In M. L. Arkava and E. C. Brennen (Eds.), *Competency-Based Education for Social Work: Evaluation and Curriculum Issues.* New York: Council on Social Work Education, 1976.

CLUBOCK, M. "Evaluating the Effectiveness of a Helping Skills Training Program." *Journal of Applied Social Sciences,* 1978, *2,* 33–41.

COLLIER, K. *Rural Social Work—Theory and Practice.* Regina, Saskatchewan, Canada: University of Regina Faculty of Social Work, 1977.

COMMITTEE ON LOCAL AUTHORITY AND ALLIED PERSONAL SOCIAL SERVICES. *Report of the Committee on Local Authority and Allied Personal Social Services.* Command 3703. London: Her Majesty's Stationery Office, 1969.

COMMITTEE ON THE STUDY OF COMPETENCE. *Guidelines for the Assessment of Professional Practice in Social Work.* Washington, D.C.: National Association of Social Workers, 1968.

COOPER, B., and others. "Mental Health Care in the Community: An Evaluative Study." *Psychological Medicine,* 1975, *5,* 372–380.

COUNCIL ON SOCIAL WORK EDUCATION. *Relationship Between Social Work Practice and Education: A Report of the Task Force on Practice and Education.* New York: Council on Social Work Education, 1974a.

COUNCIL ON SOCIAL WORK EDUCATION. *Standards for the Accred-*

itation of Baccalaureate Social Work Programs. New York: Council on Social Work Education, 1974b.

COUNCIL ON SOCIAL WORK EDUCATION. *Summary of Discussion and Action by Board of Directors at Its Meeting of January 20–21, 1975.* New York: Council on Social Work Education, 1975.

COUNCIL ON SOCIAL WORK EDUCATION. *Teaching for Competence in the Delivery of Direct Services.* New York: Council on Social Work Education, 1976.

COUNTRYSIDE COUNCIL. *Report on Human Services Integration.* Marshall, Minn.: Countryside Council, 1975.

COYLE, G. L. *Group Work with American Youth.* New York: Harper & Row, 1948.

CRANE, J. A. *Interpersonal Competence and Performance in Social Work.* Vancouver: School of Social Work, University of British Columbia, 1974.

CREBOLDER, E. "The 'Home-Front' as the Extra-Mural 'Discipline'." *Huisarts en Wetenschap,* 1976, *19,* 108–109.

CREWS, J. W., and DICKERSON, Z. S., JR. (Eds.). *Curriculum Development in Education for Business.* Reston, Va.: National Business Education Association, 1977.

CUMMINS, D. E. "The Assessment Procedure." In M. L. Arkava and E. C. Brennen (Eds.), *Competency-Based Education for Social Work: Evaluation and Curriculum Issues.* New York: Council on Social Work Education, 1976.

CUNNINGHAM, R. M., JR. *The Holistic Health Centers: A New Direction in Health Care.* Battle Creek, Mich.: W. K. Kellogg Foundation, 1977.

CURRAN, J. P. "Skills Training as an Approach to the Treatment of Heterosexual-Social Anxiety: A Review." *Psychological Bulletin,* 1977, *84,* 140–157.

DALTON, R. F., SUNBLAD, L., and HYLBERT, K. W. "An Application of Principles of Social Learning to Training in Communication of Empathy." *Journal of Counseling Psychology,* 1973, *20,* 378–383.

DANISH, S. J., D'AUGELLI, A. R., and BROCK, G. W. "An Evaluation of Helping Skills Training: Effects on Helper's Verbal Responses." *Journal of Counseling Psychology,* 1976, *23,* 259–266.

DANISH, S., and HAUER, A. *Helping Skills: A Basic Training Program*. New York: Behavioral Publications, 1973.

D'AUGELLI, A. R. "Nonverbal Behavior of Helpers in Initial Helping Interactions." *Journal of Counseling Psychology*, 1974, *21*, 360–363.

D'AUGELLI, A. R., DANISH, S. J., and BROCK, G. W. "Untrained Paraprofessionals' Verbal Helping Behavior." *American Journal of Community Psychology*, 1976, *4*, 275–282.

DAVIES, I. *Competency Based Learning: Technology, Management, and Design*. New York: McGraw-Hill, 1973.

DE BONO, E. *PO: A Device for Successful Thinking*. New York: Simon & Schuster, 1972.

DE GROOT, M., and MAERTENS, N. "The Difficult Practice at the Hoensbroek Health Center." *De Eerste Lign*, Nov./Dec. 1975, pp. 8–13.

DE MARCO, J. P., and RICHMOND, S. A. "Justice, Respect for Persons, and the Scientific Method." Unpublished manuscript, Cleveland State University, 1975.

DEMBART, L. "Experts Argue Whether Computers Could Reason." *New York Times*, May 8, 1977, p. 34.

DOLGOFF, R. "Basic Skills for Practice in the Human Services: A Curriculum Guide." In F. M. Loewenberg and R. Dolgoff (Eds.), *Teaching of Practice Skills in Undergraduate Programs in Social Welfare and Other Helping Services*. New York: Council on Social Work Education, 1971.

DU BOIS, V. "The Hoensbroek-North Health Care Center Illuminated from Another Side." *Huisarts en Wetenschap*, 1971, *14*, 137–138.

DU BOIS, V. "The Shaky Equilibrium of the Team of a Health Care Center." *Huisarts en Wetenschap*, 1976, *19*, 178–180.

DUEHN, W. D., and MAYADAS, N. S. "Entrance and Exit Requirements of Professional Social Work Education." *Journal of Education for Social Work*, 1977, *13*, 22–29.

EGAN, G. *The Skilled Helper: A Model for Systematic Helping and Interpersonal Relating*. Monterey, Calif.: Brooks/Cole, 1975.

ELLIS, H. C. *The Transfer of Learning*. New York: Macmillan, 1965.

ELLIS, J. A. N., and BRYANT, V. E. "Competency-Based Certification for School Social Workers." *Social Work*, 1976, *21*, 381–385.

EMERY, F. E. (Ed.), *Systems Theory Thinking: Selected Readings.* New York: Penguin Books, 1969.

EPSTEIN, L. "Task-Centered Treatment After Five Years." In B. Ross and S. K. Khinduka (Eds.), *Social Work in Practice.* Washington, D.C.: National Association of Social Workers, 1976.

ETZIONI, A. *Modern Organizations.* Englewood Cliffs, N.J.: Prentice-Hall, 1964.

EVANS, R. I. "Smoking in Children: Developing a Social Psychological Strategy of Deterrence." *Preventive Medicine*, 1976, *5*, 122–127.

FALKLIND, H., and others. "The Tynnered Project: Integration of Primary Health Care and Social Welfare Activities." *Lakartidningen*, 1974, *74*, 596–598.

FEDERICO, R. *The Social Welfare Institution.* Lexington, Mass.: Heath, 1973.

FIEDLER, D. "The Decision to Be Assertive." *Journal of Consulting and Clinical Psychology*, 1978, in press.

FINE, S., and WILEY, W. *An Introduction to Functional Job Analysis: A Scaling of Selected Tasks from the Social Welfare Field.* Kalamazoo, Mich.: W. E. Upjohn Institute for Employment Research, 1971.

FINKEL, A., and NORMAN, G. R. "The Validity of Direct Observation in Assessment of Clinical Skills." In *Research in Medical Education: Twelfth Annual Conference.* Washington, D.C.: Association of American Medical Colleges, 1973.

FISCHER, J. *The Effectiveness of Social Casework.* Springfield, Ill.: Thomas, 1976.

FISCHER, J. *Effective Casework Practice: An Eclectic Approach.* New York: McGraw-Hill, 1978.

FISCHER, J., and GOCHROS, H. *Planned Behavior Change: Behavior Modification in Social Work.* New York: Free Press, 1975.

FLEMING, J. B., and WASHBURNE, C. K. *For Better, For Worse—A Feminist Handbook on Marriage and Other Options.* New York: Scribner's, 1977.

FOOTE, N. N., and COTTRELL, L. S., JR. *Identity and Interpersonal Competence.* Chicago: University of Chicago Press, 1955.

FOX, P. D., and RAPPAPORT, M. "Some Approaches to Evaluating Community Health Services." *Archives of General Psychiatry,* 1972, *26,* 172–178.

FREIRE, P. *Pedagogy of the Oppressed.* New York: Seabury Press, 1970.

FREIRE, P. *Education for Critical Consciousness.* New York: Seabury Press, 1973.

FROMM, E. *Escape from Freedom.* New York: Holt, Rinehart and Winston, 1941.

GAGE, R. W. "Integration of Human Services Delivery Systems." *Public Welfare,* 1976, *34,* 27–33.

GAMBRILL, E. D. *Behavior Modification: Handbook of Assessment, Intervention, and Evaluation.* San Francisco: Jossey-Bass, 1977.

GAMBRILL, E. D., and RICHEY, C. A. *It's Up to You: Developing Assertive Social Skills.* Millbrae, Calif.: Les Femmes Publishing, 1976.

GARDNER, L. "Humanistic Education and Behavioral Objectives: Opposing Theories of Educational Science." *School Review,* 1977, *86,* 376–394.

GARRETT, A. *Interviewing: Its Principles and Methods.* New York: Family Association of America, 1942.

GENERAL MILLS. *The General Mills American Family Report 1974–1975: A Study of the American Family and Money.* Minneapolis: General Mills, 1975.

GIJSMAN, J. B. "Five Years' Registration of Current Research in and on First-Line Health Care." *Huisarts en Wetenschap,* 1976, *19,* 303–305.

GILBERT, N., and SPECHT, H. "The Incomplete Profession." *Social Work,* 1974, *19,* 665–674.

GILBERT, N., and SPECHT, H. "Advocacy and Professional Ethics." *Social Work,* 1976, *21,* 288–293.

GILBERT, N., and SPECHT, H. *Coordinating Social Services: An Analysis of Community, Organizational, and Staff Characteristics.* New York: Praeger, 1977a.

GILBERT, N., and SPECHT, H. "Social Planning and Community

Organization: Approaches." In J. Turner (Ed.), *Encyclopedia of Social Work*. Vol. 2. Washington, D.C.: National Association of Social Workers, 1977b.

GLASER, B. C., and STRAUSS, A. L. *The Discovery of Grounded Theory*. Chicago: Aldine, 1967.

GLICK, L. (Ed.). *Undergraduate Social Work Education for Practice: A Report on Curriculum Content and Issues*. Washington, D.C.: U.S. Government Printing Office, 1972.

GLICK, L. J. "Social Work Education: Traditional or Competency-Based?" Paper presented collaboratively with G. Gross and W. Ehlers at the Southern Regional Educational Board, Atlanta, Ga., Feb. 1974.

GOLDBERG, H., and LEWIS, R. G. *Money Madness: The Psychology of Saving, Spending, Loving, and Hating Money*. New York: Morrow, 1978.

GOLDSTEIN, A., HELLER, K., and SECHREST, L. *Psychotherapy and the Psychology of Behavior Change*. New York: Wiley, 1966.

GOLDSTEIN, A., and SORCHER, M. *Changing Supervisor Behavior*. Elmsford, N.Y.: Pergamon Press, 1974.

GOLDSTEIN, H. *Social Work Practice: A Unitary Approach*. Columbia: University of South Carolina Press, 1973.

GOODWIN, M. *Correlates of Career Choice: A Comparative Study of Recruits to the Health Professions and Other Professional Fields*. Vancouver: School of Social Work, University of British Columbia, 1972.

GORDON, W. E. "A Critique of the Working Definition." *Social Work*, 1962, 7, 3–13.

GORDON, W. E., and SCHUTZ, M. L. *Final Report: Field Instruction Research Project*. St. Louis, Mo.: George Warren Brown School of Social Work, Washington University, 1962.

GORMALLY, J., and HILL, C. E. "Guidelines for Research on Carkhuff's Training Model." *Journal of Counseling Psychology*, 1974, 21, 539–547.

GOTTMAN, J. M., and LEIBLUM, S. R. *How to Do Psychotherapy and How to Evaluate It*. New York: Holt, Rinehart and Winston, 1974.

HACKMAN, J. R., and OLDHAM, G. R. "Development of Job Diagnostic Survey." *Journal of Applied Psychology*, 1975, *60*, 159–170.

HACKMAN, J. R., and OLDHAM, G. R. "Motivation Through Design of Work: Test of a Theory." *Organizational Behavior and Human Performance*, 1976, *16*, 250–279.

HACKNEY, H., and NYE, S. *Counseling Strategies and Objectives*. Englewood Cliffs, N.J.: Prentice-Hall, 1973.

HALL, P. B. *Family Credit Counseling: An Emerging Community Service*. New York: Family Service Association of America, 1968.

HANSON, D., and others. *Wisconsin Career Executive Program and Executive Assessment Center: A Comprehensive Management Review*. Madison: Wisconsin Department of Administration, 1976.

HASENFELD, Y. "People Processing Organizations: An Exchange Approach." In Y. Hasenfeld and R. A. English (Eds.), *Human Service Organizations: A Book of Readings*. Ann Arbor: University of Michigan Press, 1974.

HEIMLER, E. *Survival in Society*. London: Wiedenfeld and Nicolson, 1975.

HERSEN, M., and BARLOW, D. N. *Single Case Experimental Designs: Strategies for Studying Behavior Change*. Elmsford, N.Y.: Pergamon Press, 1976.

HERTZBERG, H. W. "Competency Based Teacher Education—Does It Have a Past or a Future?" *Teachers College Record*, 1976, *78*, 20–21.

HILL, R. *Family Development in Three Generations: A Longitudinal Study of Changing Family Patterns of Planning and Achievement*. Cambridge, Mass.: Schenkman, 1970.

HO, M. K. "Evaluation: A Means of Treatment." *Social Work*, 1976, *21*, 24–27.

HOLLIS, E. *Casework: A Psychosocial Theory*. New York: Random House, 1964.

HOLLIS, E., and TAYLOR, A. *Social Work Education in the United States*. New York: Columbia University Press, 1951.

HOOKEY, P. "Education for Social Work in Health Care Organizations." *Social Work in Health Care*, 1976, *2*, 337–345.

HOOKEY, P. " 'De Eerste Lign': A Dutch Pressure Group of International Significance." Paper presented at the annual meeting of the American Public Health Association, Washington, D.C., Nov. 1977a. (Available from the author at the School of Social Work, University of Illinois, Urbana.)

HOOKEY, P. "The Establishment of Social Worker Participation in Rural Primary Health Care." *Social Work in Health Care*, 1977b, *3*, 87–99.

HOOKEY, P. "Social Work in Group Medical Practice: An Introduction to Developments in Ten Countries." *International Social Work*, 1977c, *20*, 24–29.

HOOKEY, P. "Social Work in Primary Health Care." *Social Work in Health Care*. 1978, *4*, 241–254.

HOSHINO, G., and WEBER, S. "Outposting in the Public Welfare Services." *Public Welfare*, 1973, *31*, 8–14.

HOUSTON, W. R. (Ed.). *Exploring Competency Based Education.* Berkeley, Calif.: McCutchan, 1974.

HOUSTON, W. R., and ALLEN, R. W. "The Competency-Based Movement: Origins and Future." *Educational Technology*, 1977, *18*, 14–19.

HOWARD, A. "An Assessment of Assessment Centers." *Academy of Management Journal*, 1974, *17*, 115–134.

HOWE, M. W. "Casework Self-Evaluation: A Single-Subject Approach." *Social Service Review*, 1974, *48*, 1–23.

HUCK, J. R. "Assessment Centers: A Review of External and Internal Validities." *Personnel Psychology*, 1973, *26*, 191–212.

HUDSON, W. "Elementary Techniques for Assessing Single Client/Single Worker Interventions." Paper presented at the annual program meeting of the Council on Social Work Education, San Francisco, Feb. 1975.

HUETT, D. L. *The Structure of Final Ratings Rendered at Wisconsin's Executive Assessment Center.* Madison, Wisc.: State Bureau of Personnel, 1975.

HUNTER, F. *Community Power Structure: A Study of Decision Makers.* Chapel Hill: University of North Carolina Press, 1953.

HUYGEN, F. J. A. "The Home-Team." *Huisarts en Wetenschap*, 1962, *5*, 119–123.

HYER, A. L., and others. *Jobs in Instructional Media Study.* Washington, D.C.: National Education Association, 1971.

INGHE, G., and ROLANDER, A. "Social-Medical Experiment in Luleå." *Lakartidningen,* 1974, *71,* 2627–2630.

IVEY, A. E. *Microcounseling: Innovations in Interviewing Training.* Springfield, Ill.: Thomas, 1971.

IVEY, A. E., and AUTHIER, J. *Microcounseling: Innovations in Interviewing, Counseling, Psychotherapy, and Psychoeducation.* Springfield, Ill.: Thomas, 1978.

IVEY, A., and GLUCKSTERN, N. *Basic Attending Skills, Leader and Participant Manuals.* North Amherst, Mass.: Microtraining, 1974.

IVEY, A., and GLUCKSTERN, N. *Basic Influencing Skills, Leader and Participant Manuals.* North Amherst, Mass.: Microtraining, 1976.

JACKSON, B. W., III. "Black Identity Development Theory." Amherst: University of Massachusetts, 1973.

JANIS, I. L. *Victims of Groupthink.* Boston: Houghton Mifflin, 1972.

JARRETT, H. H., JR. "Implications of Implementing Competency Based Education in the Liberal Arts." *Educational Technology,* 1977, *17,* 21–26.

JARRETT, H. H., KILPATRICK, A., and POLLANE, L. P. "Operationalizing Competency-Based BSW Field Experience." Paper presented at the annual program meeting of the Council on Social Work Education, Phoenix, Ariz., Feb. 1977.

JENSEN, T. A., and others. *The Devils Lake Comprehensive Human Services Center.* Devils Lake, N.D.: Devils Lake Human Services Center, 1973.

JONES, J. E., and PFEIFFER, J. W. *The 1973 Annual Handbook of Group Facilitators.* La Jolla, Calif.: University Associates, 1973.

JOYCE, B., and WEIT, M. *Models of Teaching.* Englewood Cliffs, N.J.: Prentice-Hall, 1972.

KADUSHIN, A. *The Social Work Interview.* New York: Columbia University Press, 1972.

KADUSHIN, A., and KELLING, G. *Final Report: An Innovative Program in Social Work Education: The 3-2 Program.* Madison: School of Social Work, University of Wisconsin, 1973.

KAGAN, N. *Influencing Human Interaction.* East Lansing: Michigan State University Press, 1972a.

KAGAN, N. "Observations and Suggestions." *Counseling Psychologist,* 1972b, *3,* 42–45.

KAGAN, N. *Interpersonal Process Recall: A Method of Influencing Human Interaction.* East Lansing: Michigan State University Press, 1975.

KAGAN, N., KRATHWOHL, D. R., and MILLER, R. "Simulated Recall in Therapy Using Videotape—A Case Study." *Journal of Counseling Psychology,* 1963, *10,* 237–243.

KAGAN, N., and others. "Interpersonal Process Recall." *Journal of Nervous and Mental Diseases,* 1969, *148,* 365–374.

KAHN, A., and KAMERMAN, S. *Social Services in the United States.* Philadelphia: Temple University Press, 1976.

KANE, R. "Look to the Record." *Social Work,* 1974, *19,* 412–419.

KAPLAN, A. *The Conduct of Inquiry: Methodology for Behavioral Science.* Scranton, Pa.: Chandler, 1964.

KATZ, D., and others. "Starting Out in Television: A Student Centered Approach to Media." *Journal of Education for Social Work,* 1975, *11,* 83–88.

KELLEY, E. L., and FISKE, D. W. *The Prediction of Performance in Clinical Psychology.* Ann Arbor: University of Michigan Press, 1951.

KIESLER, D. J. *The Process of Psychotherapy.* Chicago: Aldine, 1973.

KIRESUK, T. J., and SHERMAN, R. E. "Goal Attainment Scaling: A General Method for Evaluating Comprehensive Community Mental Health Programs." *Community Mental Health Journal,* 1968, *4,* 443–453.

KIRK, S. A., OSMALOV, M. J., and FISCHER, J. "Social Workers' Involvement in Research." *Social Work,* 1976, *21,* 121–124.

KIRSCHENBAUM, H. "Clarifying Values Clarification: Some Theoretical Issues and a Review of Research." *Group and Organization Studies,* 1976, *1,* 99–116.

KLENK, R., and RYAN, R. *The Practice of Social Work.* (2nd ed.) Belmont, Calif.: Wadsworth, 1974.

KNOTT, W. Personal communication. Faculty of Social Welfare, University of Calgary, June 1978.

KOHLBERG, L. "Stage and Sequence: The Cognitive Development Approach to Socialization." In D. A. Goslin (Ed.), *Handbook of Socialization Theory and Research*. Chicago: Rand McNally, 1969.

KOHLBERG, L. "Moral Education for a Society in Moral Transition." *Educational Leadership*, Oct. 1975, pp. 46–54.

KORBELIK, J., and EPSTEIN, L. "Evaluating Time and Achievement in a Social Work Practicum." In *Teaching for Competence in the Delivery of Direct Services*. New York: Council on Social Work Education, 1976.

KRUEGER, L. "An Evaluation of Consumer Credit Counseling Service in Butte, Montana." Unpublished master's thesis, Montana State University, 1970.

KRUZICH, J. "Working Paper 1: Job Analysis of Minnesota Public Welfare Administrators." Social Welfare Administration Project. St. Paul: Minnesota Department of Public Welfare, Nov. 1975.

KURZMAN, P. A. (Ed.). *The Mississippi Experience*. New York: Association Press, 1971.

LAKEIN, A. *How to Get Control of Your Time and Your Life*. New York: New American Library, 1974.

LAMBERT, M. J., and DEJULIO, S. S. "Outcome Research in Carkhuff's Human Resource Development Training Programs: Where Is the Donut?" *Counseling Psychologist*, 1977, *6*, 79–86.

LARSEN, J., and HEPWORTH, D. H. "Skill Development Through Competency-Based Education." *Journal of Education for Social Work*, 1978, *14*, 73–81.

LATHROPE, D. E. "The General Systems Approach in Social Work Practice." In G. Hearn (Ed.), *The General Systems Approach: Contributions Toward an Holistic Conception of Social Work*. New York: Council on Social Work Education, 1969.

LAUGHLIN, J. L., and BRESSLER, R. "Family Agency Programs for Heavily Indebted Families." *Social Casework*, 1971, *52*, 617–626.

LEE, P. *Social Work as Cause and Function and Other Papers*. New York: Columbia University Press, 1937.

LEVIN, A. M. "Private Practice Is Alive and Well." *Social Work*, 1976, *21*, 356–362.

LEVINE, T. "Skill in Practice as a Problem in Public Welfare." In

F. D. Perlmutter (Ed.), *A Design for Social Work Practice*. New York: Columbia University Press, 1974.

LEWIN, K. *Field Theory in Social Science*. (D. Cartwright, Ed.) New York: Harper & Row, 1951.

LEWIS, H. "Morality and the Politics of Practice." *Social Casework*, 1972, *53*, 404–417.

LEWIS, J., and LIBERMAN, H. "Use of Videotape to Diagnose and Treat an Exceptional Child." *Social Casework*, 1970, *51*, 417–420.

LINDBLOM, A. "Social Care and Health Care at Tierp with a Corridor in Between." *Social Forum*, 1974, *9*, 545–548.

LINN, B. S., AROSTEQUI, M., and ZAPPA, R. "Peer and Self-Assessment in the Quest for Evaluative Techniques That Predict Delivery of Quality Care." In *Research in Medical Education: Twelfth Annual Conference*. Washington, D.C. Association of American Medical Colleges, 1973.

LITWAK, E. "Extended Kin Relations in an Industrial Society." In E. Shanas and G. Strieb (Eds.), *Social Structure and the Family: Generational Relations*. Englewood Cliffs, N.J.: Prentice-Hall, 1965.

LOCKWOOD, T. D. "Point of View." *Chronicle of Higher Education*, 1977, *14*, 32.

LOEB, M. "Social Class and the American Social System." *Social Work*, 1961, *6*, 12–18.

LOEVINGER, J., and WESSLER, R. *Measuring Ego Development*. Vol. 1: *Construction and Use of a Sentence Completion Test*. San Francisco: Jossey-Bass, 1970.

LOEWENBERG, F. M. *Fundamentals of Social Intervention*. New York: Columbia University Press, 1977.

LOSONCY, L. E. *Turning People On*. Englewood Cliffs, N.J.: Prentice-Hall, 1977.

LUBOVE, R. *The Professional Altruist*. Cambridge, Mass.: Harvard University Press, 1965.

LUCAS, W. *The Case Survey Method: Aggregating Case Experience*. Publication No. R-1515-RC. Santa Monica, Calif.: Rand Corporation, 1974.

MC CORMICK, E. J., JEANNERET, P. R., and MECHAM, R. C. *The Development and Background of the Position Analysis Question-*

naire (*PAQ*). Lafayette, Ind.: Occupational Research Center, Purdue University, 1969.

MC FALL, R. M., and TWENTYMAN, C. T. "Four Experiments on the Relative Contributions of Rehearsal, Modeling, and Coaching to Assertion Training." *Journal of Abnormal Psychology*, 1973, *81*, 199–218.

MACKNOWIAK, R., and GONNELLA, J. "Clinical Competence as Measured by the National Board." Part III. In *Research in Medical Education: Twelfth Annual Conference*. Washington, D.C.: Association of American Medical Colleges, 1973.

MC PHEETERS, H. L., and RYAN, R. M. *A Core of Competence for Baccalaureate Social Welfare and Curricular Implications*. Atlanta, Ga.: Southern Regional Education Board, 1971.

MADISON, B. *Undergraduate Education for Social Welfare*. San Francisco: Rosenberg Foundation, 1960.

MAGER, R. F. *Preparing Instructional Objectives*. Belmont, Calif.: Fearon, 1962a.

MAGER, R. F. *Preparing Objectives for Programmed Instruction*. Belmont, Calif.: Fearon, 1962b.

MALUCCIO, A., and MARLOW, W. "The Case for the Contract." *Social Work*, 1974, *19*, 28–36.

MARCUS, G. F. *Some Aspects of Relief in Family Casework: An Evaluation of Practice Based on a Study Made for the Charity Organization Society of New York*. New York: Charity Organization Society, 1929.

MARLATT, G. A., and others. "Effect of Exposure to a Model Receiving Evaluative Feedback upon Subsequent Behavior in an Interview." *Journal of Consulting and Clinical Psychology*, 1970, *34*, 104–112.

MARSHALL, E. K., CHARPING, J. W., and BELL, W. J. "Training in Basic Interpersonal Helping Skills: An Adaptation of the Micro-Teaching Model." Paper presented at the annual program meeting of the Council on Social Work Education, Phoenix, Ariz., Feb. 1977.

MASLANY, G. W., and WIEGAND, C. F. "The Reliability of a Procedure for Selecting Students into a Bachelor of Social Work Program." *Canadian Journal of Social Work Education*, 1974, *1*, 33–45.

MASLOW, A. H. *Motivation and Personality.* New York: Harper & Row, 1954.

MASLOW, A. H. *Toward a Psychology of Being.* New York: D. Van Nostrand, 1968.

MASWELL, W. D. "PBTE—A Case of the Emperor's New Clothing." *Phi Delta Kappan,* 1974, *55,* 306–311.

MATTARAZZO, J. D., and others. "Speech and Silence Behavior in Clinical Psychology and Its Laboratory Correlates." In J. M. Schlien (Ed.), *Research in Psychotherapy.* Washington, D.C.: American Psychological Association, 1968.

MAYADAS, N. S., and DUEHN, W. D. "Videotape Instructional Techniques for Teaching Specific Facilitative Interpersonal Behaviors." Paper presented at the annual forum of the National Conference on Social Welfare, Cincinnati, 1974.

MAYADAS, N. S., and O'BRIEN, D. E. "Teaching Casework Skills in the Laboratory: Methods and Techniques." In *Teaching for Competence in the Delivery of Direct Services.* New York: Council on Social Work Education, 1976a.

MAYADAS, N. S., and O'BRIEN, D. E. "Technology and Social Casework: A Review of the Literature." In *Teaching for Competence in the Delivery of Direct Services.* New York: Council on Social Work Education, 1976b.

MEICHENBAUM, D. "Cognitive Modification of Test Anxious College Students." *Journal of Consulting and Clinical Psychology,* 1972, *39,* 370–380.

MELTZOFF, J., and KORNREICH, K. M. *Research in Psychotherapy.* Chicago: Aldine, 1970.

"MERCHANTS OF DEBT." *Time,* Feb. 28, 1977, p. 36.

MEYER, C. H. "Quality and Accountability in the Service Structure." In B. Ross and S. K. Khinduka (Eds.), *Social Work in Practice.* Washington, D.C.: National Association of Social Workers, 1976.

MEYER, H. H. "The Validity of the In-Basket Test as a Measure of Managerial Performance." (In A. Howard, "An Assessment of Assessment Centers.") *Academy of Management Journal,* 1974, *17,* 115–134.

MICHIGAN BELL TELEPHONE. *Personnel Assessment Program: Evaluation Study.* Detroit: Michigan Bell Telephone, 1962.

MIDDLEMAN, R. R. "Generalists and Specialists." *Social Work*, 1977, *22*, 143.

MILGRAM, S. "The Perils of Obedience." *Harper's*, 1973, *247*, 62–77.

MILLS, C. W. *The Sociological Imagination*. New York: Oxford University Press, 1959.

MITCHELL, H. E., BULLARD, J. W., and MUDD, E. "Areas of Marital Conflict in Successfully and Unsuccessfully Functioning Families." *Journal of Health and Human Behavior*, 1962, *3*, 88–93.

MORRIS, R. *Towards a Caring Society*. New York: School of Social Work, Columbia University, 1974.

MUEHLBERG, N., PIERCE, R. M., and DRASGOW, J. A. "A Factor Analysis of Therapeutically Facilitative Conditions." *Journal of Clinical Psychology*, 1969, *25*, 93–95.

MUELLER, J. *Systems of Service*. Report 2 of the Cornell Studies of PL 92-603. Albany: New York State Office of Planning Services, 1974.

MUELLER, J., and MORGAN, H. *Social Services in Early Education*. New York: MSS Information Corp., 1974.

NATIONAL ASSOCIATION OF SOCIAL WORKERS. *Social Casework: Generic and Specific*. Washington, D.C.: National Association of Social Workers, 1974.

NATIONAL ASSOCIATION OF SOCIAL WORKERS. *Official Position on Recommendations of Council on Social Work Education Task Force on Structure and Quality in Social Work Education and Task Force on Practice and Education*. Washington, D.C.: National Association of Social Workers, 1975.

NATIONAL BOARD OF HEALTH AND WELFARE. *Programme of Principles for Open Medical Care*. Stockholm: National Board of Health and Welfare, 1970.

NATIONAL COUNCIL ON SOCIAL WELFARE. *The Future for Social Services in the United States*. Columbus, Ohio: National Council on Social Welfare, 1977.

NATIONAL LEAGUE FOR NURSING. *Evaluation: An Objective Approach*. New York: National League for Nursing, 1972.

NATIONAL LEAGUE FOR NURSING. *Coping with Change Through Assessment and Evaluation*. New York: National League for Nursing, 1976a.

NATIONAL LEAGUE FOR NURSING. *Criteria for Developing Clinical Performance Evaluation.* New York: National League for Nursing, 1976b.

O'CONNELL, W. R., JR., and MOOMAW, E. *A CBC Primer.* Atlanta, Ga.: Southern Regional Education Board, 1975.

OFFICE OF STRATEGIC SERVICES (OSS) ASSESSMENT STAFF. *Assessment of Men.* New York: Holt, Rinehart and Winston, 1948.

OKUN, B. F. *Effective Helping: Interviewing and Counseling Techniques.* North Scituate, Mass.: Duxbury Press, 1976.

OLSON, N. "A Study of the Effectiveness of Debt Counseling Service in Seattle, Washington." Unpublished master's thesis, University of Washington, 1968.

ORNSTON, P. S., CICCHETTI, D., and TOWBIN, A. P. "Reliable Changes in Psychotherapy Behavior Among First Year Psychiatric Residents." *Journal of Abnormal Psychology,* 1970, *73,* 240–244.

OSWALD, I. "Through the Looking Glass: Adventure in Television." *Journal of Education for Social Work,* 1965, *1,* 47–55.

OSWALD, I., and WILSON, S. *This Bag Is Not a Toy: A Handbook for the Use of Video Recording in Education for the Professions.* New York: Council on Social Work Education, 1971.

"OUT OF CONTROL—COMPULSIVE SPENDERS ARE HELPED TO REPAY BY CREDIT COUNSELORS." *Wall Street Journal,* Aug. 1, 1977, Sec. 1, p. 5.

OXLEY, G. B. "The Method Lab: An Experiment in Experimental Classroom Teaching." *Social Work Education Reporter,* 1973, *21,* 60–63.

PAPELL, C. B., and ROTHMAN, B. "Social Group Work Models: Possession and Heritage." *Journal of Education for Social Work,* 1966, *2,* 66–68.

PATTI, R. J. "Patterns of Management Activity in Social Welfare Agencies." *Administration in Social Work,* 1977, *1,* 5–18.

PAUL, G. L. *Insight vs. Desensitization in Psychotherapy: An Experiment in Anxiety Reduction.* Stanford, Calif.: Stanford University Press, 1966.

PAUL, G. L. "Strategy of Outcome Research in Psychotherapy." *Journal of Consulting and Clinical Psychology,* 1967, *31,* 109–118.

PAWLAK, E. J. "Organizational Tinkering." *Social Work,* 1976, *21,* 376–380.

PAYNE, P. A., WEISS, S. D., and KAPP, R. A. "Didactic, Experiential, and Modeling Factors in the Learning of Empathy." *Journal of Counseling Psychology,* 1972, *19,* 425–429.

PERELMAN, C. *The Idea of Justice and the Problems of Argument.* London: Routledge & Kegan Paul, 1963.

PERLMAN, H. H. *Social Casework: A Problem-Solving Process.* Chicago: University of Chicago Press, 1957.

PERLMAN, H. H. "The Role Concept and Social Casework: Some Explorations. II: What Is Social Diagnosis?" *Social Service Review,* 1962, *36,* 17–31.

PERLMUTTER, M. "Videotapes for Graduate Instruction." In *New Horizons in Social Work Education and Training Through Videotapes and Loop Films.* New York: Council on Social Work Education, 1966.

PERLMUTTER, M., and GUMPERT, G. "Field Instruction and Group Process: An Experiment in the Use of Television." *Social Work Education Reporter,* 1967, *15,* 26–29.

PERLMUTTER, M., and others. "An Analysis of an Instructional Television Approach to the Teaching of Social Work Methods." *Social Work Education Reporter,* 1966, *14,* 19–21.

PERLMUTTER, M., and others. "Family Diagnoses and Therapy Using Videotape Playback." *American Journal of Orthopsychiatry,* 1967, *37,* 900–905.

PETER, L., and HULL, R. *The Peter Principle: Why Things Always Go Wrong.* New York: Morrow, 1969.

PETTIGREW, L. "Competency-Based Teacher Education: Teacher Training for Multicultural Education." In *Multicultural Education Through Competency-Based Teacher Education.* Washington, D.C.: American Association of Colleges for Teacher Education, 1974.

PIAGET, J. *The Moral Judgment of the Child.* New York: Free Press, 1948.

PIKE, V., and others. *Permanent Planning for Children in Foster Care: A Handbook for Social Workers.* DHEW Publication OHDS 77–30124. Washington, D.C.: U.S. Government Printing Office, 1977.

PINCUS, A., and MINAHAN, A. *Social Work Practice: Model and Method.* Itasca, Ill.: Peacock, 1973.

PINS, A. M. "Changes in Social Work Education and Their Implications for Practice." *Social Work,* 1971, *16,* 5–15.

POTTINGER, P. S. "Competency Assessment at School and Work." *Social Policy,* 1977, *8,* 35–40.

PURCELL, F. P., and SPECHT, H. "The House on Sixth Street." *Social Work,* 1965, *10,* 69–76.

QUIRK, T. J. "Some Measurement Issues in Competency-Based Teacher Education." *Phi Delta Kappan,* 1974, *55,* 316–319.

RAPPAPORT, J., and CHINSKY, J. M. "Accurate Empathy: Confusion of a Construct." *Psychological Bulletin,* 1972, *77,* 400–404.

RAWLS, J. *A Theory of Justice.* Cambridge, Mass.: Harvard University Press, 1971.

REID, W. J., and EPSTEIN, L. *Task-Centered Casework.* New York: Columbia University Press, 1972.

RICHAN, W. C. "A Common Language for Social Work." *Social Work,* 1972, *17,* 14–22.

RICHARDS, S. "An Analysis of the Efficacy of Group Counseling on Changing Financial Planning Behaviors." Unpublished master's thesis, Pennsylvania State University, 1975.

RICHARDS, S., and TOMDRO, M. *Consumer Budget Counseling Research—A Pilot Study.* Milwaukee: Family Service Agency, 1975.

RICHEY, C. "Interpersonal and Assessment Skills Inventory." Unpublished manuscript, University of Washington, 1976.

RICHMOND, M. *Social Diagnosis.* New York: Russell Sage Foundation, 1917. (Rev. ed., 1930a.)

RICHMOND, M. *What Is Social Casework? An Introductory Description.* New York: Russell Sage Foundation, 1922.

RICHMOND, M. "Some Next Steps in Social Treatment." In J. C. Colcord and R. S. Z. Mann (Eds.), *The Long View.* New York: Russell Sage Foundation, 1930b.

RICHMOND, S. A., and BUTLER, H. "Concrete Comparison Generalization and Validation in Social Research and Practice." *Philosophy in Context,* 1977, *6.*

RICHMOND, S. A., BUTLER, H., and ABELS, S. "The Logic and Justice of Practice." Paper presented at the annual program meeting of the Council on Social Work Education, Chicago, March 1975.

RISLEY, T. R., and WOLF, M. M. "Strategies for Analyzing Behavior Change Over Time." In J. Nesselroade and H. Reese (Eds.), *Lifespan Development Psychology: Methodological Issues.* New York: Academic Press, 1972.

RITTER, B. "Treatment of Acrophobia with Contact Desensitization." *Behavior Research and Therapy,* 1969, *7,* 41–45.

ROBINSON, V. P. *A Changing Psychology in Social Case Work.* Philadelphia: University of Pennsylvania Press, 1930.

ROGERS, C. *On Becoming a Person.* Boston: Houghton Mifflin, 1961.

ROGERS, C. "Learning to Be Free." In G. Haas, K. Wiles, and J. Bondi (Eds.), *Readings in Curriculum.* (2nd ed.) Boston: Allyn & Bacon, 1972.

ROSE, S. D. *Treating Children in Groups: A Behavioral Approach.* San Francisco: Jossey-Bass, 1972.

ROSE, S. D. "In Pursuit of Social Competence." *Social Work,* 1975, *20,* 33–44.

ROSE, S. D. *Group Therapy: A Behavioral Approach.* Englewood Cliffs, N.J.: Prentice-Hall, 1977.

ROSE, S. D., CAYNER, J. J., and EDLESON, J. L. "Measuring Interpersonal Competence." *Social Work,* 1977, *22,* 125–129.

ROSEN, A., and LIEBERMAN, D. "The Experimental Evaluation of Interview Performance of Social Workers." *Social Service Review,* 1972, *46,* 395–412.

ROSENBLATT, A. "The Practitioner's Use and Evaluation of Research." *Social Work,* 1968, *13,* 53–59.

ROSNER, B. *The Power of Competency-Based Education: A Report.* Boston: Allyn & Bacon, 1972.

ROSS, M. *Community Organizaton: Theory Principles and Practice.* New York: Harper & Row, 1955.

ROTHMAN, J. *Planning and Organizing for Social Change: Action Principles from Social Service Research.* New York: Columbia University Press, 1974.

SAMOFF, Z. "The Affective Component of Social Welfare Content." In L. J. Glick (Ed.), *Undergraduate Social Work Education for*

Practice: A Report on Curriculum Content and Issues. Vol. 1. Washington, D.C.: U.S. Government Printing Office, 1971.

SANDOZ, E. "CBTE: The Nays of Texas." *Phi Delta Kappan,* 1974, *55,* 304–306.

SAXON, L. *The Individual, Marriage, and the Family.* Belmont, Calif. Wadsworth, 1972.

SCHINKE, S. P., and others. "Interviewing-Skills Training: An Empirical Evaluation." *Journal of Social Service Research,* 1978, in press.

SCHRIESSHEIM, C., and SCHRIESSHEIM, J. "Development and Empirical Investigation of New Response Categories to Increase the Validity of Multiple Response Alternative Questionnaires." *Educational and Psychological Measurement,* 1974, *34,* 877–884.

SCHULMAN, E. D. *Intervention in Human Services.* St. Louis, Mo.: Mosby, 1978.

SCHWARTZ, W. "Small Group Science and Group Work Practice." *Social Work,* 1963, *8,* 39–46.

SELZNICK, P. "The Law of Nature and the Nature of Law." *Center Magazine,* 1977, *10,* 34–48.

SHAPIRO, M. "Reflections on the Preparation of Social Workers for Executive Positions." *Journal of Education for Social Work,* 1971, *7,* 55–68.

SHEEHAN, P. H., and BROWN, K. W. "Two Models of Competency-Based Business Teacher Education Programs." In J. W. Crews and Z. S. Dickerson (Eds.), *Education for Business.* Reston, Va.: National Business Education Association, 1977.

SHORT, R. R. "Competency Education and Evaluation: Issues and Dilemmas." *Group and Organization Studies,* 1977, *2,* 75–87.

SHULMAN, L. *A Study of the Helping Process.* Vancouver: University of British Columbia Press, 1977.

SILK, S. "The Use of Videotape in Brief Joint Marital Therapy." *American Journal of Psychotherapy,* 1972, *26,* 417–424.

SIMON, S. B., HOWE, L. W., and KIRSCHENBAUM, H. *Values Clarification: A Handbook of Practical Strategies for Teachers and Students.* New York: Hart, 1972.

SIPORIN, M. *Introduction to Social Work Practice.* New York: Macmillan, 1975.

SMALL, M., and REAGAN, P. F. "An Evaluation of Evaluations." *American Journal of Psychiatry*, 1974, *131*, 51–55.

SNYDER, B. *The Hidden Curriculum*. New York: Knopf, 1971.

SPECHT, H. "Casework Practice and Social Policy Formulation." *Social Work*, 1968, *13*, 42–52.

SPECHT, H. "The Deprofessionalization of Social Work." *Social Work*, 1972, *17*, 3–15.

SPECHT, H. "Dimensions of Generalist and Specialist Conduct at Different Levels of Educational Continuum." Paper presented at the Big Sky Symposium, Big Sky, Mont., Aug. 1977.

SPOONER, S. E., and STONE, S. C. "Maintenance of Specific Counseling Skills Over Time." *Journal of Counseling Psychology*, 1977, *24*, 66–71.

SPORES, J. C., and CUMMINGS, M. "Toward a Competency-Based Baccalaureate." In M. L. Arkava and E. C. Brennen (Eds.), *Competency-Based Education for Social Work: Evaluation and Curriculum Issues*. New York: Council on Social Work Education, 1976.

STANGE, K. H. *Experiential Learning in Social Work Education*. Regina, Saskatchewan, Canada: Faculty of Social Work, University of Regina, 1977.

STEIN, T., and GAMBRILL, E. D. *Decision Making in Foster Care: A Training Manual*. Berkeley: University Extension Publications, University of California, 1976.

STEVENS, E. W., JR. "Alternatives in Competency-Based Teacher Education." *Educational Forum*, 1976, *41*, 37–48.

STONE, G. L., and VANCE, A. "Instructions, Modeling, and Rehearsal: Implications for Training." *Journal of Counseling Psychology*, 1976, *23*, 272–279.

STREAN, H. "For the Severest Cases, the Best Therapist: A First-Year Social Work Student." *Behavior Today*, Aug. 1, 1977, pp. 4–5.

STUART, R. B. *Trick or Treatment: How and When Psychotherapy Fails*. Champaign, Ill.: Research Press, 1970.

STUART, R. B. "Research in Social Work: Social Casework and Social Group Work." In R. Morris (Ed.), *Encyclopedia of Social Work*. Vol. 2. Washington, D.C.: National Association of Social Workers, 1971.

SUNDEL, M., and SUNDEL, S. *Behavior Modification in the Human Services*. New York: Wiley, 1975.

TEARE, R. J., and MC PHEETERS, H. L. *Manpower Utilization in Social Welfare*. Atlanta, Ga.: Southern Regional Education Board, 1970.

TEN HAVE, T. T. "On Agology." *New Themes in Social Work Education*. New York: International Association of Schools of Social Work, 1973.

THOMAS, E. (Ed.). *Behavior Modification Procedure: A Sourcebook*. Chicago: Aldine, 1974.

THOMAS, E. J. "Uses of Research Methods in Interpersonal Practice." In N. A. Polansky (Ed.), *Social Work Research*. Chicago: University of Chicago Press, 1975.

TOUKMANIAN, S. G., and RENNIE, D. L. "Microcounseling Versus Human Relations Training: Relative Effectiveness with Undergraduate Trainees." *Journal of Counseling Psychology*, 1975, 22, 345–352.

TOWLE, C. "Review of a Changing Psychology in Social Case Work." *American Journal of Orthopsychiatry*, 1931, 1, 545–553.

TROPP, E. "The Challenge of Quality for Practice Theory." In B. Ross and S. K. Khinduka (Eds.), *Social Work in Practice*. Washington, D.C.: National Association of Social Workers, 1976.

TRUAX, C. B., and CARKHUFF, R. R. *Toward Effective Counseling and Psychotherapy: Training and Practice*. Chicago: Aldine, 1967.

TUBESING, D. A. *Holistic Health—A Whole Person Approach to Primary Health Care*. New York: Human Sciences Press, 1977.

U.S. DEPARTMENT OF COMMERCE. *Statistical Abstracts of the United States, 1976*. Washington, D.C.: U.S. Government Printing Office, 1976.

U.S. DEPARTMENT OF COMMERCE. *Handbook of Cyclical Indicators, May 1977*. Washington, D.C.: U.S. Government Printing Office, 1977.

VINSON, A. "Television and Group-Centered Learning." *Social Work Education Reporter*, 1968, 16, 32–33.

VINTER, R. D. "Analysis of Treatment Organizations." In Y. Hasenfeld and R. A. English (Eds.), *Human Service Organizations:*

A Book of Readings. Ann Arbor: University of Michigan Press, 1974.

VON BERTALANFFY, L. "An Essay on the Relativity of Categories." *Philosophy of Science,* 1955, *22,* 243–263.

VON BERTALANFFY, L. "General Systems Theory—A Critical Review." In L. Von Bertalanffy and A. Rapoport (Eds.), *General Systems.* New York: Society for General Systems Research, 1962.

VON BERTALANFFY, L. *General Systems Theory.* New York: Braziller, 1968.

WARD, J. H. "Hierarchical Grouping to Optimize an Objective Function." *Journal of the American Statistical Association,* 1963, *58,* 236–244.

WARD, J. H., and HOOK, M. E. "Application of an Hierarchical Grouping Procedure to a Problem of Grouping Profiles." *Educational and Psychological Measurement,* 1963, *23,* 69–81.

WARD, S., WACKMAN, D. B., and WARTELLA, E. *How Children Learn to Buy.* Beverly Hills, Calif.: Sage, 1977.

WASSERMAN, H. "Early Careers of Professional Social Workers in a Public Child Welfare Agency." *Social Work,* 1970, *15,* 93–101.

WEINSTEIN, G. W. *Children and Money: A Guide for Parents.* New York: Schocken Books, 1976.

WEISS, C. (Ed.). *Evaluating Action Programs: Readings in Social Action and Education.* Boston: Allyn & Bacon, 1972.

WEISSMAN, H. "The Social Worker in Educational Television." *Social Work,* 1963, *8,* 96–100.

WEIZENBAUM, I. *New York Times,* May 8, 1977, p. 38.

WELLS, R. "Training in Facilitative Skills." *Social Work,* 1975, *20,* 242–243.

WELLS, R. A., and MILLER, D. "Developing Relationship Skills in Social Work Students." *Social Work Education Reporter,* 1973, *21,* 68–73.

WESTBERG, G. "The Parish Pastor's Finest Hour." *Journal of Religion and Health,* 1970, *9,* 170–177.

WESTRIN, C.-G. "Cooperation Between Medical and Social Services." *Scandinavian Journal of Social Medicine,* 1973, *1,* 115–123.

WHALEN, C. "Effects of a Model and Instructions on Group Verbal Behavior." *Journal of Consulting and Clinical Psychology*, 1969, *33*, 509–521.

WHITE, R. W. *Ego and Reality in Psychoanalytic Theory*. New York: International Universities Press, 1963.

WHITE, R. W. *Lives in Progress*. New York: Holt, Rinehart and Winston, 1966.

WHITTAKER, J. K. *Social Treatment*. Chicago: Aldine, 1974.

WIEGAND, C. F. "A Procedure for Granting Credit for Non-Academic Experiences." Regina, Saskatchewan, Canada: Faculty of Social Work, University of Regina, 1976.

WILLIAMS, F. E. *A Total Creativity Program for Individualizing and Humanizing the Learning Process*. Englewood Cliffs, N.J.: Educational Technology Publications, 1972.

WILSON, G., and RYLAND, G. *Social Group Work Practice: The Creative Use of the Social Process*. Boston: Houghton Mifflin, 1949.

WILSON, M. *Job Analysis for Human Resource Management: A Review of Selected Research and Development*. Manpower Research Monograph No. 36. Washington, D.C.: U.S. Department of Labor, 1974.

WISCONSIN STATE BUREAU OF PERSONNEL. "Reliability Estimates and Internal Validity." Unpublished report. Madison: Wisconsin State Bureau of Personnel, 1975.

WOLF, M. M. "Social Validity: The Case for Subjective Measurement of How Behavior Analysis Is Finding Its Heart." *Journal of Applied Behavior Analysis*, 1978, *2*, 203–223.

WOLFE, D. M. *Toward Competency-Based Learning in Organizational Behavior*. Cleveland: Cleveland Department of Organizational Behavior, School of Management, Case Western Reserve University, 1976.

WOLFENSBERGER, W. *Normalization*. Toronto: National Institute on Mental Retardation, 1972.

WOLLOWICK, H. B., and MC NAMARA, W. J. "Relationships of the Components of an Assessment Center to Management Success." *Journal of Applied Psychology*, 1969, *53*, 348–352.

WOOLEY, A. S. "The Long and Tortured History of Clinical Evaluation." *Nursing Outlook*, 1977, *25*, 21–25.

YIN, R. K., and HEALD, K. A. "Using the Case Survey Method to Analyze Policy Studies." *Administrative Science Quarterly*, 1975, *20*, 371–381.

ZALD, M. N. "Demographics, Politics, and the Future of the Welfare State." *Social Service Review*, 1977, *51*, 119–124.

ZASTROW, C. "How to Counsel." In C. Zastrow and D. H. Chang (Eds.), *The Personal Problem Solver*. Englewood Cliffs, N.J.: Prentice-Hall, 1977.

ZIMBARDO, G. "The Mind Is a Formidable Jailer, A Pirandellian Prison." *New York Times Magazine*, April 8, 1973, pp. 38–52, 56–60.

Name Index

A

ABELS, P., xii, 60–75, 277
ABELS, S. L., xii, 60–75, 277, 300–301
ADDAMS, J., 4
ADLER, A., 80
AHRONS, C. R., 111, 277
AIKEN, M., 275, 277
ALAMSHAH, W. H., 87–88, 277
ALINSKY, S., 7, 278
ALLEN, R. W., 290
ALLPORT, G., 88
ANDREWS, T. E., 278
ARGYRIS, C., 278
ARKAVA, M. L., ix–xv, 31, 45, 46, 67, 92, 111, 114, 167, 185, 278
ARMITAGE, A., 31, 45, 111, 112, 278
AROSTEGUI, M., 65, 294
AUSTIN, C. D., xiv, 234–249
AUSTIN, D. M., 125, 227, 278

AUSTIN, M. J., xiii, 32–33, 132, 134, 146–160, 278–279
AUSUBEL, D. P., 93, 279
AUTHIER, J., 82, 183, 279, 291
AYLLON, T., 118, 279
AZRIN, N. H., 118, 279

B

BAER, B. L., xii, 96–110, 279
BANDURA, A., 171, 279
BARKER, B., 138n
BARKER, H., 138n
BARKER, R., 279
BARLOW, D. N., 112, 113, 289
BARR, H., 263, 264, 265, 279
BARTLETT, H. M., 2, 15, 279
BASSOFF, B. Z., 275, 279
BELL, W. J., 111, 295
BENSCHOTTER, R., 279
BERDYAEV, N., 88, 279

309

Subject Index